iPod, YouTube, Wii Play

iPod, YouTube, Wii Play

Theological Engagements with Entertainment

D. BRENT LAYTHAM

 CASCADE *Books* · Eugene, Oregon

IPOD, YOUTUBE, WII PLAY
Theological Engagements with Entertainment

Cascade Books
An Imprint of Wipf and Stock Publishers
199 W. 8th Ave., Suite 3
Eugene, OR 97401

www.wipfandstock.com

ISBN 13: 978-1-55635-509-7

Cataloguing-in-Publication data:

Laytham, D. Brent.

iPod, YouTube, Wii play : theological engagements with entertainment / D. Brent Laytham.

x + 210 pp. ; 23 cm. Includes bibliographical references and index.

ISBN 13: 978-1-55635-509-7

1. Popular culture—Religious aspects—Christianity. 2. Christianity and culture. 3. I. Title.

BL65.C8 L39 2012

Manufactured in the U.S.A.

For Missy, with all my love,
in hopes of many shared entertainments to come

Contents

Acknowledgments

I AGAIN OWE DAN Bell a great debt, as he pushed both me and Cascade Books together for this project. Thanks to Northbrook and Winnetke Covenant Churches, Evanston First United Methodist Church, and DePaul University for allowing me to present portions of this material. Thanks to North Park Theological Seminary for a spring 2011 sabbatical that contributed significantly to completing this project. Olaf van de Klashorst, Rusty Brian, Randy Cooper, and Jake Wilson read drafts and offered valuable feedback. Debra Dean Murphy gave me the gift of a thorough theological reading.

My family has been the most important to me in this writing process. Our children, Monica and Wesley, gave me an iPod nano (for research purposes!) and plenty of opinionated help with various cultural trends. Wesley made sure that before I wrote about video games I had actually played them (and lost resoundingly)! Monica showed me the superiority of live musical performances, whether in a concert hall or a living room. I am most grateful to my wife, Missy, who not only read the book with her sharp editorial eye, making invaluable improvements in its shape and content, but shared with me the enjoyment of its research. Watching all those movies, ball games, and television shows wouldn't have been half the fun without her companionship, so to her I dedicate this book.

one

Now *That's* Entertainment

THESE DAYS, ENTERTAINMENT SEEMS almost bigger than God. It isn't, of course, but in pop culture appearances often point to places we Christians should be asking good questions. So this book will describe some of the ways that entertainment seems big, if not BIG! And it will regularly pose questions about how we can think and live the immensity of the gospel in the midst of an entertainment culture that, while certainly big and usually fun and occasionally profound, is far too small to mend the world. (While these questions could be useful for group discussion, they are intended to advance the book's argument or the reader's insight. Therefore they appear *in* the text, not at the end of chapters.)

✣   *Does God or entertainment have a bigger "footprint" in your every-day life? Do you "naturally" imagine God and the gospel as belong-ing to one sphere of life, entertainment to another?*

In the twentieth century, entertainment became a cultural superpower. That has, inevitably, inescapably impacted Christian discipleship, though not always in the most obvious ways. Unlike so many authors that focus on the content or "message" of our entertainments, I write with the conviction that entertainment's massive impact on us is rooted mostly in its mundane everydayness: in the way it shapes our subjectivities, affects our affections, cultures our choices, and permeates our possibilities. This power isn't ac-cidental; as a commercial enterprise, entertainment intends to shape pat-terns of thinking, feeling, and acting. And yet the cumulative effect of that shaping far exceeds what any entertainer, company, or industry intends. For disciples this matters precisely because following Jesus is a journey meant to transform how we think, feel, and act. Therefore, since entertainment and discipleship are both formational processes, we need to ask how a century's journey from radio and silent cinema through the heyday of television to our brave new World Wide Web of entertainment possibilities has been shaping how we pray and praise, how we make disciples and decisions, how we feel and love, what we believe and hope.

This alone is sufficient reason for Christians to engage entertainment *critically*. Critical engagement does not mean a tirade against entertainment's ills; its tone is not essentially negative, but investigative. Critical engagement asks what entertainment is, how it works, and what it means. We mostly haven't asked such questions, nor read the kinds of scholarship that help provide some answers—cultural studies, sociology, psychology, media studies, philosophy, cultural anthropology, and communications theory. Most of us Christians don't understand how pop culture "works" any better than we understand how an iPod or a plasma TV works. That leaves us mostly focused on the smooth, inviting face of entertainment. Whether it is consuming the bits we like or rejecting the ones we don't, either way we remain focused on surface at the expense of depth, on how things appear rather than how they are, on entertainment's content instead of its conditioning structure and power. We need to be far more critical if we're going to follow Jesus faithfully.

✠ *Have you as a Christian disciple ever critically engaged entertainment? Did you focus primarily on surface and content or structures and impacts? Is there a pop culture image for your view of entertainment's power (e.g., the Pied Piper, "the Force," the Matrix, the Borg)?*

More important than engaging critically, however, is that we engage entertainment *theologically*—which means to reflect on it before God within the church in light of the gospel. What that looks like will be put on display throughout this book. Here, suffice it to say that both the Apostles' Creed and Philippians 2:5–11 offer fulsome if brief summaries of the core Christian gospel. Unfortunately, many Christians don't know the gospel story about Jesus as well as they know the story of Oprah or Michael Vick or *The Matrix*. Moreover, most of us spend more time and passion watching *The Office* or *American Idol* or [insert name of your favorite show here] than we do reasoning together about our common life as Christ's church.

In short, we've settled for a world divided between loving God and enjoying ourselves—an easy, unacknowledged truce that divides our lives into zones of sacred pursuits and secular pastimes, discipleship and fandom. But that settlement was produced by the entertainment industry, backed by massive marketing sponsorship, while we mostly failed to notice.

Typically, I should now define entertainment academically and describe its main features, then summarize various claims that you'll encounter through the rest of this book. But that wouldn't be very entertaining, so instead let's consider specific examples: some "truthiness about w00t" and the truth about worship.

TRUTHINESS ABOUT w00t

Two years in a row, Merriam Webster chose as the "word of the year" a product of the culture of entertainment. In 2006, it was *truthiness*, the quality of sounding or appearing true (without being true). Though the term was not coined by Stephen Colbert, it was certainly made famous by his repeated use of it on *The Colbert Report* on Comedy Central. In 2007, the word of the year was *w00t*, an exclamation of triumph that online gamers text to one another. w00t's combination of letters and numbers captures perfectly the digital vibe of its techy users.

The truthiness about w00t is that such matters are epiphenomenal froth on the mocha cappuccino of life. We've mostly grown accustomed to imagining our entertainments as harmless fun, refreshing recreation, our national pastime. Sure, extreme ironing (yes, it's a real sport) may be risky, but listening to my iPod usually isn't. Sure, watching six straight hours of television might leave me more numbed than invigorated, but nothing perks me up like a couple of good YouTube clips. Sure, some gamers forget to eat, sleep, and bathe, but the rest of us sanely balance work and play. The truthiness about w00t is that entertainment is fun, fun is good, and good is right. Right?

The truth about w00t, and about truthiness too, is another matter—a complex matter that requires us to notice how the structures and processes of entertainment direct perception, foster desire, generate symbols, structure activity, orient goals, shape relationships, and form community. The truth about entertainment, in short, is that it is a profoundly powerful formational process that we will misunderstand completely if we treat it as merely a collection of discrete pleasures we control by our power of choice.

Don't imagine that this means everything that follows will be a screed against entertainment. I love movies and television and music too much for that. Rather, what follows will be an attempt to invite us to understand entertainment in new ways, to ask entertainment some hard theological questions, and at times to allow it to return the favor. Let's begin with these two words of the year.

There is a lot to love about w00t. It inscribes the cleverness of the gaming community and expresses their joy at excellent play. Here are two aspects that lie at the core of many of our entertainments: they draw together a community of the like-minded, and they orient toward enjoyment. Community and joy are both things that Christians should w00t about.

There is also a lot to love about the word *truthiness*, at least when it is deployed to skewer the lies that masquerade as truth. The Colbert comedy routine that introduced the term (October 17, 2005) satirized an American preference for feelings over facts in regard to our political decisions. Here is one of the things that entertainment can do best: invite us to laugh at our foibles and failings as a kind of therapy for improvement. By adding *truthiness* to the national lexicon, Colbert may have invited us to care more about truth.

But the truth about truthiness and w00t isn't entirely positive. Consider that in addition to signifying community and joy, w00t also signifies several ambiguous or negative trends: w00t evokes the mass migration that is underway from embodied to virtual community; w00t presupposes the corporatized scripting of play and imagination; w00t accepts the societal consensus that "free time" is mine to enjoy, and that fun is whatever I prefer. In short, w00t can remind us that entertainment has become a way of life that encompasses and (re)shapes our understanding of community, ritual, responsibility, joy, and authority. Because Christian faith is the embodiment of core convictions about the cruciform shape of each of these, we need to ask about the compatibility of entertainment and discipleship.

Truthiness is equally ambiguous. Consider, for example, that it was added to the national lexicon through a comedy routine that was two minutes and forty seconds long. While that was plenty of time to make a good joke about our culture of lies, it wouldn't begin to be enough time for careful reflection on the complexities of truth. This is an example of anthropologist Victor Turner's point about satire more generally: it is essentially conservative in effect, because even as it skewers a particular social folly or political peccadillo, it is implicitly affirming the larger social and political structure that makes both the stupidity and the satire possible.[1] Moreover, consider how attention to an entertainment—in this case *The Colbert Report*—cedes a kind of moral authority to the show, permitting it to direct our attention and focus our concern. Finally, encountering *truthiness* on TV can remind us of a fifty-year-old habit of allowing television to frame reality and determine truth. Because Christian faith has traditionally situated moral discourse, authority, and perception in the church's mission to worship, witness, and serve the risen Christ, we need to reflect on the degree to which our entertainments have now distorted or displaced a properly ecclesial—that is, church-centered—ethic.

Finally, and perhaps most subtly, we should note the ambiguity of Merriam Webster selecting a "word of the year" at all. In doing so, Webster joins the ranks of commercial entities that announce an annual superlative: *Time* magazine gives us a "person of the year." The Academy of Motion Picture Arts and Sciences hands out Oscars® each year to the "best" this and that, although the Hollywood Foreign Press Association beats them to the punch with its Golden Globes®. Each of these is an example of what Daniel Boorstin calls a "pseudo-event," the manufacturing or staging of an award or event for the purpose of getting desirable coverage in the media.[2] Let's face it, the primary rationale for having a "word of the year" is to get some attention. Capturing attention is one of the most basic components—perhaps the most basic—of the business of entertainment, for in the entertainment economy, attention equals dollars. So Webster's word of the year, and all the other "of the year" awards, are happenings that matter only if and because we pay sufficient attention. Again, because Christian faith proclaims that the world's fate turned on a singular event that happened away from media attention, we need to grapple with the significance of media that constantly require and manufacture the next new thing. And we must ask whether our entertainment media are constantly suborning the attention, acclamation, and praise that rightly belong to this one who is worthy, the Lamb that was slain (Revelation 5).

---

1. Turner notes that "satire exposes, attacks, or derides what it considers to be vices, follies, stupidities, or abuses, but its criterion of judgment is usually the normative structural frame of officially promulgated values. Hence satirical works . . . often have a 'ritual of reversal' form, indicating that disorder is no permanent substitute for order." Turner, *Ritual to Theatre*, 40.

2. Boorstin, *Image*, 1962.

TRUTH ABOUT WORSHIP

So entertainment raises the question of attending to truth, which is finally a question about worship. Let's consider the recent public confession of Walt Kallestad. Longtime pastor of the Phoenix megachurch Community Church of Joy, Kallestad is best known for his book *Entertainment Evangelism*.[3] He says the idea for the book "came together for me while standing in a line at a Dallas Cineplex waiting to see the Batman premiere. *The only way to capture people's attention is entertainment*, I thought. *If I want people to listen to my message, I've got to present it in a way that grabs their attention long enough for me to communicate the gospel.*"[4] The implementation of the book's central idea—that the weekly Christian gathering should be a highly produced form of entertainment—quickly grew Community Church of Joy's weekly worship attendance from two hundred to twelve thousand. As a student once asked me in a worship course, "What more proof than that do we need that entertainment evangelism is a good idea?"

As it turns out, Kallestad himself now claims to have been on the wrong track. Coming back from a three-month sabbatical, he noticed that his congregation's worship "was shallow," indeed, that it "was a *show*." Participating in his congregation's life with new eyes, he saw that entertainment was drawing in *spectators* rather than forming and sending forth "transformed, empowered disciples." Put another way, Kallestad discovered that entertainment couldn't be used *for* evangelism, because it already *was* evangelism: a set of processes and activities that shaped how people felt, thought, and acted. The entertainment form wasn't a neutral container into which Kallestad could load content intended to convert. This is because entertainment already has a converting intention and effect—it conditions us to want more of the same. The most common and basic effect of entertainment is that people want more, want to be continually entertained; call it the "will to pleasure." Moral theologian Paul Waddell says, ". . . there is a dangerous deception behind entertainment once it becomes culturally baptized as a fitting way of life, namely the suggestion that to be human is to be continually distracted and amused. In a culture in which entertainment is approached with religious zeal, everyone, including God, has an obligation

---

3. Kallestad, *Entertainment Evangelism*, 1996. For an excellent critique suggesting that Kallestad exemplifies America's worshiping at the altar of the 'god of Change,' see Mohrmann, "Megachurch, Virtual Church."

4. Kallestad, "'Showtime!'"

to please us."[5] Of course, God truly is pleasing and enjoyable, but on God's terms, not ours, and certainly not Hollywood's!

At Community Church of Joy, Kallestad finally recognized that entertaining worship fosters enjoyment, but gets in the way of "joy in the Holy Spirit" (Rom 14:17). Entertainment evangelism gathers an audience, but not a congregation of the "communion of saints" (see Heb 12:1). His story tempts someone like me, who favors more liturgically structured worship, to shout, "I told you not to mess with the liturgy!" But that is not the lesson to draw here. Indeed, Christian worship of every sort faces the same challenge in the American context: practicing a formational process resilient enough to resist the ubiquitous, powerful, flashy counter-formation of entertainment (and consumerism).[6] Perhaps the central lesson in what transpired at Community Church of Joy is that when it comes to entertainment, the medium is almost always the most important message.[7]

✣ *Was Kallestad's failure one of conception (the mistake of assuming that the content of faith can be packaged in the form of entertainment) or execution (a good, relevant idea that wasn't executed well enough)? Do you believe that entertainment's power and reach require us to adopt, adapt, or resist?*

So Kallestad's lesson for us is that we'll need to be far more theologically critical in our engagement with popular culture than he was. And that will require us to give some thought to what theology is and isn't. For help with that, we need to introduce two Georges.

---

5. Wadell, *Becoming Friends*, 20.

6. Saliers, "Afterword," 216–18.

7. Media theorist Marshall McLuhan coined and popularized this phrase in the 1960s (see his *Understanding Media*). Its central point was to refocus attention from media content to form. When it comes to technological media, the frame may be more important than the picture. McLuhan was suggesting that different forms of mass media have different social effects. Print technologies shaped the world one way, broadcast technologies another, and digital technologies are now clearly reshaping our imaginations and relationships yet again. So McLuhan's bumper sticker invites us to worry less about the body count in the latest action flick or the sexualization of prime time television, and to worry more about how cinematic and television technologies capture and engage our attention, how they structure our perception and imagination, and how they restructure social and political life.

MR. LINDBECK MEETS MR. LUCAS

In 1984, George Lindbeck published a book that created almost as big a stir in theology as George Lucas's *Star Wars* trilogy had just done in film (1977, 1980, 1983). Lindbeck's *The Nature of Doctrine* offered a typology of three ways Christians have understood theology.[8] The first sees theology as the propositional articulation of what Christians believe, implying that our core mode of being Christian is cognitive—*believing* key truth claims about God and the world. The heart of being Christian, you might say, is in the head. The second way sees theology as the expression of fundamental religious experiences, implying that our core mode of being Christian is experiential—*feeling* certain things about God and God's world. Here, the center of being Christian is certainly the heart. Lindbeck suggests that while our beliefs are true, and the life of faith is inevitably experiential, both of these understandings of theology fail to address the full scope of being Christian, which is finally a matter not just of thinking/believing or feeling/experiencing, but of *being/doing*.

So theology explicates practice. It articulates faith's way of living, not just ideas in my head or feelings in my heart. Lindbeck therefore proposed a third way of understanding theology: as the grammar of Christian language—the language that forms and performs Christian living. Here, the heart of being Christian is a kind of cultural fluency and agency: knowing what and how to say the gospel, *and saying it*; knowing what to do in order to do God's will, *and doing it*. So just as learning to be French involves learning to use the French language with all of the cultural meanings, values, patterns, habits, obligations, aspirations, and actions that it entails, so being Christian is also about learning all of the culture-like meanings, values, patterns, habits, obligations, aspirations, and actions that hearing and speaking the Christian gospel entails.

Let's leave Mr. Lucas on Tatooine a bit longer in order to notice how the two inadequate approaches to theology Mr. Lindbeck identifies inevitably lead to inadequate theological engagements with entertainment. In the first approach, where theology is a propositional articulation of cognitive truth claims about God, you get one of two extremes. *Either* this conceptual approach compels us to assess how well entertainment content agrees with our doctrines and whether its "worldview" comports with ours.[9] *Or* limit-

---

8. Lindbeck, *Nature of Doctrine*.

9. An example of this approach is Godawa, *Hollywood Worldviews*.

ing faith primarily to adherence to propositional truth allows us to watch and do whatever we want, so long as we continue to believe the right doctrines.[10] Neither of these is adequate to theology's intended role of turning us toward, training us in, and transforming us with the gospel.

In the second approach, where theology is deemed an expression of religious experience, engaging entertainment will be considerably fuzzier, partly because "experience" is less precise, and partly because (as we saw in the last section) our continual experience of being entertained powerfully shapes what we want and expect experientially. Some in this camp view entertainment pleasure as a direct competitor with religious experience, producing a stance of avoidance and denunciation that is only slightly caricatured by the dictum "If you're having fun, it's wrong; stop immediately!" Others see individual entertainments as expressions of a particular artist's *experience* of truth or beauty, which should be evaluated in light of "Christian experience"—usually construed monolithically.[11] Others will investigate the effects of entertainment on us, looking for "sacramental moments" that bear some semblance to our experience of real sacramental moments.[12] So though less precise, this second understanding of theology produces engagements with entertainment that are just as inadequate as the first approach, because in the end, God intends to transform and beatify us, not just make us tingle. Theology exists to serve that Holy Spirit agenda.

Now the third approach, in which being Christian entails a kind of cultural competency, or linguistic fluency, or normative practice. In it, theology is a governing wisdom, a guiding grammar, a reflective rubric for training in faith, hope, and love. In other words, real theology is inherently practical—truthful convictions that organize and undergird how we live and love (not just how we think and feel), because faith is a way of living in, with, and for the God-who-is-love.

Note how closely Mr. Lindbeck's cultural-linguistic account of theology as forming competent disciples resembles Mr. Lucas's dramatic depiction of Obi Wan Kenobi's forming Luke Skywalker to be a competent Jedi. Obi Wan uses his wisdom not to impart truth or cultivate experience

10. William Romanowski points out the disconnect between doctrinal beliefs and entertainment behaviors in *Eyes Wide Open*, 39.

11. This approach suffers not only from a too narrow view of theology, and a culturally and historically myopic notion of normative Christian experience, but also from a romantic sentimentalization of the individual artist.

12. E.g., Fraser, *Images of the Passion*. For a spirited argument that although movies move us, they aren't sacraments, see Byassee, "God Does Not Entertain."

(though he does both along the way), but to form character and nurture ability and rework identity. For Luke to become what he is not—a Jedi—he needs Obi Wan to use that Jedi wisdom to orient, guide, train, and critique him. The sign that he has become a Jedi (in *Return of the Jedi*) is not that he professes Jedi doctrines or emotes Jedi feelings, but that he acts *as* a Jedi (*as* not *like*!).

I don't usually use pop-culture analogies for matters theological, since they often invert the comparison in tail-wagging-the-dog kinds of ways. We too easily feel greater affinity for the pop-culture reference than for the primary theological point or idea, and we too quickly preempt depth and subtlety by stopping with the analogy, as if reflection were completed rather than just begun. Nevertheless, I've risked introducing such an analogy here, and introducing Mr. Lucas to Mr. Lindbeck, because of a news story I remember from 1983. A Christian essayist reported that while waiting in line for the premier of *Return of the Jedi*, another fan said to her, "May the Force be with you," to which she immediately replied, "And also with you."

On the one hand, and without the help of Lindbeck, we might celebrate this as nothing more than a cute story of a pop-culture serendipity, an illustration of how easily some entertainments create communities of affinity among strangers. On the other hand, and still absent Lindbeck, we might bemoan this as a dangerous parody of the traditional Christian call to corporate prayer, seeing in the exchange a sign of creeping secularism (or sacrilege), or a call to culture wars or the like.

Lindbeck offers three more angles on the incident. His "cognitive-propositionalist" type would ask what beliefs and worldview are implicit in "the Force"—that is, to what does the exchange ("May the Force be with you," "And also with you") ask us to give intellectual assent? His "experiential-expressivist" type might consider what feelings the incident encourages or evokes, or how it is symbolic or expressive of an inner experience. Lindbeck's third approach, however, sees here a powerful formation at work, one that is constantly constituting identity, shaping agency, communicating sentiment, regulating speech, and providing intelligibility. In other words, the real "Force" at work in Star Wars is one that tells us who we are, guides what we do, and renders it all in meaningful language and practice. (See the discussion of entertainment media as "superpowers" in the next chapter.)

Mr. Lindbeck helps us see the force of entertainment as idiomatic: the discursive structures, habituating activities, shared norms and rituals, and communicative processes of entertainment are more fundamental and transformational than is the content or subject matter. *That* we go to movies is more basic than *which ones* we see. *That* we watch TV is more important than *what* we watch—even if it's far less than the U.S. average of thirty-plus hours a week![13] *That* we listen to recorded music shapes us far more powerfully than whether it's country, jazz, rock, rap, or classical. So we must ask how widely disparate entertainments shape our sensibilities, cultivate our desires, form our feelings, discipline our bodies, pattern our actions, and determine our relationships.

✤ *If theology is more a matter of living the Christian life fluently than of thinking Christian ideas or feeling Christian experience, how might this complicate your theological engagement with entertainment? Which George symbolizes the most powerful formational forces in your life—Lindbeck or Lucas?*

Knowing that our "life is hidden with God in Christ" (Col 3:3), theology recognizes three things: first, entertainment isn't theology, even if it is ripe for theological reflection; second, in this culture, saturated with entertainments and overwhelmed with amusements, theology must engage entertainment; and third, entertainments will variously converge toward, complement, compete with, confuse, or confute Christian conviction. Therefore, we must make discerning theological judgments whose purpose is neither to condemn nor celebrate entertainment per se, but to help ourselves imagine more fully the shape of fidelity to Christ, to embody more completely fellowship in God's Spirit, to live more steadfastly our faith in the triune God. We begin that process by essaying five theological dimensions of entertainment.

THEOLOGICAL DIMENSIONS OF ENTERTAINMENT

Whether it's iPod or YouTube, ballet or *SmackDown*, there are a number of categories and themes woven through our entertainments that invite theological engagement. Let us consider the theological dimensions of pleasure, play, attention, leisure, and audience. As mnemonic devices, I will connect these dimensions to signifying body parts or relationships, and use italic typeface for the plethora of terms that help us understand them.

Heart. We seek entertainment for *pleasure, fun, excitement.* These aren't trivial or peripheral matters, however; *desire* and its *fulfillment* lies at

---

13. See this statistic and others summarized in Dill, *Fantasy Becomes Reality*, 38–40.

the very core of our humanness. Augustine began his *Confessions* by noting that we are made for God, and thus our hearts restlessly quest for rapturous rest in God. The Westminster Catechism begins by affirming that our "chief end is to worship and *enjoy* God forever." John Wesley summarized earlier Christian tradition by affirming that God intends for us holiness and *happiness*, two sides of the same coin. And Jewish philosopher Emmanuel Levinas says that enjoyment is when we are most fully ourselves, most completely human.

Obviously, popular *amusements* are not spiritual disciplines like prayer, Bible study, or meditation. But we must ask whether entertainment can sometimes evoke, direct, or shape our God-given desires. In a culture shaped by and saturated with entertainment, do we desire *diversions* from, or directions toward, God? Social psychologists Kubey and Csikszentmihayli point out "how easily organisms can be harmed by that which they desire. The trout is caught by the fisherman's lure, the mouse by the cheese. . . . Realizing when a diversion has gotten out of control is one of the great challenges of life."[14] So is recognizing where a diversion might actually be directing us toward our heart's true home—the triune God.

✤ *Do your entertainments provide pleasures that make you more human, more happy, more holy, or less? Are they more likely to thrill you or stupefy you? Do we expect God to play the role of minstrel, comedian, entertainer?*

Head and shoulders, knees and toes. Entertainment roots in and satisfies our human impulse to *play*. Play is activity that stretches the *imagination* even as it sharpens the mind and engages the *body*. You can hear traces of entertainment's connection to play in our language: we watch our favorite team play ball, or listen to our favorite artist play the banjo, or see our child in the school play. Athletes and actors are players, and so are iPods and BlueRays. The most important button on these machines is "play," and likewise for the YouTube and iTunes interfaces. Movies play at the cinema, music plays on the radio. Although play is often denigrated as immature, insignificant, or "not real," it is actually crucial to personal development, essential to human culture, and engaged with reality.

✤ *Do we denigrate play as immature, unserious, or fictional, and then transfer those attitudes to entertainment, to ritual, to worship?*

14. Kubey and Csikszentmihalyi, "Television Addiction," 48–55; cited in Dill, *Fantasy Becomes Reality*, 24.

In play, *freedom* marries *form, creativity* partners with *repetition*, time and space are reconfigured, and individual and social *performances* weave worlds, identities, and meanings. Although the play of children doesn't seem to get anything done, it is actually a core task of becoming human. Although the play of adults might seem a childish regression, it is actually a core expression of our humanity. Although play doesn't figure prominently in Scripture, it is nonetheless a positive image of God's relation to and delight in creation. Therefore, Christians probably shouldn't worry about the playful dimensions of entertainment per se. (For a fuller discussion, see chapter 6, "We Play.")

But we certainly should worry about the way play's freedom is increasingly captured by commodity forms, the way play's creativity is increasingly constrained by corporate scripts, the way play's performances are increasingly limited by capitalist interventions.[15] Because our entertainment culture is also a consumer culture, entertainment industries exist to serve profit, not play. It is more profitable to manufacture imagination's completed edifice than its raw materials, even when this constrains play in damaging ways. For example, there's no profit if I build with sticks and rocks, some if I purchase original Legos® (generic shapes), but maximum profit if I am drawn into the unending purchase of every new Lego® set—since each one has a singular, unrepeatable form. Whereas traditionally child's play has involved pretending to do adult things like work, parent, or teach, now child's play is increasingly imitative of entertainment, since self-referentiality is more profitable. So the *Star Wars* movies morph into Saturday morning cartoons, Happy Meal prizes at McDonald's, video games, coloring books, comic books, books, Halloween costumes, Lego® sets, and Lego® Star Wars video games. Somewhere along that profit-seeking continuum lies the demise of play's essential creativity.

Finally, can you imagine a world in which children must pay a fee every time they want access to playmates? That's our world, where digital playmates (shows, songs, movies, games, apps) must be rented or purchased, and where technological appliances (gaming stations, computers, smartphones), programs/platforms (Facebook, YouTube, 4G, Web 2.0) and services (Internet, phone, data, gaming networks) act as the intermediaries of our social play. There's little profit for corporations in face-to-face play,

---

15. In "Royal Juggernaut," 33, Linn writes, "For twenty-first century little girls, commercialized play manifests in repetitive, media-driven scripts in which female characters are characterized by entitlement, helplessness, and dependence—the same rigid roles that triggered rebellion in the women's movement of the 1960s."

plenty in MMORPGs (massive multiplayer online role-playing games), in social networks, in network-ready gaming stations, smartphones, and all the rest. It isn't leftist politics, but Christian vision, that lets us see how child's play is being marketed to the highest bidder, to the detriment of human freedom, imagination, and sociality.

✥ *Have entertainment products and experiences constrained play's freedom? Have corporate scripts for entertainment colonized play's imagination? Have entertainment appliances and services isolated us from play's inherent sociality?*

Eyes and ears. Entertainment is an activity rooted in our capacity to give *attention* to something or someone. So entertainment is intimately bound up with, and depends on, our capacities for *watching* and *listening* to others. Entertainments actively *engage* us by capturing our *interest* and holding our attention; relatedly, we actively *give mind to*, attend to, *consider*, or *entertain* their performance, beauty, *message*, or revelation. All this intersects directly with Christian faith and life. Christians can describe the *goal* of discipleship as an optimal *seeing* of God's glory—now we see through a glass darkly, but then we shall see God face to face (1 Cor 13:12)—and the *way* of discipleship as an obedient *listening* to God's Word—as God says at Jesus' transfiguration, "listen to him!" (Matt 17:5). Thus paying attention to God in Christ, and to everything else in its God-relatedness, is both our calling and our true home.

Since our life of faith is about paying attention faithfully to God, entertainment practices—as modes of paying attention—are necessarily part of that picture. First, notice how our verbs of attention have become metonyms for being entertained: I am *watching* the play, or television, or YouTube; I am *listening* to the comedian or the radio or my iPod. Because entertainment focuses on core capacities of attention, it has everything to do with our engagement with God. One enduring concern of the church has been whether some or all entertainments are *distractions* from God, or whether some (probably not all) entertainments can be *attractions* toward God. Second, notice how many of our entertainment habits diminish our capacities for actively reflecting, considering, and attending. Increasingly, our entertainments condition us as passive recipients (physically immobile, mentally numbed) capable of only partial attention (e.g., multitasking, television or music as background) or fleeting attention (e.g., channel surfing).

Finally, since the business of entertainment is an "attention economy," profiting only by the ongoing capture of our attention, competition continually expands and escalates. It expands to permeate every dimension of life with entertainment. Its relentless effort to monopolize our gaze habituates us to expect everything and everyone to be entertaining, which fosters in us an addiction to *spectacle*, an antipathy to *boredom*, and an anxiety that reality itself is boring. Entertainment must escalate and proliferate continuously because it is increasingly difficult to capture and sustain attention in a supersaturated entertainment environment. To be seen or heard in the ever-escalating visual clutter and sonic din, and to capture and keep our attention, entertainments get faster, louder, and more extreme.[16] This habituates us to be anxious about *relevance*, vulnerable to *hype*, and addicted to *novelty*. In a culture dominated by entertainment, the Christian calling to worship God in all things—which means first and foremost to attend to God in God's own beauty, goodness, and truth—is considerably harder.

✤ *Do you approach entertainment as a distraction, a way to take your mind off challenges and anxieties? In what ways, positive or negative, are you and your church impacted by the "attention economy"? Are there particular entertainments that invite you to attend more fully to God, to creation, to love of neighbor?*

Calendars and Clocks. Entertainment is increasingly central to how we structure, experience, and imagine *time*. It has reshaped dramatically our *patterns* of work and play and even our *rhythms* of day and night. The industrial revolution manufactured not only products but *leisure* itself, giving us *free time* that we fill with *pastimes* to stave off *boredom* (which is experienced as the burden of unentertaining time). Broadcast media and mass entertainments took things further, colonizing our evenings as *prime time* for television, *scheduling* our *weekends* for sports contests and movie premiers, and ordering our years with *seasons* (television series, individual sports), championships (Super Bowl, World Series, March Madness, World Cup), *festivals* (Oscars, Grammies), *finales* (*American Idol*, *Friends*) and *pilgrimages* (to Disneyworld or other themed entertainment environments). In all of these ways, entertainment doesn't just fill up our days and nights, it qualitatively changes our experience of, and relation to, time.

---

16. Gabler, *Life the Movie*, 189.

All this should give Christians considerable pause, since we are people called to relate "to time in a way that is unique and peculiar."[17] We are heirs of a faith that orders our days (Ps 55:17; Acts 3:1), weeks (Exod 16:27–30; Acts 20:7), and years (Exod 12:6–8; 1 Cor 5:7–8) to the purposes and promises of God. We are freed from anxiety about death by our sharing in Christ's resurrection. We can take time for God because God has made time for us in creation, redeemed time for us in resurrection, and given time to us in the future-bringing Holy Spirit. Our clocks, schedules, and calendars can bear witness to a living hope that even time has been redeemed to serve God's eternal love.

Unfortunately, in the deluge of entertainments, we all too easily feel and keep time like all the other fans. At one level, this can be as simple as asking the quantitative question whether our calendar is so full of entertainments that pastimes are displacing core *practices* like worship, devotion, witness, and service. There is no doubt that the average Christian in the United States more regularly watches *The Biggest Loser* than feeds the hungry, more faithfully follows *Law & Order* than visits the prisoner. It's not that we reject these traditional "works of mercy" as no longer germane to discipleship, only that as "works" they are alien to our rhythms of labor and leisure, and as "mercies" they are foreign to how we imagine and schedule free time. (In an entertainment culture, free time is me time.) At a deeper, qualitative level, we must ask whether our best times—of expectancy and hope, of rejoicing and celebrating, of lamenting and consoling, of stillness and satisfaction—are typically provided by the church or by the entertainment industry. In sum, entertainment's calendar threatens to crowd out God, its schedule threatens to reimagine discipleship, its temporal flow threatens to displace or replace the experience of eternity in our midst.

✢ *How many calendars, schedules, and clocks structure your sense of everyday life? Does your sense of the flow of the week derive more from worship, work, or entertainment? Does your daily rhythm orient toward prayers and praise, chores and obligations, or particular entertainments? Are the highlights of your year family events (birthdays, anniversaries), liturgical events (Easter, Christmas, Pentecost), or entertainment events (the Super Bowl, the Oscars)?*

---

17. Smith, *Desiring the Kingdom*, 156. Though some traditions of Christianity reject calendrical celebration outright, most have structured not only the week but the year with ritual remembrance of the gospel story.

Family, friends, and fans. Entertainment is intrinsically *social* activity (solitaire and *Angry Birds* notwithstanding). It requires various kinds of *communication*, and it promises not only a *shared* experience but an experience of *community*. A live entertainment *audience* is something more than a collection of individual spectators. The audience is really some*thing* more than the sum of its parts; it is a social body comprised of constituent *members*. The social dynamics of entertainment have strong parallels with the church. Just as being entertained constitutes an audience as a social body, so gathering in Jesus' name constitutes a congregation as his body, the church. Just as entertainment communicates a shared, communal experience, so worship communicates the communal experience of really sharing in Christ's body and the Holy Spirit's fellowship. Unfortunately, too often these structural parallels between entertainment and worship are treated as material equivalences, as if the power drawing us together were expectation of enjoyment, as if the reality that makes us one were sharing the same agreeable amusement rather than our experience of sharing in Christ.

Over the last hundred years, these confusions have only gotten worse as cultural changes affecting where and how we are entertained have profoundly impacted entertainment's *"who?"* To begin, over the course of the twentieth century, nearly all our entertainments became commercial in origin, which means they needed a large enough audience to pay the bills. Enter *mass media*, technologically sophisticated possibilities for dramatically extending the reach and scale of entertainments. Paradoxically, broadcast media aggregated ever larger audiences by isolating us from one another. First radio, then television, and now the World Wide Web have migrated entertainment's *public* from the social community to the domestic sphere, where further migration from living room to family room, kitchen, and finally bedroom indicate ongoing fragmentation, culminating in isolated audiences of one.[18] The drive toward mass audiences led to a "massification of society," in which local art forms and regional distinctives were overpowered by the drive to create a global audience for Coca Cola ads. Again, paradoxically, mass-mediated entertainments have now created *communities of affinity—fans—*whose bonds of unity are experienced and treated as more real, valid, and powerful than are the bonds of mutual presence (family), common activity (coworkers), and shared geography (neighbors). The capacity to record and distribute performances as repeatable entertainment

---

18. This latter migration represents a transition from family listening to generally segmented viewing, often while multitasking, to isolated entertainment consumption.

commodities (e.g., albums, DVDs, MP3s) along with appliances designed for privatized reception (transistor radio, Walkman, mobile media player, earbuds) has further valorized individual taste in ways that aggregate global audiences (markets) by isolating the entertained from bodily sociality. A final paradox: Web 2.0 and its much ballyhooed "social media" offer a technologically mediated solution to a problem that those same media helped create—the isolation of human bodies through the intervention of entertainment screens.

So in the midst of this massive cultural transformation the Christian church, called to gather around the One who is worthy of all adoration and praise, struggles to form a people willing and able to assemble bodily as Christ's body.

✤ *Do we believe that audience size is a measure of significance or value? Does participation in various entertainment audiences form us to ascribe worth—to worship—what isn't God? Do we feel or imagine a greater connection with those who share our entertainment tastes and habits than we do with the people of God around the world? Do you recognize the power of the three paradoxes of mass-mediated commercial entertainments: 1) entertainment creates larger audiences by extracting us from social settings, 2) it shapes a common culture of taste by eviscerating local bonds, and 3) it manufactures repeat business by alienating us from our bodies and each other?*

In describing entertainment theologically, this section has implicitly offered a "theological anthropology"—an account of our humanity as created by God. Each of the five dimensions of entertainment presented here is "very good" (to echo Gen 1:31), because each one is intrinsic to our destiny of fellowship with the triune God: hearts desiring happiness in God; eyes looking for God's true beauty; bodies playing toward heavenly freedom; temporality pulsing with eternity's rhythms; and sociality gathering us into God's triune life. These dimensions of human creatureliness are inherently good, but presently distorted and disordered by sin—in entertainment as in every other realm of human living. So engaging entertainment theologically will require from us a consistent dialectical movement of refusing all that diminishes or denies our true humanity, while affirming all that expresses and enhances it. That dialectic of saying "yes" and saying "no" is the focus of the next chapter.

two

No *Via Media* between Superpowers and Trivial Pursuits

TECHNOPHOBIC PROPHETS AND POP-CULTURE PRIESTS

MANY CHRISTIANS WHO ENGAGE with entertainment stand squarely in one of two opposing camps. There are critics on one side who believe, on the whole, that the entertainment industry is dangerous and that our practices of entertainment are damaging. The critics regularly catalog the problematic content, pervasive use, and pernicious effects of entertainment in order to indict it. For example, they claim that "Hollywood is smutty," "Facebook is addictive," or "Television breeds apathy." These critics sound like the prophets of old, warning against the encroachments of culture on the fidelity of God's people. While some of their criticisms may not be wrong, that doesn't mean their warnings are all that helpful. In the end, these critics can leave us lacking a thick enough theological understanding of entertainment to guide our faithful response.

On the other side stand the fans, eager exponents of a popular culture in which secular spiritual longings connect with traces of divine revelation. These proponents regularly laud the permeating spirituality, pervasive use, and positive effects of entertainment. Their work seems almost priestly, commending an "entertainment theology" to the faithful, and calling them to veneration at the altar of popular culture.[1] I think these priests of pop culture are wrong—wrong to give up on the elect people of God as the central medium through which God continues to reveal and redeem. But being wrong does not make them unimportant or unhelpful. In the end, they can offer us a deepened awareness of the power of mediated entertainment, and a closer look at its particular formations. In the end, a theological engagement with entertainment will require us to be neither doomsday prophets nor utopian priests of pop culture.

Of course, there are wise observers who try to find a balanced, middle way between the prophets and priests. Quentin Schultze is one. In *Communicating for Life*,[2] he offers the cautionary tale of David Puttnam. As a film producer, Puttnam succeeded in bringing *Chariots of Fire* to the silver screen, yet a few years later, as head of Columbia Pictures, Puttnam tried to reform the movie industry and got fired instead. This story leads to Shultze's effort to temper notions "that the latest medium is either going to save the world or doom it" (112–13). He warns that we should chart our course between *media idolatry* and *technophobia*.

Media idolatry is "a belief that the latest media can solve practically all of our social and individual problems" (118); it is part and parcel of the technological optimism that has attended the rise of modern science.[3] Americans have been especially eager to believe that we can discover salvation in a laboratory, engineer hope in the drawing room, and build a utopia—or at least its raw materials—in a high-tech factory. That kind of hope translates into hype about each new generation of entertainment technology; lately it's been BlueRay and now 3-D technologies, promising to transport us to a leisure Xanadu.

American Christians regularly transpose that optimism into a theological key. From the telegraph, through radio and television, to tweeting, Christians in the United States have trumpeted the arrival of the kingdom

---

1. This is my reading of Taylor, *Entertainment Theology*, and Detweiler and Taylor, *Matrix of Meanings*. Though the authors claim to be value neutral, merely showing us what is going on, in fact their books constitute an ongoing assertion that the primary locus of divine revelation has shifted from the church to popular culture. For an example of a theologically nuanced interpretation of pop spirituality that avoids hyperbole and resists credulousness, see Dark, *Everyday Apocalypse*.

2. Schultze, *Communicating for Life*, cited parenthetically through the rest of this section.

3. Albert Borgmann has recently suggested that technological optimism is the only kind of optimism we have left. *Power Failure*, 35.

of God on the wings of the latest communications technology. Here's a recent example: Live B.I.G., a multimedia Sunday school curriculum marketed by a denominational publishing house. Its promotional video looks like an episode of Barney minus the purple dinosaur.[4] Live B.I.G. promises that children will "come to know and love Jesus and want to live out their belief in God" and "develop faith that will last a lifetime." Making disciples is, of course, an utterly worthy goal. But remembering Kallestad's entertainment evangelism lesson (see chapter 1), we should immediately see that handing disciple-making over to entertainment is more likely to produce kids who like to watch Live B.I.G. than kids who like to follow Jesus.

The media idolatry is evident in the promise that Live B.I.G. "reaches your children with *cutting-edge teaching tools*" like "cool music" videos and "*DVD-enhanced*" story time (emphasis added). Schultze helps us notice the media idolatry implicit in claims that successful Christian formation is guaranteed by using the right communications technology. The technologies we idolize never live up to the hype (119), but instead of curing us, using these technologies continually leads us to project our hope onto the next new thing.

✢ *Has your church been tempted to media or entertainment idolatry? How did/will you resist? Has your church exhibited technophobia? How did/will you respond?*

Besides his historical claim that the kingdom of God does not arrive on the wings of media technology, Schultze makes a second point: we and our media inhabit "a sinful world with broken institutions" (119). That claim ought to lead him to discuss media institutions as powers and principalities that seek to captivate our gaze, colonize our imaginations, and capture our allegiance. In other words, besides our tendency to idolize media technologies, there is also the tendency of those powers to divinize themselves—to elicit loyalty, trust, and hope that transgress proper limits. Because Schultze does not adequately develop that argument,[5] I will do so in the next section.

---

4. Protestants aren't the only Christians prone to media idolatry (though there is probably some correlation between infrequency of mediated sacramental encounters with Christ and anxiety for culturally "relevant" mediations of grace). A Catholic priest in the United States was disciplined for presiding over a children's mass while wearing a Barney the Dinosaur suit.

5. There are five mentions of powers and principalities in the index, and Schultze gives two pages to the topic in a prior chapter, where he refers to the work of William Stringfellow.

At the opposite end of the spectrum from media idolatry is technophobia, an unwarranted fear of technology, in this case media technology. The problem with the label is that it easily overreaches, preventing discerning judgments about analyses and criticisms of technology. Once the term *technophobia* is deployed (along with its first cousin, *Luddism*), it will always lurk in the background, ready to sweep aside reasoned argument and nuanced analysis with a dismissive bit of polysyllabic name-calling. One doesn't even have to care enough to utter a sentence, let alone mount a truthful argument. Crying "Luddite" will end thinking as we know it. In this regard, Sherry Turkle offers wise counsel: "We have to love our technology enough to describe it accurately. And we have to love ourselves enough to confront technology's true effects on us."[6]

Schultze spends less time criticizing the technophobes, but he makes similar arguments—one historical and the other theological. Historically, the apocalyptic fears held by technophobes like Malcolm Muggeridge and Neil Postman have not come true. Technological media have done good things for us and will continue to do so, Schultze suggests. So technophobia "obscures the ways that God works through even unrefined technologies to bring grace and peace to humankind. Just as our communities can fall prey to the latest media fads, they can unnecessarily rue every new technology as the possible end of civilization" (120).

Again, Schultze's point is well taken. I'm pleased to receive my former pastor's newsletter column via email each week, saving paper and postage while keeping me in a very modest form of communicative relationship with someone I love. More to the point of this book, I'm impressed by the documentary-style video podcasts being produced by some youth missions organizations. Far from undermining zeal for servant ministry, they seem to be focusing it, perhaps even eliciting it.

Schultze's second reason for refusing technophobia is theological. He writes:

> Although we often think of the media as mere sources of entertainment, they are really extensions of our God-given ability to cocreate culture. In spite of their limitations, the media are potential resources to help us serve our neighbor by telling the truth and building communities of shalom. (121)

6. Turkle, *Alone Together*, 243.

Schultze believes that the communicative power of mass media is an embodiment of human creation in the image of God (see 18–19), and an opportunity to practice loving stewardship toward our neighbors. Again, true enough. Yet in focusing on media's power to accomplish good, Schultze risks a kind of works righteousness that justifies media through the good that it accomplishes. When he contrasts media as cocreated culture with "mere entertainment," he misses the significance of insignificance, the grace of doing nothing all that important. I'll say more about this in the final section.

Schultze helps us recognize that mass-mediated entertainment tempts us to false hopes (media idolatry) and false fears (technophobia). He means both to chasten us in the good we expect media to accomplish, and to encourage us to use it for good. He calls for us to steer a middle course between extremes—he commends to us what might be called the virtue of media temperance. The problem with this form of temperance, however, is that it fails to adequately reckon with the truth of two apparently contradictory extremes—namely, the power and triviality of entertainment.

✣   *Have you been influenced by the entertainment prophets and priests? Are you more likely to decry the spiritual dangers of entertainment, or to acclaim its spiritual power?*

OMNI-ENTERTAINMENT?

If being divine primarily meant being always and everywhere all-powerful, then entertainment has taken on godlike qualities in contemporary American culture. (Happily, being divine primarily means being the effulgent triune love who creates and redeems.) Specifically, entertainment is nearly omnipresent and omnipotent these days.

A traditional biblical trope for omnipresence is the psalmist's rhetorical question, "Where can I go from your spirit? Or where can I flee from your presence?" (Ps 139:7). The psalmist goes on to aver that whether she goes up to heaven or down to Sheol or out to the "farthest limits of the sea," God is present in all these places. If we use a similar question, the near-ubiquity of entertainment stands revealed. Where could I go to flee from the presence of entertainment? Not the heavens, for when I soar there United Airlines provides me with magazines and in-flight music and movies. Not the depths, for when I plunge there in the subway the newspaper precedes me, radio broadcasts follow me, and my personal entertainment devices—novel, Gameboy, portable DVD, laptop, MP3 player, cell phone games—accompany me. Not even beyond the settled limits of the world, for when my children work at camp in the Upper Peninsula of Michigan, even there an entertainment embargo requires the careful confiscation of two or more electronic devices per camper. All the spaces of our lives have been filled with entertaining possibilities—television waits for me not just in the living room, kitchen, bedroom, and garage, but at the school cafeteria, the gym, the hotel elevator, the grocery store checkout line, and the gas station pump; radio finds me not just in the house (including the bathroom), but in the car and the office, on the bike or the mountaintop, at the beach or the ballpark.

Concomitant with inhabiting our space is a ubiquitous filling of our time by entertainment. Mediated entertainment is now available 24/7, so that the old hawker's line "it's showtime" now means not some specific moment but all the time. Objectively, we can trace the history of media availability from cyclical to continuous distribution and accessibility. Broadcast media (radio and television) moved from partial to whole-day programming (so unlike me, my son never stared at color tuning bars on Saturday morning waiting for the first cartoon to appear). Print media (magazines, newspapers, and even books) have developed corresponding Web sites where text is continually added or updated. Movies, which had been limited by release date and projection run, are now constantly available in a variety of physical and electronic formats. The Internet has nearly completed entertainment's trajectory toward ubiquity, making entertainment available always and everywhere, transcending both space and time. And nothing demonstrates the objective omnipresence of entertainment more than ads, which have become "ubiquitious, round-the-clock backgrounds to our daily lives."[7]

---

7. Budde, *(Magic) Kingdom*, 38.

And Now a Word from Our Sponsors

Advertising is everywhere. Visa made a virtue of that for twenty years, with its slogan "It's Everywhere You Want to Be" (the new slogan is "Life Takes Visa"). Whether we want it to be there or not, advertising is everywhere we are. A typical hour of radio has fifteen minutes of commercials.[8] A normal day exposes us to an estimated "16,000 commercial messages, symbols, and reminders."[9] An average year of watching television includes 38,000-plus commercials.[10] If a quarter of the typical broadcast hour is ads, they comprise half of most magazines and 65 percent of a typical newspaper.[11] Craig Detweiler and Barry Taylor call advertising "the air that we breathe,"[12] a metaphor intended to communicate both the pervasiveness and the taken-for-grantedness of advertising. So our lives become supersaturated with advertisements, a phenomenon that industry analysts call "clutter." There are so many messages that we pay less and less attention, which means that advertisers must try even harder to draw us in. So they make their ads and commercials and jingles and mascots as entertaining as possible. And they're not afraid to shout to be heard.

Subjectively, entertainment powerfully shapes our imagination in multiple ways. Most people—Christians included—take it for granted that they should own the appliances and subscribe to the services that make ubiquitous, on-demand entertainment really present. William Romanowski reports on Barna Group research that shows that Christians and the general population have about the same rate of access to media entertainments.[13] One of my favorite illustrations of how entertainment permeates our subjectivity is Rodney Clapp's comparison of late medieval English culture with

8. Rodman, *Making Sense of Media*, 304.

9. Budde, *(Magic) Kingdom*, 38. This includes everything from the hood ornaments on our cars to the logos on our computers and clothing, from the print, broadcast, and online ads to the giant television billboards that increasingly line our streets.

10. Rodman, *Making Sense of Media*, 319. Detweiler and Taylor, *Matrix of Meaning*, 61, place the total at forty thousand.

11. Rodman, *Making Sense of Media*, 304.

12. Detweiler and Taylor, *Matrix of Meaning*, 61.

13. ". . . almost three quarters of Americans subscribe to cable TV; just over one quarter have a satellite dish. Ninety-three percent of Americans own a VCR and 59 percent have Internet access." Romanowski, *Eyes Wide Open*, 39.

ours. In that bygone era, Clapp notes, one "could hardly make it through a waking hour of the day without encountering living manifestations of the Christian tradition."[14] Today we can pass many an hour, if not days on end, without the church's presence being obvious. Not so with the myth of romantic love, which so permeates our ubiquitous entertainments that it is being broadcast "around the clock. Escaping it would mean never turning on the television, watching a movie,"[15] seeing a billboard, surfing the Internet, listening to the radio, reading a magazine, newspaper, or novel.

So looking at the times and places of our lives, it can certainly appear as if what "fills all in all" (Eph 1:23) is not the risen Christ, but entertainment. Less obvious is my claim that entertainment is nearly all-powerful.[16] Rather than cite statistics of economic clout (a $480 billion industry) or measures of imaginative force (Mickey Mouse as global icon), I offer one small anecdote. At the beginning of a school year, I was purchasing a graphing calculator for my daughter's use in a precalculus class. With two Texas Instruments models of the same name in hand, I asked the clerk why one cost more than the other. "Oh, that one comes with games installed," she replied. Her taken-for-granted notion that it is normal for a mathematical calculator to have video games installed is an indication of the power of entertainment to capture and transform virtually every facet of our lives into amusement. For the past ninety years or so, entertainment has been aggressively colonizing our habitats, homes, vehicles, tools, bodies, schedules, and, most crucially, our habits and imaginations. Entertainment is normalized and habituated. We take it for granted that we swim in an entertainment-saturated world, that entertainments will surround us and beckon us. Correlated with this normalization is habituation, the fact that participating in mediated entertainments trains us to continue participating. We may change channels or switch media devices; we may even migrate from movies and television to video gaming and virtual worlds.

---

14. Clapp, *Border Crossings*, 119.

15. Ibid.

16. Here I will not try to make a case for how entertainment is an unstoppable force or irresistible power. For such a claim, Neal Gabler's *Life the Movie* is a good read; it expounds American history as the story of "how entertainment conquered reality." More important is Michael Budde's *The (Magic) Kingdom of God*, which argues that the global culture industries—which "account for the vast majority of the world's output of shared images, stories, songs, information, news, entertainment, and the like"—have become the most powerful cultural force in the world today. Budde, *(Magic) Kingdom*, 14.

What we won't do, almost certainly, is unplug ourselves from our mediated entertainments.

REBELLIOUS POWER!

In this regard, entertainment can be counted as one of the "principalities and powers" that exist in opposition to God. Defining the principalities and powers is notoriously difficult, but most contemporary interpreters agree that they include structures, dynamics, and institutions that are meant for God's glory and our good. They are created to give, sustain, and enrich life. In our fallen world, however, the powers regularly transgress their servant role in two crucial dimensions. They turn away from God, becoming self-referential and self-aggrandizing. They turn away from serving our good, and instead they deceive, seduce, or force us into glorifying and serving them. For our part, we are often willing accomplices in the powers' rebellion, living as if they are neither fallen nor finite but absolutely good and truly ultimate. So as the powers actively enslave us, we just as willingly submit to them, an unholy dialectic so resilient that only the cross of Jesus Christ could conquer it.

In my description of the powers I have used the language of personal agency—the powers give and serve, transgress and rebel, deceive and demand—without taking a position on their exact metaphysical status. This is because for my analysis here it makes no significant difference whether one thinks of the powers as actual personal entities, or as social structures that exhibit quasi-personal behaviors. Either way a power is far more than the sum total of its parts. A power's agency is always more than the amalgamation of its individual human actors. A power's fallenness, its capacity for and achievement of evil, is greater than the sum total of the human sinners involved. A power's resistance to grace continually exceeds the resistance of its individual participants. This means that we can expect to find a power's rebellion at work not only in the worst things it does but also in the best. It also means that we cannot expect to redeem a power by taking control of it, or by staffing it with more faithful Christians. Rather, our response to the powers is dialectical: we resist their seductive rebellions while respecting their identity as good creations; we refuse their pretensions to ultimacy while affirming their subordinate role in Christ's triumph; we reject the temptation to hope *in* their power for good while patiently hoping *for* their renewal.

Mass-mediated entertainment is obviously among the powers and principalities. On the one hand, it serves real, though limited, goods. There is a real sense in which entertainment can enrich our lives by providing us pleasure and enjoyment, beneficial rhythms, excellence worth attending to, forms of belonging, and freedom to play (see chapter 1). On the other hand, entertainment exists in constant rebellion against its properly subordinate role; indeed, the very nature of modern entertainment seems to be its constant pretension to be more important than it is, and its incessant demand that we order our lives around it. There may be more basic principalities—government, economy, and medicine come to mind—but in the shifting ecology of contemporary life, there are no powers more shiny and seductive than entertainment. Considered as a power, then, the most worrisome feature of entertainment is not its increasingly questionable content. There is a place for concern about numbing violence, demeaning sex, and empty materialism; there is a need for objection to amusements that are increasingly banal, ugly, and false. But the central concern is larger and deeper than that; it is the way entertainment regularly glorifies itself rather than the Creator,[17] the way it morphs limited goods into utter necessities, the way it incessantly demands more from us—more money, more time, more attention, more commitment.

✢ *Assess the power of this power in your life. Which of your regular entertainments (if any) draw you deeper into entertainment, and which draw you out toward neighbor, creation, or Creator? Which of your entertainment appliances could you give away tomorrow, and which do you feel you could not live without?*

In the face of such pressures and pretensions toward ultimacy, we cannot inhabit some temperate middle ground between the critics' refusal and the cheerleaders' enthrallment. Because mass media are a fallen power, the *via media* (middle way of moderation) is a dead end. There is no such thing as a balanced diet of idolatry! Instead, we are called to a more dialectical response, doing two things at the same time. One is to name entertainment as a principality, to refuse its quest for primacy in our lives, and to resist its seductive power. The other is to name entertainment as a *triviality*, and therefore intentionally to enjoy its freeing possibilities.

17. Two examples of this: the myriad self-congratulatory awards events (Oscars, Emmys, Grammys, Tonys, Clios, etc.), and the hyper-self-referentiality of entertainment content (movies about movies, musicians, or athletes; songs about songs, stars, or shows; etc.).

TAKING TIME FOR THE TRIVIAL

Quentin Schultze says that information and communication technologies can divert our "attention from the central concerns of life . . . to *relatively trivial pursuits* with little enduring value."[18] His claim echoes nineteenth-century Protestant leaders, who called "relaxation, play, amusement and idle time . . . 'diversions,' reflecting the belief that they 'divert' people from the higher tasks of life associated with work and piety."[19] If all that is true, if entertainment is diverting and trivial, then let the people say "Amen!" and "Thank God!"

I conclude this chapter with the counterintuitive claim that entertainment is trivial, or at least that we should learn to see and consume it as such. Yes, it appears to dominate our landscape and mindscape. But rather than conclude that this makes it a determining force in our lives, we would do better to remember that as creatures of the living God it is God who gives us all that we need, and God in Christ who secures our future. Thus we are not required to square off against the principality of entertainment in order to control or redeem it; the future of goodness, truth, and beauty does not depend on our grasping Hollywood by the director's seat and steering it toward the kingdom of God. In the meantime, God gives us trivial pursuits that free us from false claims to ultimacy.

I find an essay by Stanley Hauerwas extremely helpful in this regard. In "Taking Time for Peace," written nearly thirty years ago, Hauerwas took note of the way a threat like nuclear holocaust or an injustice like the Vietnam War could come to wield a totalitarian dominance over our lives. (If he were writing today, he might note the same totalitarian possibility in our fear of terrorism or of Hollywood.) Without denying that these are problems that require a response, Hauerwas insists that we notice how frequently discussion of these problems suggests that the problem now determines our entire life. Recognizing the problem and taking it seriously is said to require that every aspect of our life, every action we undertake or

---

18. Schultze, *High-Tech Heart*, 13, emphasis added.

19. Romanowski, *Pop Culture Wars*, 43. If you pay attention to the loaded adjectives we use with entertainments, they seem to fall into two groups. One group is evaluations of specific entertainments: the *best* movie of the summer, the *worst* episode ever, my *favorite* song, etc. The other group modifies entertainment as a whole, and this group is almost always demeaning and diminishing: *trivial, frivolous, escapist*, etc. These disparaging adjectives find powerful partners in a series of nouns, the most important of which is probably *diversion*.

forego, be determined by the problem. If political totalitarianism originally meant a loyalty to the state so severe that "there are, or there should be, no indifferent actions,"[20] this threat-of-the-moment totalitarianism (be it the bomb, the war, or Hollywood) similarly claims our whole life for opposition. We are given the imperative to resist in everything we think, do, and are; our whole life is claimed.

The power of Hauerwas's analysis is that he notices how this totalitarian impulse robs us of the goodness of the ordinary, the insignificant, irrelevant, unimportant, and altogether common places of our lives. Totalitarianism takes from us the grace and freedom of time for the trivial. Yet permission to spend time in trivial pursuits is something we need desperately. We need areas of our lives that are not fraught with ultimacy; we need activities that are not supposed to make a difference; we need permission and opportunity to waste time. What we need is precisely what God gives: "time to enjoy the trivial" (257). When we "take time to enjoy a walk with a friend, to read all of Trollope's novels, to maintain universities, to have and care for children, and most importantly to worship God" (257), we are living in ways that reclaim life from totalitarianism precisely by recognizing life—and especially time—as God's good gift. Taking time for these activities becomes a way to embody God's peace in a violent world.

Does any of this apply to entertainment? Hauerwas does not directly engage that question. None of his examples of taking time for the trivial involves our common forms of mass-mediated entertainment. The two entertainments he mentions are reading novels and watching baseball, and it may be telling that he affirms reading all of Trollope's novels and going to the ball game (and eating a Polish sausage there). Moreover, he says that properly trivial activities have to be more than just stopping to smell the roses; they should "give us a sense of worth, a sense of making a contribution which enriches our own life and those of other people" (259). Clearly there is no sense of "making a contribution" in the passive form of many contemporary entertainments. So the central trivial pursuits that Hauerwas is recommending here are not entertainments, and may well be the kinds of activities—like cooking and enjoying a meal—that entertainment nowadays diminishes or displaces.

Nevertheless, I believe that at least four aspects of Hauerwas's analysis are helpful in recognizing the properly trivial place of entertainment in our

---

20. Hauerwas, *Christian Existence Today*, 255, subsequent references given parenthetically.

lives. First, entertainment is everyday, common, ordinary. It is trivial, not in the sense of being utterly insignificant or trifling, but as the kind of thing you can find anywhere and everywhere. Enjoying entertainment, therefore, is an affirmation that all of life is God's good gift to us, and that our salvation is not from the world, but in it.

Second, entertainment is impotent; it cannot save the world (even if, as a rebellious power, it too often implies that it can). Enjoying entertainment, therefore, is an affirmation that Christ has freed us from the tyranny of making the world come out right. We have permission, occasionally, to waste time and make no difference at all.

✣ *In fact, for most of us, wasting time occasionally is a daily matter. Does daily, habitual entertainment express graced freedom or obligation?*

Third, entertainment can be a good time; it can bring us pleasure, sometimes even exhilaration. Enjoying entertainment, therefore, is an affirmation that even in the midst of suffering and pain, God gives us laughter, pleasures, and joy. I like the way the authors of *Dancing in the Dark* put it: "At perhaps its most minimal level, . . . popular entertainment prompts a simple relishing of the sensuous goodness of life. The gift of feeling good about being alive is no small present—nor is its acceptance a trifling thing."[21]

Finally, entertainment takes time; it has duration, pace, boundary, and rhythm. The quality of time varies incredibly from one entertainment to another; witness the difference in duration between a pop song and a symphony, or the difference in pace between baseball and basketball, or the fixed length of a sitcom versus the unbounded play of online gaming, or the patterns of recurrence in going to the movies or clubbing or watching *The Simpsons*. In all its variations, entertainment takes time and reshapes time into something different from and better than the monotonous ticking of the clock. Enjoying entertainment, therefore, can remind us that we have time in abundance as God's good gift, and that we have times—various moments and seasons—for all the goods of human living: for rest and work, for care and play, for receiving and achieving.

This chapter has suggested that it is just as dangerous to make entertainment the ultimate source of our hope as it is to make it the ultimate object of our fears. The path forward, however, is not a *via media* between these two extremes. Instead, I have suggested a more dialectical

---

21. Schultze et al., *Dancing in the Dark*, 267.

approach—both resistance to entertainment as a principality, and embrace of entertainment as a triviality. Such a dialectical engagement is tricky to practice. It will more closely resemble ever-changing tactics than settled strategy. It will enact the logic of both Lent and Easter, the rhythms of both feasting and fasting. Refusing "always" and "never," it will enact the freedom of Christ's resurrection by sometimes enjoying and sometimes eschewing entertainments.

three

iPod: Our Song Gone Wrong?

♪♪ This chapter may make more sense if you put your earbuds in and turn your iPod on, because I'm writing from the Podzone. I'll keep you informed. ♪♪

IN JULY 2004, NEWSWEEK ran a cover story titled "iPod Nation," declaring that "in just three years, Apple's adorable mini music player has gone from gizmo to life-changing cultural icon."[1] That sounds over the top to Christian ears, since our eyes are trained to see crosses or crucifixes or real icons as the true images of life-change. Yet considering how we immediately "get" words like iGeneration and poddict, *Newsweek's* claim may not be iPerbole after all. The iPod is an iCon of cultural change. This chapter engages the iPhenomenon by using four key words from *Newsweek's* caption: *icon, gizmo, player,* and *life-changing.* We'll see that the iPod is an icon of musical identity and transcendent interiority, a gizmo that commodifies music and denies limits, a player that usurps our present communal singing, and a life-changing habit that sounds better than it is.

♪♪ Sorry, I had to pause a moment to drum along with the amazing intro to Boston's "Long Time." Back to work. ♪♪

1. Levy, "iPod Nation."

iPOD AS ICON

Newsweek wasn't the first magazine to call the iPod an icon. The thirty-fifth anniversary edition of *Rolling Stone* had dozens of tributes to "American Icons"—people, inventions, and images that "make such a profound human connection it is impossible to imagine what life was like without them." Most of the icons were drawn from the world of entertainment, and many of the authors were entertainers themselves. Martin Scorsese wrote on the leading man, Courtney Love on the Blonde Bombshell, and Dale Earnhardt Jr. on the Corvette.

✛ *What does it say about our cultural landscape that most of the "icons" that populate popular imagination are rooted in entertainment? Is entertainment becoming the vernacular language even of the church?*

Though the iPod was barely nineteenth months old, *Rolling Stone* was already claiming that "it has changed how we listen to music."[2] Whether the iPod is the source of that change or just its symbol, white earbuds have certainly become iconic of two things: musical identity and interiority.

The iPod is an *iCon of musical iDentity*. Researcher Michael Bull regularly hears iPod users say, "I feel incomplete without it" and "I don't go anywhere without it."[3] Clearly, the iPod has attached iTself to personal iDenity more firmly than my earbuds stick to my ears. Why? Partly because it combines the coolness of a hip personal electronic device with the uniqueness of one's personal musical taste. We've been subtly trained by advertising to weave our purchases into our personality, and lately the ads have been telling us that personal electronic gadgets are fundamental to a person's sense of self, if not self-worth. We also self-identify through music, the styles and artists and songs we like. Each person's music "collection" becomes a unique marker of who she is. So as the personal electronic device that stores your entire music collection, the iPod "becomes the most personal of personal devices. More than a computer, a car, or a fancy pair of shoes, it's part of your makeup, your personality. What's on it—the music—tells you who you are."[4]

---

2. *Rolling Stone*, May 15, 2003, 113.

3. Bull, *Sound Moves*.

4. Kahney, *Cult of iPod*, 3.

But there is more to the relation of music and identity than our proclivity to self-define through the latest gadget and our favorite songs. In popular culture, we express and perform personal identity through music. Tia DeNora calls music a "technology of the self,"[5] because we actively use it as "a means for creating, enhancing, sustaining and changing subjective, cognitive, bodily and self-conceptual states."[6] I play certain songs to cheer up, others to concentrate, and different ones for workout versus work.

♪♪ Jack Johnson's "Bubble Toes" makes my fingers dance happily on the keyboard. ♪♪

The iPod becomes the perfect musical technology of the self, because it both requires and empowers us to create, monitor, and modulate our "musical self." I create my musical identity on the front end by consciously deciding which songs to load. I can also create "playlists" for various activities or moods. I then monitor and modulate my ongoing identity by continuous negotiations with the machine: *I choose* whether *I want* to hear this song, whether *I feel* like that playlist, whether *my mood* is better served by shuffle, genius, or full control. Thus, I am continuously assessing, constructing, and expressing my identity through engagement with my iPod. (Notice, by the way, that I'm probably not praying.)

So the iPod is an iCon of iDentity, raising some important questions for Christians whose fundamental identity is received in baptism, constructed and expressed in practices of discipleship. Let's take it to church for a moment. Over the past three decades, many American congregations have experienced considerable conflict around musical selection and style in worship. They have often found it difficult to engage that conflict in illuminating ways. It seems likely that both the severity and the intractability of these conflicts are rooted in the ways that musical entertainments (first radio and records, then Walkman and cassettes, now iPods and iTunes) have become part of our identity and subjectivity.

✣ *How important are your entertainment devices and preferences to your self-image and self-understanding? Does your musical identity enhance or diminish your identification with Christ's body, the church? How regularly do you use an iPod (or another musical technology) to shape your thoughts, mood, or behavior? Does*

5. Chapter 3 of DeNora, *Music in Everyday Life.*

6. DeNora, *Music in Everyday Life*, 49.

> *that use displace Christian practices of prayer and other spiritual*
> *disciplines?*

The iPod is also an *iCon of musical iNteriority*. Part of the beauty and power of music, and of other entertainments too, is this capacity to effect moments of transcendence, of euphoria or pathos or tranquility or joy. Before the advent of personal electronic devices, such moments were usually shared social events. The iPod allows them to become inner personal experiences.

Another Word from Our Sponsors

iPod ads are distinctive, memorable, and highly entertaining: great music accompanies dancing black silhouettes wearing white earbuds in a field of bold color. Erik Jenkins has analyzed iPod ads from the perspective of the theology of iconography, the Eastern Orthodox tradition of visual images that connect believers to God and the communion of saints. Jenkins suggests that in its signature silhouette commercials, the iPod becomes an icon of "the experience of immersion in music."[7] In the ads "the dancing, the rhythmic music, the headphones, and the neon backdrop all reference the experience of immersion in music."[8] Watching *and hearing* the commercials becomes a brief simulation of watching oneself immersed in music.[9] The neon backdrop of the ads makes it clear that the focus is not the context or environment where the iPod is used; we have literally no idea where the podster is, and it doesn't really matter, since the locus of this transcendent musical experience lies between the earbuds. Moreover, the ad is constructed to invite me to imagine myself as the podster: "the emptiness of the silhouettes allows the viewer to more easily identify with and project themselves into the image."[10] Of course, that silhouetted podster dances like I never could, but that is also the point. Apple isn't suggesting that iPods confer magical powers of physical grace and dancing prowess;

7. Jenkins, "My iPod, My iCon," 476.

8. Ibid., 477.

9. Jenkins is not as clear as I am being that this is about watching oneself. In fact, he suggests that what the ads simulate is "the experience of the world through headphones" (ibid., 477). And yet, the ads do not look out on the world through our eyes; rather, the ads look "inside" our sonic experience, evoking the freedom, authenticity, and joy that "immersion in music" promises.

10. Ibid., 482.

rather, the magic is the musical experience. That makes the extraordinary jumps, twists, flips, and spins iconic of the iPod's spiritual promise. Don the 'buds, click the wheel, give yourself over to the music, and you will leap for joy—inwardly.

Jenkins's point is more than the claim that music connects with our spirit, moves us, achieves transcendence. It is that the iPod (and similar devices) mobilize and interiorize transcendence so that it is no longer public, interpersonal, or even spatial. Musical sound conveyed through earbuds creates a sense of enclosure, a feeling that music is being delivered "inside" the boundaries of my body. The music becomes a canopy or shell that complements the physical surface of my body and the socially prescribed boundaries of my personal space. I am "within" my music. Of course, external ambient sound continues to intrude. But we experience these sounds as penetrating from the outside in, as alien, as needing to be excluded.

Unfortunately, the transcendence that the iPod promises can be entirely world-denying, other-ignoring, God-avoiding, precisely because it is sought and sensed within. Equally unfortunate, the regular experience of transcendent musical interiority can habituate us to overvalue subjective emotion.

Again, let's take it to church for a moment. Where in worship do you feel closest to God? John Witvliet has suggested that whereas Catholics and Episcopalians have normally experienced the eucharistic table as their deepest intimacy with God, and Protestants have felt similarly about the reading and preaching of Scripture, lately a number of Christians are experiencing that intimacy most profoundly in and through the church's music.[11] Perhaps this has less to do with where music fits within God's saving plan and more to do with where it fits in our culturally mediated practices of entertainment. The practice of listening to music on my iPod invites and trains me to expect that the most important moments in life come with or through a soundtrack and are personal, inner experiences that soothe, stir, and in other ways shape my own subjectivity.

So the iPod is an iCon of transcendent interiority, raising some important questions for Christians, whose central experience of divine transcendence ought to come through the embodied practices of corporate worship.

11. See Ruth, "Rose by Another Name," 48–50.

✣ *Is your typical practice of musical entertainment a private, interior experience or a communal sharing? Does your typical practice of musical entertainment turn you inward or draw you out of yourself? How does your practice of musical entertainment impact your understanding of and participation in corporate worship as Christ's church?*

GIZMOS REWIRE LIFE

♫ American Airlines just e-mailed me the joyous news that they have a free app for my iPhone that is "perfect for flying through airports." Suddenly my nano looks pretty antiquated and anemic; I grieve not owning an iPhone. Thank goodness Guns N' Roses is singing "Don't Cry" in my earbuds. ♫

The iPod has been lovingly described as a gizmo and a gadget.[12] Innocuous words like these suggest that it is relatively harmless, insignificant, and fun. This section will draw on the work of Albert Borgmann to show that iPods embody the significance of technologically mediated entertainment. It will then ask whether these gizmos are all fun and no harm.

Borgmann is a philosopher of technology who shows us what technology promises, and how it shapes the way we hope, think, and live. The basic promise of technology is to work on our behalf to liberate and enrich us. My furnace liberates me from cutting wood or digging peat, and it enriches me with abundant warmth. Likewise, my stereo "makes music" for me, freeing me from the labor of practicing the saxophone to make my own music, and enriching me with music of the tuba and tambourine.

All of this has a certain logic, which Borgmann calls the "device paradigm." We shop and live, and engineers design and build, from within this largely invisible mindset that technology ought to make us continually freer and richer by purveying commodities instantaneously, extensively, reliably, and easily. The device paradigm imagines a world free of the drudgery of manual labor, free of bodily limits, free of the constraints of time and place, free of the contingencies of circumstance. The device paradigm imagines a world in which we are continually richer in things, experiences, and opportunities, all available with less effort, less cost, less practice, less waiting.

12. Its trademarked name is "mobile musical device."

✣ *How many entertainment devices do you own? How often have you upgraded an entertainment device because it promised to increase the freedom, abundance, or availability of entertainment?*

Enter the iPod, a tiny stereo on steroids. This gadget liberates by being utterly mobile; climbers tote it up Everest, and astronauts shuffle in freefall. This gizmo enriches by making a superabundance of music (and videos and games and . . .) available almost instantly and continually. The iPod is emblematic of the device paradigm, each new version promising to make us freer and richer than the one before.

It is not technophobic to ask whether this gizmo, for all its wonder, may in some ways ensnare us even while it liberates, or impoverish us even as it enriches. While recording technology blesses us with a superabundance of recorded music, it also transforms music from a situated event to a contextless commodity. And while musical reproduction technology liberates us from the necessity of making our own music, it can also habituate us to disregard what truly matters.

First, musical devices enrich but also impoverish. There is no doubt that sound transmission and recording technologies have enriched us musically. We now have access to more music from more cultures encompassing a greater variety of genre, instrumentation, and style than our forebears could have imagined. I've heard Christmas masses from St. Peter's Basilica, folk music recorded during the Great Depression, Dizzy play and Ella scat and the Beatles sing.

But there is a subtle transformation that accompanies this abundance: music becomes more of a thing than a happening. Our primary experience of music has gone from a performative event in which we participate, to a commodity we consume and manipulate at will. So music as we typically experience it is cut off from its original production, context, and circumstance, separated from its original makers, purpose, and meaning, a reproduction ready to be re-tasked for whatever moment, meaning, or use we devise. The price of our musical enrichment is that ". . . music has become a disembodied, free-floating something. . . ."[13] We are richer in musical recordings, but poorer in musical relationship.

13. Borgmann, *Power Failure*, 31.

♪♪ Ah, here's "Sunday, Bloody Sunday" by U2. I've heard this song about a million times! Most of those times, I had no knowledge or awareness of this song's origin in and challenge to "the Troubles" in Ireland. Actually, I liked it for several years without even knowing who U2 was. ♪♪

Second, technology's liberating power too easily disengages us from what really matters. We design our devices to overcome the limits of time and space, and especially to increase control and choice.[14] That is why iPods are truly iconic as technological devices: utterly portable, they are the anytime, anywhere magic wands of musical entertainment.[15] Borgmann uses the phrase "regardless power" to name the technologically given capacity "to procure a result regardless of the recalcitrance or variety of circumstances. . . . Switches, keys, pointers, buttons, and dials are the insignia of this inconspicuous and consequential power through which we summon up, regardless of time, place, skill, or strength, whatever we need or desire."[16]

✤ *What devices do you regularly use that manifest "regardless power"?*

Technology promises this kind of regardless power, offering us an endless procession of "magic wands" that provide an infinite stream of the commodities, products, experiences, and outcomes that we desire. And we become so habituated to the exercise of regardless power that we expect to exercise it everywhere and all the time.

The iPod is a freeing device because it maximizes regardless power. Earphones ensure musical entertainment regardless of the sonic environment or the musical preferences of those around us.[17] The click wheel instantly procures the music I want anywhere, anytime, regardless of the contingencies of circumstance.[18] The regardless power of the iPod promises near total control. No annoying DJs, commercials, playlists, or tests of

14. Ibid., 43.

15. "Magic phone" is what our friend Christine calls her iPhone, with its thousands of apps for reshaping the world. Bull notes that "technology, precisely in its miniaturization . . . acquires a magical quality." *Sound Moves*, 3.

16. Borgmann, *Power Failure*, 88.

17. Ibid., 88–89.

18. In the development of the iPod, Steve Jobs was particularly adamant about the speed of the menu system and the click wheel. Now, the touch screen interface of the iPhone and iTouch are an even greater kind of regardless power, as advertisements show persons shaping virtual reality with an effortless, magical flip of their finger.

the emergency broadcast system. No limits on storage, selection, sequence, location, or timing. No awkward conversations with strangers on the train, no intrusion of ambient sound while I run, no meaningful eye contact with the beggar on the corner. Just total control—all provided by the regardless power of my iPod.[19] All this control brings an exhilarating sense of freedom.

♪♪ I skip "Welcome to the Jungle." Nano shuffles me "Stairway to Heaven." That's so much better. What a curious juxtaposition is "jungle" and "heaven." Who sings "Welcome to the Jungle"? Push the back button. Oh, it's Guns N' Roses. Forward to "Stairway." Ahh, that's nice: great music, *total control*, I'm in heaven! ♪♪

But there is a problem with too much regardless power: using it continually can habituate us to disregard. The regardless power of the iPod can diminish our regard for creation's goodness or our neighbor's good, our regard for the circumstance, stranger, even God that we daily encounter. I'll say more about that below under "podding." Here, notice how the regardless power of technology invites us to disregard limits. Because technology continually transcends and overcomes the limits of our finitude, it can seduce us into imagining that true freedom is life without limit, rather than life within human limits. I am suggesting that the ultimate logic of technology tempts us toward inhumanity. That's the kind of apocalyptic claim that might have a place in a discussion of bioengineering, but seems radically exaggerated if applied to an entertainment gizmo like the iPod. Except that coming to terms with our finitude is a primary school for developing key virtues like prudence, temperance, and patience. The regardless power of my iPod (and my cell phone and my Netflix subscription and all the rest) invites me to habitually ignore the limits where God's love waits to make me whole.

✣ *Does the regardless power of the iPod (or TiVo or streaming media) seduce you into forgetting your finitude, thereby short-circuiting the formation of virtue?*

If it does, don't think I'm suggesting you throw your iPod away. (If you do, please tell me which dumpster it's in!) I would suggest that instead of

19. Michael Bull, who has done extensive research on iPod use, says, "it's a generalization, but the main use [of the iPod] is control. People like to be in control. They are controlling their space, their time, and their interaction. . . ." (cited in Kahney, *Cult of iPod*, 26).

an iPod purge or embargo, we need to be more prudent about when and where we won't 'bud up, more temperate about how frequently we pod on, and more patient with a world that groans more than it sings (Rom 8:22). Regarding the goodness of finitude while recognizing the iPod's amazing power, such an approach courageously takes time to enjoy the trivial pleasures of music.

+ *Has the "device paradigm" habituated you to expect technology to do the work of providing entertainment? Do you prefer commodified entertainments over participatory or live ones? Can you entertain yourself without machines?*

+ *Are there technological devices in your life whose design (or logic) structures or shapes your behavior? (A friend cancelled TiVo service because he felt so obligated to record and watch all the "good shows" that he didn't have time for the good things that were already in his life—playing with his child, meals with his wife, walks in his neighborhood. The device logic of abundant availability was distorting the life logic of enriching engagements.)*

iPLAYER REPLACES OUR SONG

Music is the soul of the little music player we call iPod. Focusing for a moment on the word *player* might help us notice that music's journey through the twentieth century has changed both music and us. In the 1800s, a music player was some*one*, a person who was making music on the spot. The advent of broadcast and recording technology (beginning in 1877) meant that machines could now do that work for us. A player can now be some*thing*. With the advent of solid-state technologies, that player now fits in my pocket.

A hundred years ago, a Methodist Christian like me would also have had music in her pocket. Not a miniature musical device, however, but a hymnal.[20] If we trace music's twentieth-century journey from pocket hymnal to iPod in three broad strokes, we'll discover that the changes the iPod represents and fosters aren't healthy for Christians. Why? Because music has gone from being our *performed social communication* to my *passive solitary consumption*.

20. I owe this insight to Taylor Burton Edwards.

First, the iPod symbolizes music's journey from performance to passivity. In 1900, music was sold only as musical scores (e.g., sheet music or songbooks); in 2000 it was musical recordings (mostly CDs). The implication is startling: rather than being passive listeners whose primary responsibility is to spin the click wheel for volume control or to skip an unfortunate shuffle selection, music consumers a century ago were active performers who intended to sing or play, to bring the music into existence. Sure, some people in the room merely listened, but *being in the room* was itself a form of engagement. Active listening is a powerful bodily and mental engagement. Stephen Webb compares the bodiliness of listening to live music with the artificiality of recorded music.

> . . . instrumental music is always the product of people and objects in motion—vibrating, sliding, blowing, and banging. The instruments are masks of sound that point beyond themselves to the humans who play them, a point that is demonstrated by the fact that seeing music performed, where one can watch the musicians at work, is more satisfying than hearing a disembodied recording. Recordings, in fact, can become too perfect, removing the all-too-human sounds that make a concert so immediate and powerful.[21]

In addition to "perfection," recording and transmission technologies like the phonograph and radio "liberate" us from the active burden of performance to the passive possibility of listening.[22] So most music listening these days is passive—an auditory accoutrement to other activities. The iPod epitomizes music's journey from "we play" to "I listen."

Second, the iPod symbolizes music's journey from social to solitary. Music has an amazing variety of social uses and contexts, only some of which are related to entertainment. Live musical performances are nearly always social interactions of some sort—people making and hearing music together (the exceptions are singing in the shower and whistling while you work). What the first music players precipitated was a transition from public venues to domestic spaces; people more often listened to musical entertainments in their homes than in the concert hall.[23] With the advent

21. Webb, *Divine Voice*, 228.

22. "Instead of having to perform music oneself, or pay others to do it, people were given easy access to a range of music. . . . [music listening] went from a participatory skill or special event to a background activity that could be integrated into the rhythm of daily life. These changes . . . contributed to the passive reception of culture as an object of consumption." Miller, "The iPod," 175.

23. This transition affected all broadcast entertainments—music, theater, sports.

of mobile music players (beginning with car radios, but climaxing with the iPod), there came a further shift to "private space" and personalized musical envelopes. Note that this is not just the argument that the iPod is an icon of interior musical ecstasy; it is the claim that music players have created "audiences of one" who use the equipment and activity of musical entertainment to create utterly private spheres, and to negotiate social space as anonymously as possible. Apple's mobile music player completes musical entertainment's journey from our music to my tune, from we sing to iPod.

Third, the iPod symbolizes music's journey from communication to consumption. Anthropologists note that music has had a communicative role in the "organization of healing, war, work, political process, ideologies of identity, the recording of history, the relationship of human beings to one another," worship,[24] and, of course, entertainment. As music players became some *thing* rather than someone, so music itself was transformed from personal communication to commodity, a product to purchase and consume. We can use musical commodities as a means of communication if we want (ever give someone a mixtape or a playlist?), but their basic purpose has become personal pleasure rather than interpersonal communication. We still occasionally communicate musically—identity with the national anthem or "Take Me Out to the Ballgame," security with a lullaby, intimacy with a love song. But we mostly consume music according to product preference rather than engage music as communicative presence. The iPod typifies music's journey from we commune to I like.

❖   *When and where do you engage with music that is not commercially produced as mass-mediated entertainment? Are these engagements influenced by your regular consumption of music as entertainment? Another way to ask the question is this: do you think that a congregation's capacity for musical worship is enhanced or diminished by the members' extensive consumption of commodified, technologized musical entertainments?*

Notice that these three trends make the musical dimension of Christian worship profoundly atypical, for worship is always a performed social communication, never a passive, private consumption. So regular engagement

---

"The withdrawal of audiences from public venues into private spaces not only changed the nature of entertainment, it also changed how we live our lives." Sayre and King, *Entertainment and Society*, 11.

24. Herzfeld, *Anthropology*, 279.

with music as entertainment (recreational listening) may make us less fit for the musical work of worship. At a minimum, we should carefully differentiate between recreational listening (music as entertainment) and doxological communicating (music as worship). That won't be easy, since God can touch us through musical entertainment, and since even pop songs can be used to praise God (last Sunday I sang U2's "One" in church). But it is utterly necessary.

In light of these three changes, let's return to my nineteenth-century Methodist layperson and her pocket hymnal. Her hymnal held at most a few hundred songs. It could "shuffle" if she fanned the pages, but remained utterly mute and entirely inert without her effort, her inputs as user. Lacking any form of musical notation other than suggested tune names, the hymnal required her to know the melodies, harmonies, rhythms, and tempos for each song; it was the very antithesis of plug and play. Yet in spite of its limited technological capacities, her hymnal was superior in significant ways to my iPod.

With it, she could sing the communal songs of faith while sitting, walking, or riding, thereby joining with the communion of saints, even if none was visibly *or audibly* present. Thus the hymnal implicates and assumes relationships with fellow Christians and with God; one doesn't sing hymns by oneself or to oneself. Even if I'm the only person in the room, I sing praise with all Christ's saints. Even when I love the song, I sing it not for myself, but for and to God. And the hymnal invites action, a bodily practice learned in community and shaped by tradition. Apart from active performance by the "user," a hymnal cannot make music.

Today, that same Methodist is more likely to have a much smaller iPod, filled not with the communal songs of faith, but with the commoditized songs of pop culture. Hearing them involves not active performance but passive consumption. The iPod is far less relational than the hymnal was; indeed, it is a personal device that—once loaded with my songs—is not interchangeable with any other iPod. It doesn't inherently connect me with a particular community or with God, though it does establish a commercial and emotional relationship with particular artists. If there is an invocation of communal feeling, it is the feeling of connection with the shared fan base of each artist or musical style, rather than connection to my brothers and sisters in the church. But more likely, the music simply evokes in me particular feelings, ones that I engineer myself by selecting the songs that will evoke them.

To put the contrast as starkly as possible: the music of the hymnal requires an active practice that is learned in community, directed toward God, and oriented to an open musical future (and thus to God's eternity); the music of the iPod allows passive consumption, is directed toward myself, endlessly seeking the reproduction of a past musical closure (the recorded song is completed and unchangeable). Thus the music contained in my iPod is not a communicative engagement with God; it is not, in the best sense of the word, prayer. Listening to my iPod is a reflexive engagement with myself, one into which the Spirit of God can certainly break. But whereas the pocket hymnal was a device for praise and prayer, the iPod is a device for private entertainment.

What this extended explanation reveals, I hope, is the degree to which we now divide the geography and chronology of our lives between the sacred and the entertaining, with separate soundtracks for each. When Christians gather to worship each Sunday, we could almost certainly use our sophisticated sound systems to play recordings of sacred music that are technically excellent and acoustically beautiful. Indeed, such recordings would likely be far more excellent and beautiful than the music we actually make together. Yet like the street-corner musician busking for change, we choose the vitality of our live performance rather than the "virtuality" of someone else's recording. That is the right choice (no matter how poorly we sing), and it preserves a certain wisdom about the performative, communal, and communicative dimensions of music.[25] Together, these dimensions sustain the possibility of musical practices that are genuinely celebrative and divinely engaged.

iLIFE

Newsweek called the iPod a "life-changing" device. That's a large claim, though there is plenty of sentiment to support it. This section first describes ongoing changes in lifestyle in which the iPod participates and symbolizes. The iPod has not caused music to permeate our lives, but it could certainly

---

25. Webb, *Divine Voice*, 217, says, "Except for the qualitative difference in hearing sound 'live' as opposed to hearing it recorded, the church would have little to offer in competition with the Kingdom of Entertainment that is America." Webb overstates with the "except." In addition to the importance of "live" there is the importance of the communal and the communicative.

be indicted as an accessory after the fact. Second, this section will describe a particular imPact of the iPod.

Nowadays, music accompanies our lives almost ceaselessly. Think for a moment about how much of your day is "accompanied" by music. Technology has long made music available in your home, car, workplace, elevator, gym, and store. We take it for granted that our days and our activities will and should be filled with music, and we habitually seek and select music to surround and accompany us. It is certainly pleasant to be continually immersed in music, but that gain comes with several losses.

We're losing silence. Worse, we're losing the capacity to attend to silence. Where silence is unavoidable, it is endured rather than enjoyed or engaged. But it makes us nervous or bored, so we banish it with music. The iPod is a perfect weapon to defeat silence.[26] There is gain in that: with music, time passes differently, usually more enjoyably. But silence can also be a gift, offering space for encounter with God, with self, with creation. We've nearly lost the gift of silence and the skills to engage it faithfully and creatively.

✛ *How often do you experience silence? What is your capacity for engaging it? Has doing so deepened your relationship with God, yourself, or creation?*

We are also losing the desire and ability to attend actively to music. Hearing music mostly as background for working and shopping, as soundtrack to shows and ads, or as energy boost for workouts habituates us to give music only "continuous partial attention." That's fine for music created to accessorize other activities, but for music that rings true or sounds out beauty or riffs goodness, complete attention is better than partial attention. Perhaps some uses of the iPod increase our capacity to give music our full attention, while others diminish it.

✛ *How often do you give music your full attention? What is your capacity for actively engaging music? Has doing so deepened your relationship with God, yourself, or creation?*

Finally, we may be losing the capacity to enjoy life "straight." Instead, we increasingly aestheticize our lives, intentionally choosing a soundtrack

---

26. Bull suggests that "contemporary consumers invariably feel a sense of discomfort when confronted with silence," a silence the iPod overcomes. *Sound Moves*, 5.

for this activity or that environment.[27] The most shocking image of aesthe-citization I have ever seen is a photo in the *Newsweek* article mentioned at the beginning of this chapter. It shows a thirtysomething mother cradling her infant, each smiling at the other. The mother clearly has her earbuds in, and looking closer, we see that her left hand cradles not only the baby's bottom, but an iPod! Thus, mother's engagement with child is now experienced "through" her iPod; her mothering has a soundtrack. While I imagine an iPod would be priceless for coping with colic, I am disturbed by its presence in an already joyous engagement. Surely some relational moments are so rich and complete that they lack nothing, not even a soundtrack!

✢ *To what degree is your daily life aestheticized by music? Are there any boundaries to where or how music should envelop you?*

✢ *Are there any situations or activities that should be kept music-free?*

There is one change in lifestyle that has virtually coincided with the iPod invasion. Call it "podding" or "cocooning." The iPod is most commonly used to separate or insulate an individual sonically, socially, and psychically from surrounding persons, circumstances, and environment. Michael Bull calls it a "privatized auditory bubble."[28] Podding insulates the self against environment, place, the passage of time, circumstance, and contingency, ambient sound, and social interaction with or obligation to other people.[29] I pod myself against noise (but also silence), boredom (but also serenity), overstimulation (but also discovery), ugliness (but also compassion), awkwardness (but also serendipity), strangers (and thus perhaps also Christ).

♪♪ I'm reading Sherry Turkle's claim that "tethering technologies" (cell phones, MP3 players, PDAs, etc.) can disrupt our psychological and emotional development. The instantaneity of cell phones facilitates quick and frequent emoting, which gets in the way of cultivating "the ability to be alone, to reflect on and contain one's emotions."[30] I would find this really disturbing except for the fact that Godsmack is wailing "I need serenity" in my earbuds. ♪♪

---

27. Simun, "My Music, My World," 931.

28. Bull, "No Dead Air!," 344.

29. Turkle, "Always-on/Always-on-You," 3, says, "Our media signal that we do not want to be disturbed by conventional sociality with physically proximate individuals."

30. Ibid., 10.

So podding cuts us off from all kinds of potential goods. There is one more good that podding certainly excludes—shared listening. It is, after all, an *i*Pod, not a *we*Pod. The social enjoyment of musical entertainment has been in decline for years, but the iPod has accelerated that exponentially. Anyone who has traveled across the country with teenagers knows they would rather sit in the back listening to their iPods than negotiate what gets played on the radio. So we are losing both the practice of and capacity for shared listening, and with it the adult skills of negotiation, compromise, and empathy.

✣ *How would you differentiate between appropriate and inappropriate "podding"? Does podding risk isolating us from gracious encounters with God's glory (Exodus 3) or neighbor's need (Luke 11)?*

iPOPE AND HOPE

On March 3, 2006, the staff of Vatican Radio gave Pope Benedict XVI a white 2G iPod nano. "Computer technology is the future," the pope is reported to have said. Perhaps we should qualify that a bit. Almost thirty years earlier, in his book *Eschatology: Death and Eternal Life*, he reminded us Christians that in spite of all that we don't know about our future, we certainly do know that our future is Jesus. His "livingness" as the resurrected one is our future hope and our present help.[31] That can free us from the tyranny of cutting-edge technology, and the terror that we are falling behind the times.

This chapter has described numerous ways in which the tiny iPod is massively influential. It is part of the principality we know as the entertainment industry. As such, we will often need strategies to resist it, but we need never fear it. The chapter has sometimes hinted at ways that the iPod is also a triviality that can enrich us through encounters with beauty, goodness, and truth, that can free us from the necessity of making every moment count. As such, we can strategically embrace it, but we must never serve it.

✣ *In light of this chapter, should you change your practices of musical entertainment?*

---

31. See Ratzinger, *Eschatology*.

four

Youtube and U2charist

Community, Convergence, and Communion

LIVING ROOM, AEREOPAGUS, OR VANITY FAIR?

YOUTUBE IS A PHENOMENON that elicits hyperbole from all sides. One reason is its phenomenal success. Perhaps a more basic reason is that it is not entirely clear what YouTube is, both because it is growing exponentially and because it is continually evolving. (For example, while I was drafting this chapter, YouTube began offering online rentals of feature films from Sony, Universal, and Warner Brothers, making it a direct competitor of Netflix.) So let's begin with five different images of YouTube, none entirely satisfying.

Clean out the attic of someone who parented in the 1950s or 1960s and you might find a cardboard box containing old canisters of fading 8mm home movies. So, is YouTube the massive cardboard box in our global attic, brimming with footage from family life and domestic spaces? If so, it is also our global living room, the place where we record and watch home movies. Plenty of YouTube videos are shot in living rooms—one of my favorites shows a Japanese preschooler crooning the Beatles' "Hey Jude" while strumming his oversized guitar. Unfortunately, this image of YouTube as global cardboard box and living room is misleading in several respects. First, this box contains mass quantities of material that is corporately produced—music videos, movie and television clips, commercials; homages to and parodies of that material; and "channels" showcasing the talents of hoping-to-be-discovered directors, bands, and actors. Its structural logic is profitability (of corporations and persons) rather than preservation of cherished memories. Second, this "living room" uses algorithmic search logic to draw together strangers, not family and friends. Its structural imperative is toward celebrity (recognition by strangers) rather than intimacy (deeper relationship with family and friends).

Robert Barron calls YouTube "a virtual Areopagus, where every viewpoint—from the sublime to the deeply disturbing—is on display."[1] Barron is referring to Saint Paul's stay in Athens (Acts 17), where Paul's daily arguing in the marketplace won him an invitation to speak with the philosophers gathered at the Areopagus. Just as Paul referenced the surrounding culture in his presentation of the gospel, so Barron posts reflections on movies, music, and cultural trends. He has seen clearly that YouTube is a social medium, not a one-way broadcast. YouTube allows and invites viewers to comment, so that Father Barron can use it to try to initiate conversation with those he describes as "mostly young opponents of religion." While I appreciate his work, and invite my students to engage it, it seems to me that he has fundamentally misconstrued YouTube's place in our postmodern cultural landscape. As the prior paragraph indicated, YouTube's commercial structure makes it more like the marketplace where Paul first argued than like the Areopagus where philosophers held court about truth. Indeed, what catalyzes YouTube is not the search for truth, but quests for pleasure.

If YouTube is neither living room nor Areopagus, perhaps it is more like Vanity Fair in John Bunyan's *Pilgrim's Progress*, where life's debaucheries are constantly on display: ". . . there is at all times to be seen Jugglings, Cheats, Games, Plays, Fools, Apes, Knaves, and Rogues, and that of all sorts. Here are to be seen too, and that for nothing, Thefts, Murders, Adulteries, False-swearers, and that of a blood-red colour." If YouTube were only a techno-version of Vanity Fair, and if entertainment were always a distraction from the path of discipleship, then Pilgrim's response should become ours: to close our ears and avert our eyes, crying, "*Turn away mine eyes from beholding vanity. . . .*"[2] But there is more to YouTube than devilment and dissipation, and more to entertainment than diversion from our proper ends.

---

1. Barron, "YouTube Heresies," 21. His channel is wordonfirevideo.

2. Bunyan, *Pilgrim's Progress*, 88, 90.

Media theorists are also divided over YouTube. For Alexandra Juhasz, YouTube "is really good for wasting time"; it is "our *private postmodern TV of distraction*" masquerading as media democracy.[3] Though people share favorite clips, typical engagement with YouTube is *private*—one pair of eyeballs per screen. YouTube is not *postmodern* because its videos are so new, but because all of them, regardless of era, are decontextualized from their original circumstances and context in a way that allows them to become flotsam in a sea of cynicism or raw material for endless recontextualizations. Juhasz calls YouTube "TV" not merely because a screen is involved, but because the most popular clips look and feel like television, and because we bring TV habits like channel surfing to the experience, allowing YouTube to do what television has been doing for sixty years: "expertly delivering eyeballs to advertisers."[4] Whether it is primarily a *distraction* from matters that matter is the agenda for the rest of this chapter.

In contrast to Juhasz, Jean Burgess and Joshua Green hope that YouTube might become the "site of cosmopolitan cultural citizenship—a space in which individuals can represent their identities and perspectives, engage with the self-representations of others and encounter cultural difference."[5] For them, the invitation to "broadcast yourself" is not an imperative for narcissists, or an enticement for voyeurs, but an opportunity to do the important political work of noticing global neighbors and negotiating cultural difference. Whether their aspirations for YouTube are truly suited to its developing trajectory is, again, a question requiring closer attention.

What we can say for sure is that both these latter perspectives may be both right and wrong. Yes, YouTube can be a colossal waste of time. But it can also bring hilarity, wonder, sympathy, and righteous indignation in concentrated doses. Yes, YouTube may be one more way for corporations to make us feel empowered while they capitalize on our attention (seen *The Matrix* lately?). But YouTube is also where we can poke politicians, prod governments, and parody consumerism. So YouTube critics are right but also wrong. The same goes for the lovers of YouTube. Yes, it can connect persons who are geographically distant and culturally diverse in ways that lessen prejudice and deepen understanding. But it can just as easily facilitate the transmission of ideas and attitudes that are profoundly prejudiced or incredibly ignorant.

3. Juhasz, "Five Lessons of YouTube," 147, emphasis mine.

4. Ibid., 146, 147.

5. Burgess and Green, *YouTube*, 81.

In this chapter, I will neither damn YouTube as civilization's end, Vanity Fair, or the death of the living room, nor will I praise it as the kingdom's coming, the agent of cosmopolitanism, or the newest Areopagus. Instead, I will suggest that YouTube invites the dialectical engagement discussed in chapter 2. Because YouTube is both an entertainment principality and an entertaining triviality, we must refuse its pretensions and distortions with a Lenten ascesis while we embrace its serendipities with an Easter freedom. Along the way, YouTube will help us understand larger trends called "vernacular culture" and "media convergence." That will allow us to conclude by questioning entertainment's impact on Christian worship in two ways: what happens when video culture becomes our vernacular language for prayer and praise, and what happens when pop music converges with communion?

THE BIG AND SMALL OF IT

By almost any measure, YouTube is big. Invented in 2005, it was purchased sixteen months later for $1.65 billion. A year after that, the Web site's name was doing double duty as both noun and verb. More than likely, you've "youtubed" your share of videos, even if you never have and never will "broadcast yourself." By 2010, YouTube had become the third most popular Web site in the world. On its sixth birthday, YouTube announced that forty-eight hours of video are uploaded to the site every single minute (that's nearly eight years of video added each day). Thus YouTube's temporal immensity makes it genuinely incomprehensible to our finite minds; we couldn't take it all in if we had a thousand lifetimes to do nothing else. That makes it a kind of parody of the triune God, whose love is infinitely abundant and whose nature is incomprehensibly immense. YouTube also announced that it was handling three billion views per day, suggesting that it handles almost as many petitions each day as God does![6]

Yet in another sense, YouTube retains a certain feeling of smallness. Visually, we select from thumbnails, and the standard display is less than a quarter of the computer screen. Temporally, the average video runs a few minutes, and most of us watch for less than an hour at a time. Sociologically, much YouTube content is intimate in scale (close-ups are common, wide-angles rare); intimate in focus (many video blogs, or vlogs, are quite introspective); and intimate in originating context (family life, domestic

6. Wauters, "YouTube Turns 6," para. 2.

space, "ordinary life"). It has the stature of television (before giant screens), not cinema.

Both big and small, YouTube is something of a paradox. That may stem from its dual structure as "both a 'top-down' platform for the distribution of popular culture and a 'bottom-up' platform for vernacular creativity."[7] From the corporate end, YouTube looks like one more entertainment principality. Yet from the participant end, it looks like a benign and amusing triviality. In addition to that paradox, YouTube is also tricky to understand because it is a moving target. It is continually growing and changing; it has too much material to study, and what's there is incredibly diverse. For all these reasons, I will not make grand claims here that purport to capture what YouTube is, nor will I suggest a singular strategy for engaging it. Instead, I offer four assessments of dimensions of YouTube that require a dialectic of affirmation and negation.

"LOOK AT THIS!"—PRECIOUS MOMENTS AND GIFT EXCHANGE

Unless you have adopted a screenless lifestyle in a computer-free zone, you almost certainly have someone who invites you to watch a favorite new video from time to time. Most likely, you occasionally return the favor. My kids say, "Dad, watch this," so I do. I say, "Kids, you've got to see this"—they usually watch. Video sharing has become a normal part of our *entertainment ecology*.

Note three things about this new form of entertainment. First, YouTube can be wonderfully fun (in small doses), a "legitimate" way to spend a little time. I put legitimate in scare quotes because plenty of people think that watching YouTube videos is a waste of time. They're right! Watching YouTube is not an efficient way to feed the hungry or to read the Bible. Watching YouTube doesn't accomplish any of our most noble goals; it's just trivial. We can take time for this sort of pleasurable triviality precisely because Christ's resurrection has freed us from the grim necessity of always striving to make a difference, and because laughter is a divine gift and shared laughter a spiritual joy. (But we must never forget that YouTube, despite dispensing its pleasures in small doses, intends to capture our attention for as long a time as possible. Before, during, and after each video, YouTube suggests what to watch next; it is "an endless chain of immediate

7. Burgess and Green, *YouTube*, 6.

but forgettable gratification that can only be satisfied by another video."[8] Our freedom to enjoy this stream of trivialities far too easily becomes an enslavement—of our time, attention, bodies, and pleasures.)

Second, a significant amount of what people watch on YouTube is also trivial: tips on baking and knitting, laughing babies and cute puppies, amazing talents and precious moments. A fair amount of what we enjoy on YouTube is domestic in origin, silly or whimsical, surprising or serendipitous. This entertainment can remind us that life is full of small pleasures that are not spectacular in scale, not corporately generated, mass produced, or commercially distributed. In other words, some of the most entertaining videos on YouTube can remind us that life's best entertainments are not necessarily produced and distributed by Hollywood or mediated by mass electronic technologies. (However, when watching YouTube results in our baking or knitting less, playing less with babies and puppies, or being less able to notice instances of serendipity, then it has become a power that holds us captive, rather than a trivial form of real freedom.)

Third, a good deal of the fun is in the sharing. We enjoy "gifting" family and friends with the discovery of a wonderfully entertaining clip. Usually this continues the circulation of a gift that has first come to us: someone shares a fun favorite with me; I watch it, and like it so well I share it with my friends. This last point explains why "Charlie bit my finger—again" has more than a third of a billion views! But my emphasis is not on the process by which a video goes viral, but rather on how the size and accessibility of YouTube videos makes them perfect for sharing with people we like. Ideally, we watch it together—and I not only enjoy the video again, I also enjoy watching *you* enjoy it for the first time.

✣ *This section affirms YouTube's potential to entertain us, its celebration of life's trivial pleasures, and its ecology of sharing. Which of these has been most important to you? How are these three interrelated for you?*

---

8. Juhasz, "Five Lessons of YouTube," 147.

"DON'T WATCH THAT!"—STARING DOWN
MORAL UGLINESS

Of course, sometimes someone invites us to enjoy something that is unseemly, repugnant, or contemptible. YouTube holds a massive store of persons behaving badly. It offers to entertain us with brutality, hatred, mental illness, sexualized children, addictions, and mass quantities of stupidity. For example, a teen posts videos of his mentally ill brother's fits of rage; a tween films her mother's drunken stupor; bullies video and then broadcast their violence. These morally repugnant clips captivate our attention in the same gruesome way that a car wreck does, but they should not entertain us. Yet, too often, they do. Worse, the "us" being entertained by YouTube are predominantly children![9]

It would seem to go without saying that Christians should not find pleasure in the tragedy, misery, and evil that others suffer. But that claim requires nuance. Entertainments that are unrealistic about human fallenness are often shallow, false, or tepid. In our novels, films, and plays, we want honest evocations of the human condition—in its brokenness as well as its beauty—that can foster empathy, insight, even conversion. But there is something different about the naked display of real human ugliness. Being entertained by such spectacles demeans the persons who are put on display, while simultaneously diminishing those who watch and weakening the common good. In other words, there are three intertwined dimensions of harm in being entertained by degradation: it's bad for them, bad for us, bad for the world. Let's see why.

Let's begin with how such degrading spectacles diminish us. The early church had to think through the morality of entertainment in the context of spectacle. Should they go to the gladiatorial games (which were free) or stay away? Early Christians chose to stay away because they understood that our entertainments shape our hearts. What we watch, attend to, and enjoy shapes how we perceive, think, and feel. They recognized that the thrill of watching mortal combat would school one to see, think, and feel in ways that are antithetical to the thrill of worshiping the crucified messiah.

That is just as true of our contemporary forms of spectacle, even though our context has shifted from the coliseum to *The Jerry Springer Show* and its YouTube equivalents. Of course, watching these tragic, mean,

9. "YouTube is the favorite online destination for children two to eleven years old. Children under eighteen view more YouTube clips than any other age group." Strangelove, *Watching YouTube*, 60.

or ignorant people make a spectacle of themselves might sound like good moral formation. Their disasters might serve us as cautionary tales. And the pleasure we take in experiencing and expressing moral censure toward them might seem to reinforce our own values and commitments. In the end, however, we are not ennobled, but diminished by participating in such spectacle. Our apparent pleasure in remonstration ("How could they?" or "For shame!") is derived not only from satisfaction with our own moral rectitude, but also from our vicarious enjoyment of their transgressive behavior. In other words, we run a con game on ourselves when we watch such entertainments, subconsciously enjoying what we are consciously rejecting. The result cannot help shaping how we see our neighbors, how we think about the good life, how we seek happiness. Here's an example of the debasement we experience: after participants in a study were shown an episode of *The Jerry Springer Show* that depicted "promiscuous women," their ability to recognize accurately a situation of sexual harassment was measurably diminished.[10] In other words, their capacity for accurate moral perception was weakened by observation of a degrading spectacle.

That example shows not only how spectacles of degradation diminish us who watch, but also weaken the fabric of our common good. Increased acceptance of harassment and stereotyping of women is a tragically high price to pay for the "fun" of trashy talk shows or raunchy YouTube videos. Rather than exhaustively catalog the social harms attributable to degrading video (who but God could accurately do that?), I will instead point out a dynamic of escalation that exacerbates harms.

YouTube is part of the massive and growing attention economy, which has simultaneously fostered in many people a desire to be "seen" and thereby validated in the mediascape, while proliferating and cluttering media outlets such that it is increasingly difficult to be noticed. This "cocktail party effect" generates a dynamic of escalation that rips at the very fabric of civility. Actively seeking to be seen on *Springer* and now YouTube, people adopt and display Springeresque behaviors. But to get noticed they have to stand out, which requires even greater rudeness, more exaggerated deviancy, and over-the-top vulgarity.

Of course, most of the guests on *Springer* willingly demean themselves for the joy of being televised. YouTube, on the other hand, includes both those who willingly video and upload their own degradation, and those who are unwillingly, often unknowingly, degraded by someone filming and

---

10. Dill, *How Fantasy Becomes Reality*, 109.

then broadcasting them. Is there a moral difference between victims of vicious voyeurism and exhibitionist, boorish autovideographers? Yes, when it comes to their culpability, but no, when it comes to ours. We must learn to look away, to turn it off, to refuse to see and be entertained by such degraded and degrading displays. Not only because it diminishes us, not only because it decreases our common good, but also because it demeans the people we are watching. Whether they want to be demeaned or not is finally irrelevant. Whether they actively demean themselves by their behavior is irrelevant. The one relevant claim is that God has created them in God's own image, establishing an irrevocable dignity. We who are disciples of one unjustly reviled are called to acknowledge and honor the dignity of every human person, even and especially where others do not. We do that best, in these cases, by looking away.

In a culture of spectacle, we need to develop a sense of decorum that knows when to look away. The church must develop a proper moral repugnance rather than a prudish one. Call it the cultivation of taste *against* what demeans human dignity, diminishes proper desires, and weakens the common good. In our entertainments, we must not only develop a taste *for* what is ennobling, but a taste *against* what debases. As we do, "Look at this!" and "Don't watch that!" become more than expressions of entertainment preferences; they become moral counsel.

✤ *This section calls for development of a proper moral repugnance that turns away from video that demeans its subjects, diminishes us who watch, and weakens community. How will you cultivate that moral sensibility? What examples of such harm have you experienced?*

"BROADCAST YOURSELF" SPARINGLY

YouTube's motto, "Broadcast yourself," invites us to consider how it has become a medium for constructing and communicating self-identity. Notice first that decades of mass-mediated entertainments have schooled us to consider it natural to want to be seen and recognized by an audience. One aspect of this is the transposition that occurs in videoing special moments: what was at first a desire simply to *record* such special moments for later viewing has increasingly become an urge to *stage, produce,* and *edit* such moments in order for them to be truly and fully special or real. Increasingly, video doesn't capture significance, but creates it.

✢ *Think about worship services in your context that mark significant life transitions in our Christian journey—baptisms, weddings, funerals, and perhaps ordinations, dedications, first communions, quinceañeras. Do they look more like a "paparazzi mob" or like a "sacred moment"? Have we unconsciously accepted the idea that video makes something better, "real," or meaningful? Does a "video culture" seduce us into valuing the replay more than the event itself?*

"Broadcast yourself" captures and helps fulfill the widespread aspiration to be seen in the mediascape. In entertainment culture, it seems like nearly everyone wants their fifteen minutes of fame. YouTube and the availability of webcams make it possible for tens of thousands of video diarists (vloggers) and YouTube performers to fulfill that ambition. They express themselves, display their talents (or lack thereof), profess their opinions, and confess their foibles to "whoever is out there."

Notice several things about this. First, YouTube is more than just a digital medium through which people show off. There's plenty of that, but there's also plenty that is more significant—poignant or piquant sharings of self, witty or wonderful observations of life, graceful or gladdening performances. All that is good, and it may grow out of a deep human desire for respect and affirmation. The ancient Greeks thought that this impulse for recognition by the community inculcated a positive form of pride (*thymos*), which in turn was the seedbed of all the other virtues.[11]

✢ *So, is the imperative to "broadcast yourself" good moral advice, drawing us into a medium that inculcates integrity, courage, justice, prudence, and temperance?*

Hardly.

Unfortunately, in an attention-seeking culture, getting noticed usually requires excess rather than moderation. That inserts a certain pressure for the individual to become entertaining—not to broadcast yourself, but to broadcast a more outrageous, bizarre, extreme, noticeable version of your *self*. There is plenty of evidence that vloggers and 'tubers feel that pressure, and that many of them give in to it. Thus, the ecology of entertainment in which YouTube is situated encourages, even insists on, excessive performances rather than temperate behavior, and it rewards rash actions rather than prudent decisions.

---

11. Gardella, *Domestic Religion*, 72.

Even where participants don't hype themselves for broadcast, there is a second pressure that is almost unavoidable—*reflexivity*. Reflexivity is heightened awareness of being perceived and taking greater care in managing those perceptions. Reflexivity is already a significant cultural ill for us, given the way advertising pressures us to create and manage our identities through practices of consumption. We already inhabit a world in which every purchase is fraught with implications for self-image and group identity. YouTube exacerbates this in two ways, one technological, the other sociological. To "broadcast yourself" requires a range of decisions about perception that cannot be avoided because the technology demands it. You are determining how to present yourself as you decide matters like camera position and lighting, as you decide whether and how to edit, and as you select what to upload and what to call it. All of this will inevitably exaggerate reflexivity. To "broadcast yourself" on YouTube also relocates where reflexivity is happening, from an existing, embodied community to a virtual one called into existence by the video. For example, the typical high school show-off does his showing off in front of people he knows and with whom he has an ongoing relationship. If that same high schooler broadcasts himself, he is now showing off in front of a "community" drawn together by nothing more than the act of observing and recognizing him. As Michael Strangelove observes, "YouTubers are their own paparazzi."[12]

Second, the self you broadcast isn't just being *communicated* through YouTube, it is also being *constructed* by it. YouTubers are not simply expressing their identity; they are actively constructing that identity within media-world—an environment of values, relationships, and practices structured for entertainment. The first sign of this constructive effort is the username. My given name is part family inheritance and part parental gift, both prior to my active participation or control. My username, on the other hand, is something I create and give to myself. The center of self-construction on YouTube is the video. The self broadcast on YouTube gets constructed through self-reflexive performance that can include all the elements of a TV show or movie: staging, costuming, scripting, multiple takes, editing, and the addition of a soundtrack, graphics, and special effects, as well as linear "episodes" through time. Even video diaries that are (or seem to be) unedited, and thereby suggest "authenticity," remain captive to entertainment culture's "script" for everything from reality to rebellion, as well as to its stock of characters, its styles of humor, intimacy, and concern, and

12. Strangelove, *Watching YouTube*, 75.

its constant need for and evocation of spectacle. So while the vlogger is working out her identity "in front of" the invisible YouTube "community," she is doing it "in" a medium instantiating profoundly distorting pressures on wholeness.

The church should think carefully about the dangers of allowing identity construction to migrate from embodied to virtual community. Traditionally, identity gets created, negotiated, and sustained in embodied "theaters" such as home, neighborhood, school, workplace, and church. Like live theater, identity gets worked out in embodied, communal, and interactive ways: I show, speak, and act who I am as you watch, listen, and respond; and I see, hear, feel, and sense your response immediately. For Christians, the primary theater of identity is the church, where we are identified as *children* of God, *siblings* of Christ and therefore one another, and spiritual *members* of the one ecclesial body. The Christian practice of baptism suggests that this identity is both an originating gift and a lifelong journey of transformation. Both dimensions are thoroughly relational, rooted in embodied presence and participation.

Virtual environments, on the other hand, create what theorists call "context collapse." In YouTube, the "community" is neither here nor now; it is *whenever* and *wherever* strangers watch. I can't see, hear, feel, or sense these relational others, unless and until they "respond" with a comment or even a video reply. Worse, YouTube's metric logic (counting viewings) invites participants to value quantitative feedback as much as, or more than, qualitative. The goal of "broadcasting yourself" becomes less about establishing reciprocal relationships or receiving wise counsel, more about the number of views or "likes." The goal is to "go viral," not to become virtu-ous. Thus performing one's identity for an invisible, asynchronous audience enhances existing cultural tendencies toward narcissism and solipsism. "Broadcast yourself" may not be a counsel of despair, but it inherently pro-motes isolation, self-interest, and relativism.

✣ *Our baptismal journey is one of identity transformation toward Christ. Do you think the reflexivity induced by social media like YouTube is helpful or harmful in that process? Do you think the ac-tive self-construction and context collapse intrinsic to vlogging are helpful or harmful to that process? Does this chapter give you pause when it comes to videoing significant family or church events?*

ENJOY VERNACULAR VIDEO, BUT LOVE YOUR FOLKS!

In 1966, Woody Allen made *What's Up, Tiger Lily?* Allen took a Japanese action movie and overdubbed it with dialogue (in English, of course) about gangland warfare over an egg salad recipe. What took major studio muscle to accomplish four and a half decades ago can now be done by any clever teen with a computer and access to the Internet. The proof is all over You-Tube—everything from a *Mary Poppins* trailer recast as a horror movie to *The Shining* transformed from ultimate horror to heartwarming family drama. There are also plenty of original shorts showcasing the talents of budding filmmakers. Then there's "machinima"—movies made using the video capture feature of online gaming. And don't forget "mashups," unique new songs created by blending together the audio tracks of two different songs. It takes creative genius to recognize that Radiohead's vocals in "15 Steps" can be laid over the smooth instrumentals of "Take Five" by the Dave Brubeck Quartet.

These are all examples of what media theorist Henry Jenkins calls "vernacular culture."[13] He uses this term to identify the vast and growing level of participation in the creation, modification, and distribution of entertainments through contemporary media. Exactly when passive audiences passed away is unclear, but in an era of *Survivor* spoilers (fans devoted to discovering outcomes on *Survivor* before they are broadcast), *Idol* campaigns (fan movements to support particular contestants, or to counteract perceived corporate bias), and Facebook fan sites, it is clear that audiences are no longer mere receptors of whatever corporate media choose to distribute. Calling this "vernacular" rather than "amateur" can help us remember three things: First, some of it is as good as, or better than, what Hollywood produces. Second, some of the creators of vernacular media culture—call them *vernaculauteurs*—have found ways to make a living at it (e.g., through advertising revenue for a YouTube channel). Finally, the success this vernacular culture finds in the mediascape arises as much from processes of democratic access as from corporate gatekeeping.

Jenkins chose "vernacular" to communicate his sense that this is the twenty-first-century equivalent of nineteenth-century folk culture. Folks used to get together to square dance, or to play music, or to sing. They used to gather for quilting bees, card games, or just to tell stories. In the twentieth century, the productive locus of our amusements moved from

13. See Jenkins, *Convergence Culture.*

homes, neighborhoods, and churches to New York and Hollywood. In the twenty-first century, we are seeing a digital re-democratization of cultural productivity. Pop culture is going DIY (do it yourself). YouTube (and the Internet more generally) becomes the showcase, the exhibition hall, the video variety show, of vernacular culture.

There is a powerful difference, however, between traditional forms of folk culture and the vernacular culture of our digital age. We can tease it out by remembering that the word *vernacular* literally means the "mother tongue" or shared language of a people. Looking at the vernacular culture displayed on YouTube, we can notice two language-like dimensions. First, the basic *vocabulary* of vernacular culture is mostly commercial entertainment. Instead of creating from scratch, vernacular culture mostly uses the images, phrases, characters, plots, tunes, lyrics, videos, forms, and genres of commercial entertainment. It uses them as basic vocabulary. We see quotes, parodies, satires, homages, imitations, developments, denigrations, affirmations, and critiques of pop culture, some banal and some profoundly creative and entertaining. But we don't see much original language being generated, only the recycling of existing entertainment discourse.

Second, vernacular culture regularly follows the grammar or syntax of pop culture. The stories it tells, the songs it generates, the movies it makes are usually structured like the commercial entertainments it imitates.[14] For example, watch an "original" music video on YouTube and you'll find its structure, form, length, and mood more like than unlike its MTV and VH1 equivalents.

So enjoy vernacular video. But don't let the tail of pop culture wag the dog of your cultural creativity. If you do, you are likely to discover that the focus of your affection has subtly shifted from your "folks"—the people with whom you live, work, and play—to "your" shows, playlists, celebs, and vids—entertainments that shape your imagination and command your creativity. The vernacular culture that emerges from this may be funny or poignant or acerbic—all highly entertaining. What it probably won't be is truly local, really relational (that is, requiring bodily interaction), and original to the indigenous particularities of your life. So in the end we see that "vernacular culture" is not an alternative to pop culture, but rather is pop culture's full colonization of our creativity as well as our consumption.

14. ". . . it should be no surprise that much of what the public creates models itself after, exists in dialogue with, reacts to or against, and/or otherwise repurposes materials drawn from commercial culture." Jenkins, *Convergence Culture*, 137.

❖ *When you actively make your own fun, do you draw mostly on the "language" of pop culture and commercial entertainments, or do you draw from other realms?*

Another Word from Our Sponsors

From 2006 to 2010, Apple ran a series of highly entertaining ads comparing its Mac computers to PCs. The ads consist mostly of dialogue between two actors who serve as icons for each machine, typically beginning, "'Hello, I'm a Mac.' 'And I'm a PC.'" The humor hinges on the "personality" given to each character. "Mac" is hip, yet humble and caring. "PC," underneath his clueless braggadocio, is insecure and inept. Each ad typically reveals one more way in which Macs are better than PCs.

YouTube is replete with these ads—both U.S. and British versions (fifteen of the best are conveniently collected into a single YouTube video)—as well as thousands of vernacular videos that use the ad series as vocabulary, syntax, and accent for political parody, comic satire, playful experimentation, ironic comparisons (e.g., DC Comics and Marvel), send-ups of advertising, counterattacks against Apple, etc. It's all highly entertaining vernacular culture.

Ever notice how the claim "I'm a Mac" resonates a bit with "This is my body"? These ads give us a window on a sacramental quality that inheres in a lot of advertising. They are examples of a marketing trend called "associative advertising," which works at selling us products by transforming them into a participatory sign of some higher, transcendental good. Through the hocus pocus of associative advertising, the product becomes "an outward and visible sign of an inward and spiritual reality" (one classic definition of a sacrament). In the commercials, "I'm a Mac" is language that transubstantiates the actor we see into an outward and visible sign not just of the physical reality of Mac computers (which we never see on screen), but of their "spiritual" qualities—hip, intuitive, and fun (which we see very clearly). In his hipness, he represents the Mac, which in its hipness represents the hipness we will acquire and participate in by consuming the Mac. Associative marketing makes consumption a spiritual practice, makes products promissory signs that participate in and communicate spiritual qualities, and it makes all of that go down smoothly by wrapping it in the humor of highly entertaining commercials.

✤ *Why do so many modern Christians stumble over the sacramental logic of baptism and Eucharist, but buy (literally!)* the sacramental promise of commercials?

CONVERGENCE HAPPENS

Vernacular culture is part of a larger trend that Jenkins identifies as "convergence." Convergence refers to a threefold confluence: digital technologies, media industries, and entertainment audiences all increasingly support a seamless "flow of content" and migration of attention across the entire spectrum of everyday life. Entertainment content is increasingly available via multiple media technologies, media industries increasingly work cooperatively to maximize their access to audiences, and audiences are increasingly proactive in seeking the content they want. Because technology allows it, corporations promote it, and consumers want it, you can get *Star Wars* or the Beatles (or whatever you want) everywhere, all the time.

YouTube is convergence central. It is the near-perfect confluence of corporate content, fan desire, and technological enablement. YouTube displays the fruits of convergence; here you can find channels devoted to every convergence imaginable. YouTube facilitates the communication of interests that fuels the convergence engine. And YouTube is the vast repository—that giant cardboard box—of the cultural artifacts that convergence culture endlessly recycles. But convergence is bigger than YouTube, bigger by far. It represents the whole direction and impulse of fan relation to entertainment as a whole. The rest of this chapter will turn from the specifics of YouTube to a more general engagement with convergence.

Convergence reshapes us in two powerful ways. First, convergence *normalizes* the near-total permeation of life by entertainments; increasingly, we expect (or demand) instant, constant, ubiquitous access to our entertainments. Second, convergence *valorizes* the "will to be entertained"; increasingly, we choose to be continually entertained, and this choosing creates and reinforces a powerful but hidden and unexamined drive toward entertainment. We accept and demand ubiquitous entertainment as a matter of course.

✤ *What relatively new forms, modes, or locations of entertainment have you come to accept as normal? As necessary? (For example,*

> *must your van have rear passenger DVD players to entertain the kids? Must your cell phone have multiplayer gaming functions?)*

✤ *How powerful is your "will to entertainment"? For example, if some circumstance (technology malfunction or preempting event or personal responsibility) prevents you from enjoying an entertainment, how do you feel and what do you do? Do you generally evaluate your desires for entertainment, or simply enact them? Do you work your calendar around your entertainments?*

So convergence begins to feel like something that "just happens," not a cultural effect with technological, corporate, and personal causes. If convergence is something that "just happens," then *resistance is futile*.[15] But if convergence is formed and fueled by our own participation, then we still have the capacity and responsibility to be active cultural agents, both in the degree to which we allow convergence to level all of life into a single entertainment ecology, and in the degree to which we allow pop culture to become our mother tongue. Resistance is actually faithful rather than futile. And if convergence, while delivering plenty of fun, cannot bring true happiness or true beatitude, then we will need to preserve domains of vernacular performance that invoke our best selves and our highest good. Christians have long understood this goal to be the beautiful, beatific vision, and this performance to be gathered worship. Worship, although perhaps not fun, is true enjoyment.

EDGY WORSHIP?

The church is not isolated from wider cultural trends. Given trends toward pop culture as vernacular, and convergence as vector, it is not surprising to find these trends exerting increasing pressure on Christian worship. There is not only pressure on Christian worship to adopt the *idiom* of entertainment—looking, feeling, and sounding like secular entertainments—but to adopt its *content* as well—for example, by quoting movies, TV shows, pop songs, and YouTube videos during worship. Quoting often means

15. That phrase, drawn from the pop-culture lexicon, originated on *Star Trek: The Next Generation*. It was the motto of the Borg, an aggressive techno-culture seeking galactic domination. I use the phrase 1) because its familiarity illustrates that pop culture has become our vernacular, and 2) because its content elicits our deep-seated emotional anxiety about the collectivizing effects of digital technology.

projecting part or all of the entertainment on a large screen, not merely referring to it verbally.

Some describe this shift as a faithful modulation of Christian worship.[16] At key moments in its history, the church concluded that we should hear God's Word and pray and praise in our own linguistic idiom. So the Roman church heard Scripture in their native Latin, the Reformation church praised in German, French, and English, and post-Vatican II Catholics pray in Tagalog, Mandarin, and Spanish. Paul's "I became all things to all people so that by all means I might save some" is touted as a warrant for pop-culture evangelism. Or the need for U.S. immigrant churches to switch from the mother tongue to English if they want to retain their children is taken as an analogy for transposing worship from "high culture" to "pop culture." Collectively, these arguments seem to have powerful truth on their side. Surely the introduction of vernacular and viral video into worship is faithful enculturation for a new era, capturing churchgoers' imaginations and interest. Besides, it's edgy—it keeps up, makes relevant, shows sophistication.

I'm not so sure. This claim from Henry Jenkins ought to give us pause: "media audiences . . . will go almost anywhere in search of the kinds of entertainment experiences they want."[17] On the one hand, this might suggest that since video is the *lingua franca* of our culture, the church can't afford not to use it. But on the other hand, Jenkins's observation suggests that what video is, ultimately, *is entertainment*, and what it draws is a *media audience* wanting an *entertainment experience*. While such experiences can and do grace our lives, they are not often the occasion for offering ourselves fully to God, nor for experiencing the fullness of God's self-giving to us. For that reason, I would be very leery of setting a "tone" or "theme" for worship by using the latest viral video from YouTube. I would definitely never dress as Barney the Dinosaur and then lead a children's communion service.

✤ *But what about the deeply Christian music of U2? Wouldn't that be a proper convergence, an authentic vernacular, for Christian worship? Wouldn't it be truly edgy to let The Edge join our praise band?*

16. E.g., Johnston, "Visual Christianity."

17. Jenkins, *Convergence Culture*, 2.

U2CHARIST

Perhaps nothing embodies the migration of media convergence into the church's worship more than the "U2charist." First performed in 2004, the U2charist is described by its creator, Sarah Dylan Breuer, as a "service of the Eucharist using the music of the rock band U2 for service music (e.g., the Sanctus, the Gloria) as well as for hymns, and intentionally taking up the call to engage God's mission in the world, particularly around issues of social and economic justice . . . ."[18] In other words, the music of U2 becomes the "dress" worn by Holy Communion, the message of U2 becomes its theme, and Bono becomes the troubadour for Christ's holy feast. It is hard to imagine a more powerful convergence of entertainment culture with Christian practice than this one.

Clearly Breuer and those who follow her lead have the best of intentions, with culturally relevant evangelism and passionate social justice topping their list. Moreover, the Eucharist should be sung, and it does include the call to live justly in the world. There are reports that U2charists are often more joyful and participatory than your average communion service. So what's not to like?

Four things. First, we shouldn't like the idea that an essential Christian practice needs a booster shot from pop culture, whether YouTube clips for the sermon or U2 songs for communion. In the era of the Reformation, it was recognized that the church lives by and from the Word preached and the sacraments practiced, when both are done as performances of the life-giving gospel. In other words, the church's life and vitality were given by God in these gospel-acts of preaching, baptism, and communion. The value of these acts was not conferred by how we felt about them, but was created by God who worked in and through them.

The cultural shift to an entertainment economy has reversed the flow of valuation. These days entertainment has become "the primary standard of value for virtually everything."[19] Notice how making U2 the soundtrack to the Lord's Supper seems identical to making U2 the soundtrack to iPod ads. In both cases, it is highly successful associative advertising.

❖ *But is the price of such success a subtle transformation of the Eucharist into a product that needs U2's validation, an activity whose worth now depends on their entertainment value?*

18. Breuer, "What Is a U2charist?," para. 1.

19. Gabler, *Life the Movie*, 176.

Probably.

Second, we shouldn't like the notion that an entertainment practice can become worship simply because we intend it to become one. That probably overrates the power of human intentionality. In his report on the U2charist he attended, Jason Byassee says that the lyrics of "Still Haven't Found" "almost demand to be sung in church."[20] He's probably right about that, but the reality is that if we know the lyrics, it's because we've heard and sung them repeatedly in the car and the bedroom and the concert coliseum. That is to say, we already have a history with this music, a pattern of *consuming it as entertainment.*

✧ *Can that entertainment history—and the habits of mind and heart that it has shaped—simply be offloaded at will, so that we can now sing it as corporate Christian worship?*

Probably not.

After all, there really is a divergence of direction between entertainment, which is about my receiving pleasure, and worship, which is about my offering praise to God. Of course, worship can be pleasurable, but that's not the point. If we're already struggling in our worship with audience behavior and entertainment expectation (the will-to-convergence), then risking the full-scale importation of entertainment content appears naive at best, cynical at worst.

Third, we shouldn't like the implication that the *communion* in this service is created by shared affinity for the music of U2, rather than by the power of the Holy Spirit to make us one in Christ. Christians have typically understood the *koinonia* that occurs in the Eucharist as God's work rather than our own. That is to say, communion is not a ritual that expresses a unity that we have already achieved by our own efforts; rather, it is a ritual that effects what it expresses. Keeping clear that the Holy Spirit is the source and agent of our unity is almost always difficult, but becomes nearly impossible in the context of what Arjun Appaduri has referred to as "communities of 'sentiment,' collective experiences of mass media . . . which can create solidarities of worship and charisma."[21]

20. Byassee, "What You're Looking For," 11.

21. As quoted in Barry Taylor, *Entertainment Theology*, 80.

✚ *Can the dynamics of affiliation grounded in shared taste become a subtle substitute for the reknitting work of the Holy Spirit? Does U2charist subtly refocus our unity from love of God to love of U2?*[22]

Probably so.

Finally, we shouldn't like the implication that without this kind of upgrade, the Eucharist is boring. Michael Hanby has argued that our powerful thirst for entertainment is rooted in our utter boredom with reality itself. The real fails to grasp us, to move us, to enthrall or inspire us. The fault does not lie with reality, but with us.[23] Those of us who believe that Christ is real, and really present in the Christian Eucharist (even if we can't say precisely how), ought to find it a compelling practice as it is, not one in need of a Bono boost. It is only our failure to be enthralled by what is really present in our midst that allows for the migration of entertainment culture into convergences like U2charist or video clip preaching. It isn't a boring Eucharist that needs fixing, but us; our boredom requires not the salve of a favorite tune, but the renewing of our minds.

My engagement with convergence has centered in the way it impacts Christian worship. That is probably the most important place for questioning, but not the only one. Readers of this guide are urged to give thought to ways in which they see convergence happening around them, or even to ways in which they themselves participate in a media convergence of entertainment. We should also consider carefully what entertainment convergence suggests about the centrality and importance of entertainment in our lives.

✚ *Would you attend a U2charist? Why or why not? Which of the four objections to U2charist do you find most compelling? Which seems the least plausible or important?*

✚ *Does the convergence of mediated entertainments suggest that the true connective tissue of our lives is our practice of entertainment, rather than our relationships and commitments?*

✚ *Do people dedicate themselves to pursuing entertainment convergence because they find little else to be passionate about in our culture? Are we bored with the real?*

22. In *The City of God*, Augustine identifies the church as that "city" united by its common object of love—the triune God.

23. Hanby, "Culture of Death."

five

The Trouble with Twitter[1]

OUR FATHER WHICH ART in heaven, Hallowed be thy name. Thy kingdom come. Thy will be done in earth, as it is in heaven. Give us this day our [2]

1. Yes this chapter title is an homage to one of my favorite Star Trek episodes.

2. . . . *daily tweets*? In fact, tweets don't come daily, but constantly. As my tongue-in-cheek chapter implies, the Lord's Prayer can't limbo under Twitter's 140-character limit (I stopped at exactly 140). So Twitter is an inadequate medium for some of life's most important communication. Shouldn't the diminishment of communication to 140-character micro-bursts strike an apostolic community of witness—the church—as a debasement of language that will ultimately distort or prevent faithful accounts of the hope that is in us (1 Pet 3:15)? For example, imagine if Peter, on that first Pentecost, had tweeted rather than preached. Or imagine Paul texting the churches of Rome, Corinth, Galatia, etc. We'd certainly be the poorer for it.

I treat Twitter in this book not because I think it is the next revolution in communications or politics, but because I think it is just one more mode of entertainment. Consider its invitation: "You can follow me on Twitter." Who do we follow? More than 19 million follow Lady Gaga, and 9.5 million hang on Aston Kutcher's every tweet. Clearly Twitter offers celebrities yet one more sky in which they can shine as stars. With Twitter, they can do it ceaselessly; I can know *right now* what Ashton Kucher is doing *right now.* How thrilling is that! Twitter is a fitting symbol for entertainment culture's obsession with what is now and new and next. Twitter should also help us see that entertainment culture is always looking for new ways to capture more of our attention. And there's the rub with Twitter. It is in crucial ways the opposite of prayer as the practice of attending to God. Tweeting invites reflexivity; it is a practice of attending to myself. Praying invites surrender; it is a practice of attending to God (and all things in relation to God). Twitter fosters consumerist subjectivism; it intends for us to connect to what we already find interesting. Prayer fosters discipleship; it intends to connect us to what is true, good, and beautiful—that is, to God and all that participates in God. Finally, I chose prayer as the lens for considering Twitter because the traditional Christian practice of ceaseless prayer (1 Thess 5:17) is almost certainly incompatible with the practice of continual Twitter. You can follow Ashton and Lady Gaga on Twitter, but Jesus doesn't tweet.

six

We Play

WE PLAY. IF WE didn't, entertainment would scarcely exist. We play for all kinds of reasons, but close to the heart of each one is the truth that we find play entertaining. Play captivates us—captures and holds our attention, elicits and trains our desire, structures and enriches our time, fosters or heightens positive emotion. Just beneath the surface of entertainments as diverse as theater and theme parks, bowling and ballet, sport and symphony, cards, charades, and computer games, the impulse to play roils like magma under a volcano. Far more than a stave against boredom or a diversion to pass the time, at its best play is both human need and divine gift, drawing us toward, and fitting us for, divine beatitude.

Unfortunately, "at its best" describes far too little of our playing. Like the rest of our fallen world, play too is distorted by the alienations and pathologies of sin. That alone is reason to engage play theologically. But in a society where technological mediation and corporate exploitation now hold child's play hostage, and captivate adults with glittering idolatries, there is an even greater need to consider play in light of the gospel.

✢ *Do you share the first paragraph's high view of play as the coalescence of human need and divine gift, or does that seem like a romantic overstatement? Do you already have a list of the sinful distortions that attend to play, or does that seem like a cynical overstatement?*

This chapter will engage play in four steps. First, we will work to reimagine play theologically as sign and gift. Second, we will summarize five key dimensions of play. Third, we will pause to notice why playing is properly considered a kind of entertainment. Finally, we'll consider the pleasures that attend to playing sports. This chapter prepares us for three successive chapters on spectator sports, gambling, and video gaming.

PLAY AS SIGN AND GIFT

One thing that is true about us humans: throughout our life cycle, across the generations, and despite our diversities of culture and language, we like to play. So do other creatures, apparently, everything from Leviathan playing in the ocean (Ps 104:26) to a bulldog I saw skateboarding on YouTube. G. K. Chesterton famously imagined the act of creation as God at play. Pondering a field of daisies, Chesterton envisioned God, having created one daisy, delighting in it and saying to himself, "Do it again! Do it again!"

Let me offer two quick claims that have theological significance: 1) like other animals, we also play, but 2) we don't play like other animals. There are theologians who dispute the first claim, fearing that it diminishes human uniqueness or devalues human play. It needn't have either of those effects, so long as we keep it properly paired with the second claim. The beauty of acknowledging the great variety of creaturely play is that it invites us to imagine God's creative activity as playful and joyful. What Genesis 1 describes as work followed by rest, Proverbs 8:30–31 imagines as a joyful activity of child's play (see the translation in the New Jerusalem Bible). Creation is God's good work, but it is just as truly God's joyful play. Creation happens because the *delight* of the Father in the Son, and the Son in the Father, is so abundant and full that the triune God brings forth all creation to signify and share in that delighting.[1] Attending to the breadth of creaturely play invites us to discover and participate in God's own delighting at creation's goodness, something we can do in and through our playing.

None of this mitigates the qualities that distinguish human play from that of other animals. I will shortly describe a number of significant qualities in human play. Here, however, let us notice how the fullness of human play can be a fitting symbol for the mission of Christ and his church. At first glance, it probably seems counterintuitive to suggest that play could symbolize the one who "suffered under Pontius Pilate, was crucified, dead and buried," or that his calling us to carry crosses, serve neighbors, and forgive enemies has anything playful about it. Nonetheless, in Matthew, Jesus

---

1. On "the playing of God," see Rahner, *Man at Play*, 22–23.

describes the failure to receive his ministry and message in terms of recalcitrant children who refuse to play: "We played the flute for you, and you did not dance; we wailed, and you did not mourn" (Matt 11:17). In Luke, the redemption of the prodigal son culminates in fittingly adult forms of play: music, dancing, feasting, joy (Luke 15). Therefore, it isn't a stretch to conclude, as William Thompson has, that "our experience of salvation displays something of a 'ludic' (playful) quality."[2] On this side of Easter, our playing embodies faith that the crucial work—the work of the cross—has already been done. Play is utterly unnecessary, and as such is a sign and gift of God's kingdom.

✢ *Do you agree that play itself can be a sign and gift of creation's goodness, of redemption in Christ, of the coming kingdom of God? Or do you imagine that play has to have a certain quality, shape, or goal to be sign and gift?*

PLAY'S DIMENSIONS

To unpack play's role as sign and gift, we must describe and explore it more thoroughly. That isn't easy, because play is a complex activity, notoriously difficult to define. There are, however, characteristics that are either essential to or typical of play. Drawing them together, we can affirm that play is a freely engaged, nonliteral, self-sufficient activity that is pursued for the fun of it. Let me unpack those in turn.

First, from the most sedentary to the most frenetic, play is always more of an *activity* than a passivity. To play is always to *do* something, whether mostly with the body (tag), largely with the mind (daydreaming), or with both (soccer). But play can never be just a list of specifiable, observable activities. Something might look like play yet not be. The child who is forced to play soccer isn't really playing; real play requires free consent by the player. The adult who can't distinguish his daydreams from reality is not playing but is mentally ill; real play requires a recognition of *unreality*. When an officer chases a suspect, it may look like a game of tag, but they aren't playing because the point is not the chase itself, but the outcome. So play is not just what you do, but how and why.

Before pondering these additional factors, it is worth noticing that the active dimension of playing runs counter to the connotations of passivity

2. Thompson, *Struggle for Theology's Soul*, 222.

that characterize many of our current entertainments. To play is, in some sense, actively to make your own fun. Players are entertaining themselves, whether the play is peekaboo, cards, tennis, or piano. The players are, or can be, both entertainers and audience in one. Yet nowadays most of our entertainment practices separate entertainer from audience, player from spectator. This division of labor has economic and aesthetic consequences. Aesthetically, it means that the music we hear, the sports we watch, and the stories we follow are usually "better" than we could sing, play, or narrate for ourselves. So I am habituated to want the "best" music more than music of my own making, even if I have to pay for it. This allows the profit motive to dwell at the very heart of entertainment, and it moves us from sufficiency to dependency. Entertainment has been transformed from a homegrown activity to a corporately produced commodity, making us generally more interested in entertainments we pay to consume than in entertainments we play into existence. And even if we regularly enjoy some form of active play—like running competitively, weekly cards night, or pickup basketball, it is unlikely that we spend as much time on these forms of active play as we do on being passively entertained.

Second, play is *nonliteral*. For example, child's play often involves pretending or role play, both of which—for the sake of play—adopt points of view that are not literal. Refusing the outlook ("This is not a fast car"; "You are not the teacher") makes play impossible. Accepting the outlook makes play not only possible, but real. When grown-ups play games or sports, their roles (and actions) are defined by the rules, and the pretense is that this activity in this space for this time truly matters. Play always requires a particular take on reality, a willingness to act *as if*—as if the discarded refrigerator box is a house, as if the playmate is a teacher, as if you cannot pick up the soccer ball and run with it.

This imaginative quality of play has significant theological import. First, it can fund our human capacity to allow ritual—the rules and roles and repititions of worship—to hold and shape us. Second, play can foster imaginations of how the world might be otherwise, of how Christ's kingdom might come. Third, the essentially unlimited possibilities of play's imagination can be a sign of the fecund, joyful plenitude of God's goodness, "infinitely more than we could ever ask or imagine." We experience a foretaste of that in the imaginative dimensions of play.

There is more. Play's nonliteral, "as if" quality requires not only an embrace of play's imaginative qualities, but also a release of ultimacy, of realness, of consequence. Or better yet, we might say that the consequences of action in *play* are limited to and bounded by the structures and strictures of playing. Playing "I'm the boss now" makes all the difference during the child's playtime, but no difference at bedtime. Playing trump on your opponent's ace has significance for this trick, perhaps for this game, but not for your career. Play, if it is to be truly play, must retain its "we were just playing" quality.

So play requires a zone (space and time and consensus) that is not fraught with ultimacy, consequence, or real-world risk. In one sense, playing creates this zone—what Johan Huizinga called the "magic circle."[3] But in another sense, we have to carve out and secure play's safety zone. Rowan Williams speaks of the necessary protection that adults give to playing children, allowing play to be safe, which means that what happens in/during play is not binding, permanent, or ultimately consequential.[4] This is not about wearing protective equipment while playing contact sports (always a good idea), or enforcing rules against biting (also recommended). It is the deeper reality that choices and actions during play must not bind futures, determine identities, or foreclose relationships. It is the deepest wisdom that play is only free for its as-if-ness when death is refused, however temporarily. So in this sense, play is activity that ignores mortality, play is time that *pre*-tends eternity. Mortality is the shadow that threatens to darken or defeat play; play is a brightness that can unveil death's pretense to ultimacy, hinting that God made us for eternal, joyful, playful life and living.

Third, play is *free*. Play requires and bestows freedom. As already noted, no matter what it looks like from the outside, you aren't really playing unless you consent to do so. Playing involves revocability, a choice that can be unchosen. The consent of the player includes a willingness to be present to and in the playing, engaging the choices, performing the actions, and holding the "as if" outlook of the game. Thus, the free acceptance that play requires has a wholistic quality, perhaps involving our bodily presence and movement, always requiring our mental attention to decisions and actions, and our (spiritual) intention that this be nothing but play. Play is one of life's reminders of the fullness of our creatureliness.

Paradoxically, free play is also freeing. First, note that there is a spectrum in play between free-form and rule-bound; think chase versus chess. And whatever we're playing, players may have more or less opportunity for

3. Huizinga, *Homo Ludens*.
4. Williams, *Lost Icons*.

response. If we're playing pirates and prisoners, the freedom of the "prisoner" will be more responsive rather than proactive. In football, the wide receivers respond to the prior action of the quarterback's pass. No matter how determined or indeterminate one's possibilities are (either by the rules of the game, the role one occupies, or the actions of other players), it is only play if one has some kind of freedom of response. If there are no choices to be made, no range of responses of body or mind, no way that one's decision, response, or ongoing consent is essential to the continuance of play, then one is no longer playing. You are no longer a player, but a pawn, a piece of equipment without agency. This negative formulation helps us see that play presumes not only the consent of the player(s), but also a realm or range of response (the possibility of choice), and the responding activity of the players. Playing creates its own freedom—the freedom to continue playing. As such, play is a sign of our creation for freedom, and play is also the gift of a partial realization of that freedom.

Fourth, play is *autotelic*. This strange word means that play's purpose or point is internal; play has its own reasons, its own goods and goals. Like all the best kinds of gifts, the value of play centers in what it is, not what it does. Sure, it has all kinds of effects, and they are largely salutary. But they aren't the point, only the benefit. The "what for?" of play is play. We play "for the love of the game": "In utilitarian terms, it is inherently unproductive"[5] or nonpurposive. Walter Ong says that "play is aimed at nothing outside itself."[6] In this sense, play is optional, unnecessary. Of course, some parents bribe their children to play baseball, and some major leaguers get fortune and fame for playing the game. But external rewards are not the point of play, and where they become its goal, play has become work. Play may "make a world" of fantasy, make-believe, or sport, but play does not intend to "change the world." The purpose of play is play, which has its own reasons, goals, aims, and desires. The primary motivations and objectives of play are *intrinsic*. There may also be secondary factors that attach to play *extrinsically*, such as business networking, health benefits, or financial remuneration. But wherever such extrinsic factors become primary, the activity has become work—despite the fact that it may still look like play. This suggests that play is not just a specifiable kind of activity, but that it also requires the appropriate accompanying attitude—a state of mind as well as a motion of body.

---

5. Garvey, *Play*, 4.

6. Quoted in Rahner, *Man at Play*, xiii.

There are two dimensions of the autotelic character of play that are theologically significant. We could say that play aims at nothing and at eternity. First, play aims at nothing; it is self-sufficient, and this self-sufficiency of play is a correlate to our life in, with, and for God. Play is not justified by what it accomplishes. The goods and goal of discipleship are not external to it, as if we do this in order to get that. Walking with God is its own reward. The point and purpose of new life in Christ is just that—new life in Christ. Play is not justified by the work it does, the effects it produces, the difference it makes. Players are not validated by the effect they have on "reality," but by their willingness to give themselves fully to their play, to trust that it is worthy, to entrust themselves to the activity, to believe in the process. If play is a "make-believe" that makes no difference, then it is a delightful analogue for justification by grace through faith.

Second, play aims at eternity, which is an internal aim. We can phrase the intrinsic purpose of play this way: we play just for the fun of it. And play is fun. Too often, we Christians have adopted a grim outlook that is a kind of presumption against pleasure. Admittedly, a desire for certain kinds of pleasure can draw us away from God (Genesis 3), but that does not make pleasure itself suspect, only our capacity to find and enjoy it apart from divine revelation. In this regard, the intrinsic fun of play can be a sign of our human destiny for happiness, for rejoicing in God. Hugo Rahner affirms that "play and dance . . . are an anticipation of heavenly joy."[7] This is true because play is a fitting metaphor for divine love and creation; dance is a fitting metaphor for the triune life; anticipation is a proper temporal orientation for human creatures; joy is heaven's pleasure. Until Christ renews creation, we certainly must continue to work, suffer, and weep just as creation continues to groan in eager expectation; but we may (not must, *may*) also play as a sign and foretaste that our redemption is drawing nigh.

Fifth, play is a form and force of *sociality*. Of course, there are some ways that we can play alone, but the natural form of play is social. The best play both requires and creates community. Play provides an experience of what anthropologist Victor Turner calls *communitas*, a mode of being one. Most of us have seen or experienced this in relation to playing sports, but it is a dimension of nearly all play. Play is where we experience liberative relation to others. As we play we discover the power of play to enrich our sense of belonging—to the game, to the other players or team or fans, even a deepened sense of belonging to the world. At its best, play is a salutary,

7. Rahner, *Man at Play*, 8.

creative sociality and conviviality. It limns the very best of who we can be—together. This experience of becoming "one" expresses our human destiny for solidarity. As such, play aspires to momentary figurations of the *social* dimension of the kingdom of God.

We can celebrate these moments, not only as good in themselves (brief moments of shared joy), but also as pointers to a transcendent good that lies beyond our capacity to produce and sustain (brief glimmers of eternal community with God). What we cannot celebrate is how many Christians these days have more powerful experiences of athletic community in the stadium or coliseum than they do of ecclesial community in the sanctuary. Noticing that *communitas* appears more likely to break forth at a match than a mass, we must not become unreflective or alarmed into the wrong kind of response. The last thing Christian worship should become is more like March Madness; nor should it opt for a youth league soccer ethos or a Super Bowl vibe. Rather, we should be ever attentive to the truth that worship, like every team sport, finds community as a gift received through playing your part.

✣ *This chapter has identified five key aspects of play—activity, nonliteral, free, auto-telic (or purposefully purposeless), and social. Can you name ways that each aspect connects positively with Christian faith? Does this change your understanding of play, or how you will play?*

PLAYING IS FUN, BUT IS IT ENTERTAINMENT?

Let's consider a question that this chapter has so far begged: is it "entertainment" when we are the ones playing—whether free play, games, or sports, or does it only become entertainment when we are watching someone else play? The answer is determined less by "facts" brought to bear on the question, and more by how we "feel" about the definition of terms. If entertainment is defined as whatever we do for fun with our leisure time, then play is certainly entertainment, even if we are both entertainer and audience in one. On the other hand, if entertainment is defined as whatever we "watch" for fun, as another's activity presented for our pleasurable but passive attention, then play is only entertainment if we are *being* entertained (note the passive verb) by the play of others.

I would like to avoid both the Scylla of "entertainment is whatever you do for fun" and the Charybdis of "entertainment is utterly passive consumption." Not everything we pleasurably enjoy during periods of leisure should be categorized as entertainment—that's one of the deepest distortions of the contemporary sexual ethos known as the "hook-up culture": it diminishes sexual communication into stimulation to stave off boredom. There are a host of pleasurable leisure activities—things we do for fun—that are best not categorized as entertainment: for example, gardening, baking, painting, composing music, or journaling. In the end, no matter how entertaining these sorts of activities are to us, they are more than entertainment precisely because they are productive. They bring forth the earth's bounty, the oven's goodness, the artist's insight, etc. This suggests to me that play does qualify as entertainment, precisely because of its autotelic character. The only thing play intends to produce is itself.

Of course, this presumes that not every entertainment is constituted by the division between active performer and passive spectator, or between entertainment production and consumption. Notions of entertainment as purely passive reception are culturally conditioned by a century of mass-mediated entertainment; they are not objective realities. So playing a game of cards together, or playing music together, or playing make-believe are all forms of entertainment, despite the fact that our only audience is one another. We are *being entertained* (passive construction) precisely as we *entertain ourselves* (active construction).

Entertaining ourselves is often free, usually cheap, and almost always fun. Being entertained by others is often expensive, and almost always is a for-profit venture for someone. In a culture of mass-mediated entertainments that bedazzle us with the notion that commercial entertainments are always superior to homegrown, and that bewitch us with the sense that mass-mediated entertainments are the gold standard, we are continually conditioned to become spectators that always watch but never play. The bulk of this chapter has suggested, contrariwise, that free, freeing play is the gold standard. We ought, therefore, to play something, sometimes, as long as we are able—whether that be playing daily with children, playing (or singing) music with others, enjoying games, or playing sports. "*Let's play!*" becomes a kind of holy invitation, as well as an effective countermeasure to "now watch this!"

✤ *Do you regularly play anything? Have you considered your playing to be entertainment?*

PLAYING SPORTS IS ENTERTAINMENT

In the remainder of this chapter, I want to focus on the entertaining pleasures of playing sports. (In the next chapter, we will look at watching sports
as entertainment.) Hardly anyone likes every sport; almost no one hates
them all. "Liking" a sport can mean we enjoy both playing and watching
it, or only playing or only watching. What do we like about *playing* sports?

The pleasures unique to playing sports are largely dependent on internal location, cooperative action, and physicality. Both spatially and psychically, players are *inside* the game. Objectively, they are both *on* the field,
court, or track, and *in* the game, match, or race, as players or competitors.
Their objective position means that they see, hear, feel, *and do* everything
from within the play's domain. They are at or near the center of the action—
action that they are continually creating and receiving.[8] In a culture where
many people lack a strong sense of agency (the feeling that our actions matter, or that we have some significant control over our own destinies), sports
put us *in* the game in such a way that how we play will powerfully influence
the outcome.

Subjectively, players are inside the "magic circle" of play, subject to its
structure, rules, roles, goals, clock, and contingencies, and also agents of its
actions, strategies, tempo, improvisations, and surprises. As the ones who
actually do the playing, only they experience playing. (Any child who runs
on the field crying "let me play" knows this at some precognitive level.) In
team sports, the subjective also includes the relational and psychic pleasures of cohesion with teammates, of complementary effort, of unified
endeavor, of shared success and failure. This dimension is what A. Bartlett
Giamatti means by "the happy camaraderie of competition."[9] It can include
interpersonal affection, but is most basically the sense of a corporate identity more important than oneself, of being a team. (For several decades,
churches have been tapping that dynamic when they reflect on leadership
as "team building.")

Probably the pleasures that are most central for players (but almost
completely unavailable to spectators) are physical and kinesthetic. This
involves a whole panoply of related dimensions of our bodiliness: the

---

8. The importance of this sense of spatial internality should not be underestimated.
The popularity of an entire strand of video games depends in part on the game's ability to
give the player a "first person" point of view within a three-dimensional virtual environment. That is a different pleasure than a third person, or bird's-eye view, of the action.

9. Giamatti, *Take Time for Paradise*, 78.

pleasures of intense effort, of working and striving and sweating and thirsting and enduring; the pleasures of athletic motion, of agility, coordination, precision, and speed; the pleasures (and pains) of the body's surface touching and being touched by the ball, equipment, opponents, teammates, ground, court, air, sun, wind, or rain. The physicality of playing sports brings pleasures that are not communicable or mediable; they cannot be conveyed by any technology, not even the wonders of HD television, but only undergone. Video gaming has developed full motion sensors and tactile feedback controllers in an effort to capture some of the bodiliness, the kinesthetic pleasure, of sport.

Playing sports is an opportunity for the marriage of form and function, where celebration of and thanksgiving for our bodiliness takes physical form. That may be the grain of truth in "endzone piety": sports play can be the simultaneous reception of bodily grace and offering of bodily praise. But the simultaneity is what makes the grain of truth in touchdown piety so tiny: you don't need to kneel, bow, point to God's throne or high-five Jesus as a communication of thanksgiving; the physical activity is itself already the word of gratitude. Indeed, you don't need to score a touchdown, hit a homer, or ace a serve to have cause for rejoicing; the physical play is itself both reason for rejoicing and a clear expression of it.

Ideally, then, we will never settle for always watching instead of playing sports, but will *play something, sometimes, as long as we are able.* (And if not a sport, then play a musical instrument or play our vocal chords or play daily with children.) If our culture of sports entertainment so conditions us as spectators that we always watch but never play, we will have lost more than we have gained.

✣ *Do you regularly play at anything (sport, dance, etc.) that involves your body and invokes praise? Do you play or do anything that evokes a sense of sociality or team?*

seven

We Watch Them Play (Sports)

HOSEA GOES TO THE SUPER BOWL

"Sport, a seemingly trivial facet of life, is a fundamental cultural activity in every country of the modern world."[1] Neither sport nor spectating is a product of modern culture, however. Indeed, every four years the modern Olympic Games should remind us that spectator sports are at least as old as the age of Amos, Hosea, Isaiah, and Micah. Although the emphasis of those first Olympics was on participation, there were always spectators. By the time of Jeremiah there is evidence of a stadium for the spectators who came to watch. (Athletes and spectators were all men, by the way, which suggests that gender bias in sport is not new either.) Apparently, the pleasure of watching others play runs deep enough to span time and transcend cultures.

I intentionally date ancient sport by reference to the Hebrew prophets in order to evoke theological sensibilities that problematize play, games, and sport. One could imagine a modern Amos, only slightly paraphrased, shouting, "I hate, I despise your *game* days, and I take no delight in your *Super Bowls!*" (Amos 5:21). Of course, Amos would be scandalized by the economics of professional sports—franchise profits, star salaries, corporate salesmanship, the exorbitant price of a ticket and a hot dog. But his greatest

1. Sage, *Globalizing Sport*, xiv.

invective would be aimed at sport as a recurrent ritualization of social well-being, a celebration scandalously oblivious to the economic injustice rampant in our communities. If Amos were standing by the turnstiles with a megaphone, there might be far fewer Christians going to games.

Thankfully, Amos's prophetic hyperbole against hypocrisy was never intended to stop proper ritual celebrations, but rather to start proper service of needy neighbors. So even today, his chastisement ought first to incite active discipleship, rather than a ban on enjoying spectator sports. Moreover, there are themes in the oratory of his prophetic colleagues far more amenable to sport. Isaiah's imagination of the blossoming of the desert and the joyful parade through it finds analogue in the festive creativity—indeed, the fecund craziness—of game day preparations, parades, and parties. Jeremiah's purchase of a field in Anathoth would be trivialized if we likened it to purchasing season tickets to the Cubs, but there are parallels: both are seemingly impotent acts that function as potent signs that we can hope in the future.

What is new about the modern Olympic Games, and all the rest of our sports culture, is the intervention of mass media, which impacts the experience, patterns, economy, and scale of sport spectatorship. The Dallas Cowboys' new billion-dollar stadium might give the impression that truly *grand* stadia are distinctively modern, but Rome's racetracks and Colosseum rival the capacity of our biggest sporting venues. The significant difference is that in ancient Rome, if you didn't get in, you missed it. Not so today. A major global championship, such as soccer's World Cup final, might draw close to a billion television viewers. There's no way you could build a grandstand for that many people.

✤ *Should your congregation's relation to sports call forth Amos's condemnation of hypocrisy or Isaiah's celebration of hope?*

THE FUN OF WATCHING

In the prior chapter, we considered pleasures intrinsic to play in general, and playing sports in particular. Here we will first consider a few pleasures that are available to spectators but not players, and then give attention to the pleasures spectators and players can share, before asking what difference electronic mediation makes.

Spatially, the spectator must be outside the realm of play. Depending on how space is arranged, the spectator is likely to have a fuller view of the whole field of play than does any player. Moreover, spectators will always see more of the action than will the players, precisely because they see every single player, whereas no player can see herself. Physically, spectators may experience restfulness, stasis, recuperation, or, alternatively, frenzy or even ecstasis. Whether solemn (think Wimbledon) or frenetic (think college basketball), fans experience the game largely free of the rules and regimens that govern physicality, except for rules about staying out of the field of play. Probably the purest expression of the spectator's freedom vis-à-vis that of the player's is eating and drinking while watching the game. While a cynic might suggest that "peanuts and Cracker Jacks" aren't intrinsic to the physical pleasures of watching baseball (nor is singing during the seventh-inning stretch), that insistence would miss the possibilities for enjoyment that inhere in being a spectator. If you're not going to eat and drink, or clap, whistle, shout, and cheer, or stand, stretch, and sing, then you may still enjoy many of the shared pleasures of sports, but you are missing out on a key pleasure unique to spectators—freedom from the physical rigor and discipline of the game. Exercising that freedom can be a sort of rejoicing.

Both players and spectators can enjoy seeing the splendor of playing bodies, and the beauty of excellent play—this is perhaps a core aim of spectation—but players have other priorities. Sport has the capacity to make us gasp, to thrill us in wonder at the splendor of excellent play, at the momentary perfection of human endeavor (sometimes individual and sometimes cooperative), at the exquisite beauty of physical bodies extending and expending themselves. In a wonderfully turned phrase, Denise Lardner Carmody says that beyond the ugliness of sport as business, the hype of sport as entertainment, and the violence of sport as competition, occasionally sport "can show us incarnate spirits achieving wonders."[2] She goes on to connect this with the early church theologian Irenaeus, who said that the glory of God is humanity fully alive. The beauty of athletic bodies (Carmody describes Nadia Comaneci and Martina Navratilova as "gorgeous specimens, aglow with an animal beauty") experienced *in situ* and *in tempo*—that is, in the midst and the momentum of the game—make it evident that our physicality, our bodiliness, is good, very good.

The attractiveness of sporting bodies and the thrill of athletic excellence can be a powerful antidote to gnostic forms of Christianity. Gnostic

2. Carmody, "Big-Time Spectator Sports," 109.

Christianity depreciates our bodiliness, demeans creation and materiality; it sees salvation as release from embodiment. Identified and refuted as a heresy by the same theologian, Irenaeus, gnosticism has nonetheless continued to dog Christianity throughout its existence, continually insinuating that being embodied is some kind of cosmic mistake. The cure for that kind of thinking can certainly be found in the biblical accounts of God's good creation and of Jesus's birth, healing ministry, crucifixion, and bodily resurrection, and in the church's embodied practices of worshiping God and serving neighbor. But there is also a curative quality in the utter, enthralling beauty of superlative play and stunning athleticism. Enjoying the beauty of sport can be a joyous inoculation against gnosticism.

✢ *The pleasures of spectating seem to be available whether we are present at the competition or watching via electronic mediation. Do you think one is better or worse? Do you prefer watching in person or on television? Does watching via electronic mediation open the door for gnosticism to creep back into our outlook?*

SHARED PLEASURES OF ATHLETIC DRAMA

For nearly forty years, ABC's *Wide World of Sports*, which producer Roone Arledge invented "to add show business to sports,"[3] opened with a paean to "the human drama of athletic competition." Both players and spectators participate in multiple pleasures of this athletic drama—narrative, emotional, social, and even mythic.

Sporting contests inherently follow the narrative arc of beginning, middle, and end. Moreover, the element of suspense is enhanced in sport, since the outcome of a game truly is open and undetermined. The contestants, as it were, are authors of their own drama, contending with one another to determine how the story will end. In this regard, sport offers a form of the pleasure of dramatic suspense that is superior to theater and film, precisely because the outcome is "authored" by the players themselves as the "story" moves sequentially through time. No one—neither audience nor actors—knows how this story will end. Sport is more like live theatrical improvisation inasmuch as the ending emerges out of what happens along the way. The narrative pleasures of following the story line, the pleasure of dramatic suspense about the outcome, attend to our best games

3. Ashby, *With Amusement for All*, 365.

and sporting contests. People who record a game that they can't watch live are usually determined not to learn the final outcome before they watch the recording. By the same token, a game or contest almost necessarily becomes boring when the outcome is no longer in dispute. Even amazing feats of athletic prowess—a lithe dunk, a powerful homer, a one-handed catch—lose some of their magic when they are too late to make a difference in the outcome. Contingency and suspense are key pleasures in sport. This pleasure may be felt more keenly by those who are physically present at the game, but it is also available to those who watch via media.

The drama of sport provides emotional pleasures that range far beyond enjoying a good story—everything from determination, anticipation, hope, or anxiety to fear, joy, exhilaration, even delirium and ecstasy. It isn't just the athletes who enjoy the "thrill of victory" or suffer the "agony of defeat"; their emotion is shared by spectators and often amplified by them. (Athletes are quick to acknowledge that the size and mood of the crowd makes a difference in a game.) Let's notice two exceedingly positive dimensions of this wide gamut of human emotion available through sport. First, because play is not ultimate, neither is the intensified emotion we experience through playing or watching sport. No matter how powerful our hopes and fears during the game, no matter how exuberant our exultations or crushing our disappointments, they are never a matter of life or death. Sure, you might say, "I'll just die if Duke loses to Carolina," but really you won't. Fans and players both experience the emotions of play in the protected non-ultimacy of play. Sport is emotionally safe.

Second, sport is emotionally beneficial. In addition to enjoyment per se, there is a quality called *eustress*, which is "positive levels of arousal. [Sport] is exciting to the senses. It gets your adrenaline going."[4] In a relatively riskless world, playing or watching sports is one of the few remaining ways to generate a consistent adrenaline rush. Sport arouses a society grown insipid. And better that such stimulation be incited by sport than by fascists and demagogues. But what should Christians think about living lives that ordinarily experience the rush of aroused passion primarily through vicarious identification with sports professionals, college athletes, or high school teams?

4. Sayre and King, *Entertainment and Society*, 297.

✥ *Is the* eustress *of passionate play good training for martyrdom? Does the* eustress *of spectatorship arouse us to greatness or divert us from it?*

Ever shout "we won!" when your favorite team wins? That "we" is a telling indication of the power of sport to evoke and foster a sense of affiliation, both a positive participation in the *communitas* of a particular game, and an enduring social identification with a team. Our shorthand nomenclature for these relationships is "fan." Apart from such identification, the dramatic pleasures of particular games is greatly diminished. Reflect on watching a game in which you were ambivalent about both teams; likely that made it difficult to care very strongly about the dramatic unfolding of the contest. Also, apart from such identification, the emotional pleasures of particular games are muted. Affiliation creates bonds between spectator and team/players that open a kind of emotional thoroughfare which allows vicarious participation in both directions. Fans participate, to some degree, in their team's joys (and disappointments), and players receive, and are empowered by, the emotional energy of their fans (think basketball's "sixth man"). Mediation, unfortunately, reduces this thoroughfare to a one-way street.

Finally, we continue a millennia-old practice of investing competitors with a representational quality. The team represents "us"—our school, or our race, or our town, or our state, or our nation. Their competition on the field of play is representative of off-field conflicts. Witness the mythic quality invested in Jesse Owens's victories in the Berlin Olympic Games, or how during the Cold War the Olympic Games were a kind of proxy war between the United States and the U.S.S.R., or the investment of racial identity in the victories (and defeats) of Joe Lewis. The most memorable recent movie depicting this reality is *Invictus*, based on John Carlin's book *Playing the Enemy: Nelson Mandela and the Game that Made a Nation*. Both book and movie show how, in post-apartheid South Africa, a rugby team that had represented racial division became both symbol and instrument of racial reconciliation.

Surely this is an instance of sport's mythic dimension, its capacity to connect us with one another by connecting us with "some transcendent something beyond [ourselves]."[5] In a modernity that has been evacuated of mystery, where our places and times are disenchanted and often banal, sports—especially "big games," storied careers, or propitious teams—can

---

5. Anker, "Rugby and Reconciliation," 24.

have a mythic ethos, pointing to something bigger and deeper than the mundane, routinized, disenchanted world we inhabit. This mythic quality derives from several facets of modern spectator sports: the extraordinary physicality of the athletes, who are capable of feats so dazzling they leave us speechless; the ritual creation of bounded space and time in games, which parallels the ritual encounter with mystery in religious worship and devotion; and the competition itself as deeply symbolic of human struggle for life (and happiness) and against death (and grief).

✣ *Do we identify more deeply with the "we" of a favorite team, or the "us" of Christ's holy, catholic church? Do the representational and mythic qualities of sport teach us how to experience mystery, or do they tranquilize us—the church—from engaging our representational mission of manifesting divine glory?*

THE PROBLEMS WITH MEDIATION

I am finite, and my finitude is intrinsically part of the goodness of being a bodily creature of a loving Creator. Part of the thrill of sports is watching bodies seemingly transcend their creaturely limits, even if only for a moment; to soar, run, shoot, throw, dribble, or catch beyond what seems humanly possible. Yet the truth of this thrill is that these bodies, these athletes, are displaying human limits to the fullest, presenting us with the full measure of humanity limned by finitude. Another part of the thrill of watching sports is bodily presence, the limited and limiting corporality of congregating around a bodily activity that one is able to *feel*—physically— as one watches, and that one can share in and with all the others who are physically present as well. Being part of the crowd at a game allows us to experience it in and through our body and its limits—our bodily surface, the limitations of skin and sight and self that jostle and touch and mingle and interface in order to become more than a solitary self, but less than an all-seeing "god."

Technological mediation changes the pleasures of watching sports in ways that are as subtle as they are significant. Or perhaps the alterations aren't really subtle, but just hard to notice after a century of habituation to sports broadcasting. There are at least three significant losses. First, mediated spectation trades limited, finite presence for an enhanced absence that can appear almost limitless. We can now watch a match (or several at the same time) five thousand miles away, from multiple angles, with close-ups and slow motion replays of great plays. I cannot see that far, that close, that slow, that many times from that many angles. Mediated spectation enhances my vision beyond human limitation, meaning that I lose the very thing that sports celebrates: the pleasures of pushing bodies to—but not beyond—their limits. Regularly watching sports from which we are physically absent thus has a gnosticizing effect—it alienates us from reconciliation with our bodily limits by habituating us to prefer mediated moments and modalities. (Anyone who has ever attended a game only to feel a pang of loss at not being able to watch endless replays of a contested call or an amazing score is experiencing this alienation, even if they do not recognize it as such.) Watching mediated games also habituates us not to notice that we are missing the shared pleasures of spectating together. It may even form us to prefer absence from the crowd. So technological mediation enhances sight in ways that alienate us from the goodness of bodily limits and of communal presence. We come to prefer powerful but disincarnate access to the goodness of being there.

Second, mediated spectation enhances attention while simultaneously fracturing it in dissipating ways. What looks like ultimate freedom to craft a personalized sports experience is absolutely bound to and controlled by the mediation itself. To begin with, we can only look at what the broadcasters decide to show; if they linger too long on a crowd shot, we cannot watch the fast break as it occurs. More importantly, we cannot choose to attend uninterruptedly to one game; most commercial broadcasts are riddled with advertisements and various other discontinuities of presentation (station breaks, news teasers, and promos of other television fare by the commentators). While the technological mediation of sport offers multiple ways to transcend our finitude, it simultaneously controls our gaze and fractures our attention.

Finally, broadcast media turn the emotional thoroughfare into a one-way street. Fans are no longer present and in sync with the team's emotion, but are at best voyeurs who see and hear that emotion represented digitally. Fans cannot return their own emotion to the players, project their own responses (even though we cheer, yell, or boo at our television screens). The communication loop is broken, which means that no matter how much we identify with our team, no matter how deeply we experience their play, we cannot—at a distance—participate in the *communitas* that arises among all who are present.

A quick theological reflection on each of these. First, preferring absence to presence. There is a subtle distortion of consciousness that arises when our spectation is primarily a mediated reality, especially when we come to prefer mediation. Consider these alternatives. There may be fans who "go to every game they can" (even if they can only afford to go once a year) and follow their team on television when they can't be present in the flesh. For such fans, television mediates many (but not all) of the pleasures of presence; television is the next best thing to being there. There are other fans who have never gone to a game, or having gone, acknowledge that they prefer watching on television. For fans such as this, mediation does not compensate for something that is missing, that is, being there; instead, mediation *is* their way of being there. For these fans, television mediates all the pleasures of spectation and accomplishes fully for them their sense of community. I believe that this latter practice of fan affiliation is deformative of our desire for presence—for presence with needy neighbors, for presence with our brothers and sisters in the church, for the real presence of Christ in the bread and the wine. Acceptance of the superiority (or sufficiency) of televised sport habituates us to be comfortable with forms of absence that are inimical to faithful discipleship—absence from the neighbor's need, from the gathered church, from participation in the Lord's Table.

Second, the fixed, fractured gaze. Sports television has heightened the excitement threshold considerably. Whether it is the endless instant replays of the most dramatic plays or controversial calls during the game, or the highlight reel that encapsulates a two- or three-hour game afterwards, we become more and more addicted to the spectacular, adrenalin-rush moments, rather than more and more in love with the sheer playing of the game. Mark Galli claims that this eventually trains us to watch "games for those 'moments.' You find yourself increasingly bored with every other part of the game. You'll multitask or wander off getting chores done—only to rush back into the living room to catch the instant replay of one of those 'moments.' It turns us (okay, me) into fourth-quarter junkies."[6] Galli goes on to lament the loss of the narrative arc, the unfolding story, of the game. Fixating on highlights is a way of preferring one of the pleasures of sport— the ecstasy of the athletically amazing—to the detriment of its other pleasures—the drama of unfolding competition, the emotion of its motion, the construction of its community. And notice how these highlights, these "rush moments," are often proffered precisely to concentrate our attention,

6. Galli, "Spectating as a Spiritual Discipline."

to keep us from being distracted by the enduring possibilities of attending elsewhere—changing the channel, looking out the window, texting, leaving the room, etc. Yet what the spectacle-izing of sport seeks to cure it simultaneously causes, namely, a fracturing—in this case a fracturing of the game itself. That habituation is unfortunate in relation to sport, but deadly to discipleship, precisely as it conditions us to seek highlights rather than constancy, to pursue and expect only mountaintop experiences in the life of faith.

Third, loss of localized *communitas*. Although fan identification with a team can locate loyalty in ways that contribute to the good of a particular place and community (as when civic pride waxes or wanes with the success of the hometown team), mediated sports and increased mobility have now dis-located fandom in ways that undermine the common good. Now the team you love isn't necessarily your "home team." The miracle of television means that "your" team can be anywhere; where it plays doesn't really matter. This enhances the individualistic quality of identity formation through fandom, while also diminishing the community-forming bonds of local teams; that is, where electronic mediation constructs fandom there is a correlative distancing from the common ground on which the common good is built. In addition to this geographical diminishment, consider how the proliferation of sports entertainments, while creating the possibility of being an avid fan of multiple teams all year long, makes spectation not a seasonal, but a continual activity. It is the fabric of everyday life. It never ends.

SPORT AS SOCIAL SIN

So having catalogued the pleasures of sports and some distorting effects of commercial electronic mediation, it remains to delineate the perils of forgetting that sport-become-big-business threatens to distort our faith, hope, and love. We won't see that threat clearly, however, if we imagine sin too categorically and too individualistically. A robust Christian theology must recognize two theological realities shaping the way we name and confess sin.

First, our sin isn't created *ex nihilo*, out of nothing, the way God created the world. Rather, our sin is a matter of distorting, dissolving, demeaning the goodness of God's creation. Sin is a kind of un-creation of goodness, beauty, and truth; it is faith, hope, and love gone astray, but not entirely gone. Michael Novak has suggested that sports are a kind of natural good-ness, where the grace of nature is available to anyone willing receive it.[7] While true, that certainly does not mean that sport is pristine, untainted by the degradations of sin. Some "sport" is very far gone from the goodness of creation—bullfighting comes to mind. All sport is susceptible to the cor-ruption of desire, understanding, and will that constitutes our depravity. So we cannot subscribe to the idealistic rhetoric that sees sport in general, or a particular sport like baseball, as a near perfect school of "Christian charac-ter." The true school of Christian character is the church; sport can at best be an analogue that displays the discipline and training intrinsic to trans-formation, and that inculcates some of the characteristics (virtues, habits, disciplines, outlooks, desires, etc.) of a proper Christian discipleship. Sport can never be more than this; too often, however, it is considerably less.

Second, *our* sin is more than just the sum total of *my* sin and *thy* sin. It is *ours*, woven into the social, relational, interstitial warp and woof of our institutions, organizations, communications, activities, recreations, and imaginations. This puts the identification of sin well beyond a simplistic cataloguing of misdeeds, and puts sin's eradication well outside the scope of personal resolve. So we regularly confess our sins, and our condition as socially situated sinners, crying out to the only one who truly can help: "Lord, have mercy. Christ, have mercy. Lord, have mercy."

IDLE PLAY AND IDOLATROUS MAMMON

Denise Lardner Carmody suggests that the greatest danger of sport is idola-try. Unfortunately, most of us immediately breathe a sigh of relief—because we hold a very deficient theology of idols. We tend to think of idols objec-tively as somebody else's problem—primitive cultures that worship images of wood and stone (rather than, say, modern fans slavering over the cover of *Sports Illustrated*). We tend to think of idolatry subjectively as an exces-sive internal attitude—sports fanatics who idolize their star player, favorite team, beloved sport (rather than, say, the subjective relationship all specta-tors have to the objective reality of modern sports). A more robust and nuanced theology of idolatry would recognize that 1) it is always a condi-tion of ignorance and often involves self-deceptions (see Isaiah's skewering satire in chapter 45); and 2) it has both personal and social dimensions, which require us to attend not only to our inner relation to the idolized

7. See Novak, *Joy of Sports.*

object, but also to the larger communicative network in which we and the idol exist (this is the force of Paul's discussion of eating meat sacrificed to idols in 1 Corinthians 8).

Let's take these dimensions in turn. Given the plethora of sports news available to us, we think we know just how "dirty" professional and college sports have become. Regarding the former, Mark Galli has written, "The problems of professional sports are legion—selfishness of players, greed of owners, rudeness of fans, the marketing and merchandizing, the gambling, the groupies, the steroids, and on and on and on it goes. A fan has to be a master of denial to block all that out to deeply enjoy a game, as a game, anymore."[8] Regarding collegiate sport, Shirl Hoffman writes, "Recruiting scandals, under-the-table payoffs, and academic cheating—all perpetrated in the name of athletic excellence—have become such regular features on the sports pages that we have come to accept them as the cost of a Saturday afternoon's entertainment."[9] Galli and Hoffman are naming the same phenomenon, a subjective self-deception that ignores the problems in order to enjoy the game. Because many of us bring an individualistic understanding of sin to this analysis, we can easily interpret all this as the result of individual choices: a few bad apples here, a dishonest coach there, a corrupt fan or corrupting booster club. Where we are willing to acknowledge the problem, we theologize it as individual choices, personal sins, the forward who shaved points, the slugger who took steroids (and then lied to Congress about it). What we refuse to acknowledge, and so fail to theologize, is our own role as spectators in a system that breeds, rewards, colludes with, coerces, and often requires these "sins."

So instead of rethinking, we engage in ritual scapegoating. Every year provides an almost endless parade of athletes who are sent away for their sins. In effect, they function as scapegoats who bear not only their own acknowledged sins, but also the unacknowledged sin of the system as a whole. This is where Carmody's work helps us see what we refuse to look at—our own contribution to and complicity in the system as a whole. Carmody notes how our long-standing tendency to displace Jesus with Mammon has colluded with modern sport's pervasion by monied interests. What pervades perverts, not only those who play but also us who watch. It perverts not only players who cheat, but every player who loses the joy of playing because now it's his job. And we watchers are not innocent, even though we

8. Galli, "Something Noble and Good," para. 3.
9. Hoffman, "Whatever Happened to Play?" 22.

claim the moral high ground (box seats?), because it is finally our incessant attention that is the source of all the money. If no one were watching, no one would be paying. That wouldn't turn the gridiron, pitch, court, and field back into the sinless soil of Eden, but perhaps many of the distortions of professional and college sports could be corrected. Sports would still reproduce most of the injustices and injuries of the larger society within which they are played—racism, sexism, classism, and nationalism, to name just a few. But much of what makes the sports we watch into occasions for idolatry would largely dissipate.

Does that mean we should stop watching? I haven't . . . yet, but I am open to the possibility that faithful discipleship might require that kind of renunciation. (If I did find myself compelled to give up pro football or college basketball, it would be very painful indeed.) Meanwhile, there are several good reasons to continue watching, to continue enjoying sport. As we do, we need desperately to be done with the denial of our own complicity. Spectation is inherently a participation in the seamy, selfish, scandalous dimensions of big-time sports. Watching implicates us in systemic sin. Lord have mercy.

✥ *In what ways, if at all, have you been aware of your complicity in the corruptions of big-time sports? Does praying "Lord have mercy" let us off the hook, or obligate us to be more discerning about the idolatries that hedge our lives?*

SPORTIANITY VS. CRUCIFORMITY

More than thirty-five years ago, Frank Deford coined the term "sportianity" to describe athletes who "endorse Jesus, much as they would a new sneaker or a graphite-shafted driver."[10] Deford wasn't naming a new phenomenon, but one that had been going strong for more than one hundred years. Star athletes have been lending their charisma, their attractiveness, their credibility to Jesus as far back as frontier camp meetings. Deford's point is that the constant here, the powerhouse source of meaning and attractiveness, is the endorsing athlete, not the endorsed product, whether that product be Jockey underwear or Jesus. Where Christians consent to "sportian" forms of evangelism, they evince a deep anxiety about the compelling beauty, goodness, and truth of Jesus. It's as if Jesus needs help, and Terry Bradshaw,

10. Deford, "Word according to Tom," 56.

Kurt Warner, Tim Tebow, or [fill in the blank] is the hero who can help him. Sportianity is a subtle but real demeaning of Jesus. Christ have mercy.

We can also use Deford's term to indicate those public displays of piety that are increasingly common in sports. How we think about them probably displays historic Christian divisions. For example, evangelical fans might dismiss as "superstitious" the baseball player who makes the sign of the cross before batting while approving the football player who drops to his knee after a touchdown and "points to Jesus." Catholic fans, not surprisingly, might reverse these responses. This joke begins to put Sportianity in perspective:

> A priest and a rabbi go to a boxing match. One fighter makes the sign of the cross just before each round begins. "What does that mean?" the rabbi asks the priest. "Not a thing if he can't box!" the priest replies.

Public displays of piety are no substitute for training, talent, and effort. Where Christian faith and devotional practices are treated as a means toward the end of winning, or of enhancing individual performances, they are being treated as a kind of spiritual steroid. And where these public displays of piety become part of the overall persona of a sports star, stage-managed to cultivate a "Christian" public image, they profoundly undermine the appearance of Christ in our midst. Grace is disgraced, faith loses credibility.

Similarly with end zone celebrations and all the rest. Again, such ritual "thank yous" after an amazing score draw more attention to the athlete who takes a knee or points toward heaven than to the crucified savior. Notice how such moments of "glorification" only occur after an amazing success; the cornerback who got beat doesn't kneel to give thanks that he didn't get injured, nor does the catcher point to heaven after a wild throw to second (to thank God for keeping him humble). The theology operative in the actions of Sportianity seems to be "thank God for victories, blame self for defeats." This simplistic theology of valuing success as divine validation runs afoul of what Paul calls the foolishness of the cross, which is God's power made available in the weakness of the cross, and in the midst of those who are weak, lowly, and despised (see 1 Corinthians). Christians who play sports, especially the ones who win a lot, would do well to remember Jesus's caution not to pray like the hypocrites who love to pray standing in the limelight (Matt 6:5–6). Christ have mercy.

✥ *Have you ever wondered why male athletes are so much more likely than female athletes to uncork a Sportian demonstration?*

FREE TIME VS. GAME TIME

As a form of play, we have already seen that sport constructs time in freeing ways. Because play's purpose is found neither in its *before* or *after*, but in its *now*, it frees us to enjoy the present, ideally in ways that anticipate our eternal joy.

But modern sport all too easily, almost inevitably, disorders the way we keep time. I'm after something subtle here, but it makes sense to start with something more overt: Sundays. Early on, some of the strongest resistance from the church to modern sports centered around the question of scheduling on Sundays. This was rooted in sabbatarian understandings of the Lord's Day as the Christian Sabbath, a day holy to the Lord, and thus not to be profaned by work or by worldly enjoyments. Both playing and spectating were considered unworthy pursuits for a Sunday. (The movie *Chariots of Fire* dramatizes the depth of this conviction in early twentieth-century British evangelicals.) Over a century or so, churches dropped their opposition to Sunday sports, and then even embraced them as a positive choice.

That change of mind was probably good since the original "no" rested on mistaken understandings of the meaning and purpose of the Ten Commandments. But the change of practice that followed has been far less good. How so? First, the Lord's *Day* has been, for most Christians, demoted to the Lord's hour, or at best to the Lord's morning. No longer does the way Christians keep an entire day bear witness to their hope that Jesus's resurrection from the dead on the first day of the week was the first fruits of their own future. Second, Christians have lost their grasp on Sunday's location as the first day of the week; our cycle of workweek and week*end* has made Sunday the week's conclusion, a last, carefree sigh before Monday morning's groan. Third, notice how this change has allowed a powerhouse sport like football, with its weekly rhythm, to colonize most of Sunday for its own purposes, meanings, and pleasures. Enjoying Sunday football is fraught with fallenness, as it interpolates us into what Charles Taylor calls a "social imaginary," a background understanding of our cultural and social world in which it is natural for our Sunday afternoons in the fall to be enthralled with football (and summer Sundays with baseball, etc.). Anticipation, a key dimension of hope, is in danger of being focused more on whether our team wins than on the prospects of gathering with God's people for worship.

What holds true for game day is equally true of the seasons of the year. "Hope springs eternal" at the beginning of every baseball season, as once again the future lies tantalizingly open, a horizon of possibilities that might fructify as victory. Contrast that with the Christian calendar of seasons, meant to draw us annually into the gospel drama of the promised coming, glorious incarnation, cruciform journey, and resurrection victory of Jesus. The church's calendar of seasons does not want to be the only schedule in town, but it does intend to be our core structural rhythm—the one premised on the promise that our hope is in Christ. I suspect that for many of us who affirm the goodness of the church year and try to follow it, there can nonetheless be a subjective sense in which particular sports seasons or "festivals" impinge more powerfully on our emotions, desires, hopes, and dreams. Baseball's opening day eclipses Good Friday; football season feels more real than Advent and Christmas. God help us when NCAA basketball's Final Four falls on Easter weekend. Lord have mercy.

✢ *In your own ecclesial setting, what ways have sports intruded into the observance of the Christian year? (Super Bowl parties for youth, perhaps?) What is the net effect of such overlaps?*

So being a fan of big-time sports implicates us in its banalities as well as its beauties. The love of the game can enrich our lives, but under the dominance of Mammon, modern sport can also impoverish our world. So the faithful can play and watch sports; faithfulness calls us to continually discern when and how we should.

eight

Gambling Doesn't P(l)ay

GAMING? PLAYING?

WHY INTERPOSE A CHAPTER on gambling between "we play" and "Wii play"? Because comparing gambling and video games can be mutually illuminating. Both industries have laid claim to the title "gaming," but their games are profoundly different: gambling games rest fundamentally on the vagaries of chance, whereas video games are rooted in the development of skill. Both activities can lead to destructive patterns of addiction, but generally Christians underestimate the significance of gambling addiction and overestimate the significance of gaming addiction. Both activities have socializing and isolating forms. Yet ironically, while the billboard image of gambling is robustly social—laughing adults at the craps table—a typical gambler is actually a solitary, stupefied slots player, and while our cultural caricature of video gaming is of profound isolation—a solitary gamer lost in his game—the most popular video gaming is actually robustly social. Finally, digital technologies have increasingly blurred the distinction between gambling and gaming, with modern slot machines being a sophisticated descendent of arcade video games, with video game versions of all gambling games, and with online gambling Web sites that offer the chance to play for virtual money (in hopes of eventually taking our real money).

GAMBLING GOES LEGIT

Over the second half of the twentieth century, gambling in the United States changed more dramatically than any other existing form of entertainment. It grew exponentially in popularity and profits. Now, in a given year, the number of people who go to casinos exceeds the combined attendance of Major League Baseball, the cinema, Broadway plays, and live concerts.[1] In 2010, gross box office revenues for movie theaters in the United States and Canada was $10.58 billion,[2] whereas gross gaming revenue at casinos was $34.6 billion.[3] Gambling, you might say, hit the jackpot.

Correlative with gambling's explosive growth has been an almost complete change in status. Whereas fifty years ago gambling was an unsavory activity, illegal in every state but Nevada, today it is almost universally legalized, legitimated, normalized, and, in activities like buying a weekly lottery ticket, even routinized. Gambling is largely seen and felt to be a normal leisure activity—just one more entertainment choice in the mix.

Now that gambling has gone mainstream, we Christians need to ask ourselves some important questions.

- *Does this show that the Catholics have been right all along to see temperate gambling as harmless fun—just another proper triviality? Or does it indicate that Protestant opponents of gambling (like my own United Methodists) have capitulated to entertainment principalities that seek our undoing?*[4]

1. Sayre and King, *Entertainment and Society*, 284. "Gambling is America's favorite pastime, at least when our activities are measured by revenue." Vacek, "History of Gambling," 88.

2. National Association of Theater Owners, "Total Grosses."

3. American Gaming Association, "Gaming Revenue." Gross gaming revenue is the amount wagered minus the winnings returned to players.

4. The Catholic position is that "*games of chance* (card games, etc.) or *wagers* are not in themselves contrary to justice. They become morally unacceptable when they deprive someone of what is necessary to provide for his needs and those of others. The passion for gambling risks becoming an enslavement. Unfair wagers and cheating at games constitute grave matter, unless the damage inflicted is so slight that the one who suffers it cannot reasonably consider it significant" (*Catechism of the Catholic Church*, para. 2413). The United Methodists aver that "gambling is a menace to society, deadly to the best interests of moral, social, economic, and spiritual life, and destructive of good government" ("Social Principles," para. 163.IV.G).

Answering well is not a matter of mere empirical assessment, since there is evidence to support both positions. On the Catholic side, plenty of people handle gambling just fine, enjoying it without addiction and without losing their shirts. On the Protestant side, there is equally compelling evidence of harms from gambling, both in the high personal and social cost of "problem" gamblers, and in the larger failures of gambling to promote a genuinely common good.[5] The one empirical factor that we ought to notice is that gambling takes quite diverse forms, which raises the important question of whether the pleasures of gambling are all of one sort, or whether they are diverse in ways that make a theological difference.

So let's begin with a quick but utterly necessary distinction between communal and corporate forms of gambling. On the communal side, friends might have a weekly poker game, or office workers a pool for March Madness, or retirees their weekly bingo night. Both the participants (friends, coworkers, neighbors) and the context (home, office, community, or church) of these forms of gambling are already part of everyday life. As entertainments, these forms of gambling 1) don't draw us to new places, 2) don't entice us with the possibility of dramatically different lives, and 3) don't entrust our well-being to strangers.

Things are otherwise with commercial gambling. The "gaming" industry includes casinos, state lotteries, racetracks (horse and dog) and off-track betting sites (physical and virtual), racinos (racetrack combined with slot machines), and video gambling (stand-alone machines or online play). The participants may include friends and family, but never just those we know. Participating is possible in everyday locations (lottery tickets at grocery or convenience stores, video slots at restaurants, online poker at the home computer), but in such places gambling is typically individualized, isolating, and anonymous. Apart from the lottery, however, most gambling occurs in a context exclusively devoted to it—an environment created for and sustained by gambling profits. There, corporatized gambling refuses the ordinary limits of the everyday 1) by immersing us in a total entertainment environment and experience (e.g., the theme casinos of Las Vegas), 2) by promising exceptional experiences with the potential to dramatically change our life, and 3) by allowing nonaccountable relations of pure self-interest.

5. Julia Fleming makes a compelling case that when state lotteries are considered from the perspective of Catholic social teaching, they fall considerably short of promoting the common good. See "State Lotteries."

The remainder of this chapter will explore the entertaining pleasures on each side of the fundamental divide between communal and commercial gambling. As may already be apparent, I will suggest that the Catholic position fits well with communal gambling, but that the Methodists are spot on with commercial gambling.

CAN'T WE HAVE A FRIENDLY GAME?

✢ *What are the pleasures of noncommercial gambling, and to what degree do they either instantiate or distort the positive dimensions of play?*

One of play's key pleasures is sociality or community. As with other forms of play, so with gambling—the form of sociality varies according to the shape of the gambling game. But some form of sociality is enacted by every form of noncommercial gambling. This gives us a theological lens through which to critically view gambling. As the prior paragraph has already hinted in relation to commercial gambling, wherever gambling diminishes, distorts, or preempts healthy sociality, whether by individualizing, isolating, misleading, damaging, or abandoning players, it is play that parodies rather than participates in the kingdom of God. So a fundamental theological check on every kind of "social gambling"—from office pools to church basement bingo—is how it impacts the quality of our community. Does it foster hospitable, generous, supportive, accountable sociality?

Let's begin with betting on sports teams among friends and coworkers. At its best—which means with low stakes that risk no one's economic well-being[6]—such activities are not primarily about the pleasures of winning the bet or pocketing the money, but are instead a means of identifying more fully with a particular team and of entering more completely (albeit vicariously) into the sporting contest itself. The sum wagered on the team serves as a ritual token of unity with the team, and with its performance in the game. Unable actually to exert ourselves in the contest, we bet money—which represents our labor—as a kind of symbolic proxy of identificatory participation. Not being contestants in the game ourselves, we use the wager to enter vicariously into the team's fate, its risk of victory or defeat. If these are indeed the pleasures of social forms of sports betting,

---

6. This is the wisdom of the Catholic emphasis on temperate wagers that do not deprive us or others of what we need to live.

then perhaps the Catholic admonition for temperance is more fitting than the Methodist blanket condemnation. One key criterion of temperance will be small enough stakes that neither friend can be harmed by losing. And an appropriate check on excess could be to make such wagers only if and when we can watch the game together as friends.

What about Friday night poker? Here, things are not quite so clear-cut. On the one hand, like many forms of regular group play, some of the pleasure lies in the camaraderie experienced in the playing (as also in basketball, bridge, banjo club), and some in the enjoyment of skillfully playing a game that includes an element of randomness (as also in bridge, *Risk*, or *Settlers of Catan*). Yet in the case of poker, the fun of playing seems directly tied to risking money on outcomes that are determined by a combination of chance and skill. (Few adults enjoy playing poker if money is not involved.) Unlike sports betting, where the wager is a way of getting "inside" the game, betting in poker is a way of breaking open the "magic circle" of play so that the game's consequences endure after it has ended. Remember that in other games, the joy and benefits of winning are integral to the game itself; after the game all we have are a sense of satisfaction and happy memories. But with poker and other gambling games, the fun of winning appears to be not only winning but *the winnings*, which become an extrinsic, tangible benefit. Moreover, the skills of a good poker player are not only mental abilities to compute probabilities and remember cards, but the psychological capacities to bluff and to intimidate. As one interpreter notes, "poker can be very predatory."[7] All of this suggests that great caution is warranted around poker, inasmuch as the structural logic of the game itself and the psychological skills to play it well are both oriented toward harming our neighbor (even if the harm is relatively minor and we do it in the name of having fun together).[8] In other words, it is tough to keep this friendly game friendly.

Finally, what are the pleasures associated with bingo? Unlike sports betting, which depends entirely on the skilled play of others, or poker, which depends on the interplay of players' skill and chance, bingo is an entirely random game. There are at least three distinguishable pleasures associated with bingo. One is the enjoyment some people find in the meticulous attention to detail bingo requires. This is an aesthetic pleasure

---

7. Turner, "Games, Gambling, and Gambling Problems," 51.

8. In both his Small and Large Catechisms, Luther expounded "don't steal" as not only involving not taking our neighbor's money and property, but as helping to improve and protect the neighbor's economic well-being.

of tracking numbers as they are called, keeping a card current, attending to straight rows, etc. The second, more important pleasure is a direct, intensified engagement with possibility. Win or lose, there is excitement in anticipating, expecting, and hoping. Finally, winning itself involves complex forms of pleasure. The desirability of the prize can be a motivation for playing and thus a core pleasure of winning. But for the most part, this is secondary—the prize simply needs to be good enough that the winner is glad to have it. (The more that desire for prizes motivates bingo, the less healthy it becomes, precisely because an extrinsic good has displaced the intrinsic pleasures of playing. Greed is a core danger in any form of gambling.) More central here is the pleasure of winning itself, which proffers a sense of undeserved reward, a faint analogue to the theological reality of blessing.[9] Note that some players experience this pleasure not only when they win, but vicariously when a friend or neighbor does. This momentary, surprising sense of being blessed may be an ever so modest analogue to spiritual joy. Obviously, there is a complex relationship between the second and third pleasures, between anticipation and fulfillment. The theological question for bingo is whether its engagement with possibility and realization draws us deeper into a sense of hope in God's provident goodness, or detours us into deadening flirtations with chance or luck. One touchstone for assessment might be whether players enjoy vicarious pleasure when a friend or neighbor wins, or whether my friend's win is experienced as my disappointing, displeasuring loss.

✤ *This section has suggested that friendship can constitute a healthy context and criterion for wagering games, but that there are always risks. Do you agree that social wagering can have positive value while also risking some significant harms? Do you think such forms of entertainment are "worth the gamble"?*

COMMERCIAL GAMBLING

Our entertainment culture predisposes us to expect commercialized entertainments to be better than homegrown—more fun and exciting, more intense and full, more enriching and excellent. That logic certainly pervades the commercialization of gambling. Casinos are portrayed as more

---

9. Lears, "Beyond Pathology," observes a powerful link between the gambler's longing for luck and the believer's longing for grace.

fun than a weekly poker game. Commercialized sports wagering is portrayed as more intense than the friendly sports bet. And state lotteries and
mega-lotteries are portrayed as more enriching than bingo, cakewalks, and
grade school raffles. Nonetheless, I have already hinted above at significant
ways in which commercial gambling is worse, not better, than its domestic
antecedents.

Saying precisely how this is so will require care. First, we will need to
be careful to distinguish what gambling causes from what it merely exag-
gerates or presupposes. For example, the United Methodist statement on
gambling asserts that gambling both "feeds on" and "fosters" greed. Some
forms of gambling clearly do precisely this to some people. Notice how
lottery play is fueled by and fuels the desire for money and what money
is expected to buy, and how lottery advertising almost always both assumes the inherent desirability of massive amounts of money, and works to
stimulate that desire in us. But then that same dynamic of feeding on and
fostering greed is at work in news reports about a ballplayer's multimillion
dollar contract or a movie star's $20 million deal or Oprah's net worth. Our
entertainment ecology continually offers us idealized consumers—super-
rich sports stars and hyper-affluent media celebrities whose role in life
(whatever their profession) seems to feed on and foster the normalization
of greed on a grand scale. So one has to squint quite a bit in order to vitu-
perate gambling's responsibility for greed while saying nothing about the
paroxysms of conspicuous consumption that have become both focus and
by-product of our entertainment ecology.

That doesn't mean that the Methodists' concern about the relationship
of gambling and greed is entirely misplaced, however. In his psychological
analysis of why people keep gambling in spite of threatened or real economic loss, Nigel Turner notes that it is "the dream of the big win."[10] What
that means is that while other pleasures and desires can motivate gambling,
over time they are eclipsed by the desire or drive for money. Even where
gambling doesn't "feed on" a preexisting greed, it inevitably fosters greed.
In the context of commercialized gambling, this creates a perfect marriage
between the gambler's greed for "the big win," and the gambling operator's
greed for the big profit. The clearest example of this may be casino slot
machines. In the past thirty years, slot machines have gone from occupying
45 percent of casino floor space to more than 80 percent because casinos
are greedy for their patrons' money—all of it. So modern slot machines

10. Turner, "Games, Gambling, and Gambling Problems," 35.

and their casino contexts are now psychometrically engineered to optimize length, volume, and speed of play so that each slot player will "play to extinction"—which means spending every penny she has (or can charge on a credit card).

✢ *What makes the casino different from a major league ballpark, where a family could easily spend their whole entertainment budget on tickets, souvenirs, and refreshments?*

Two things: First, consider how most commercial entertainments have an unavoidable ending: the movie credits roll, the band leaves the stage, the game clock expires, or the ninth inning comes. Casino gambling, on the other hand, has no stipulated or natural end point: the roulette wheel keeps on spinning, the blackjack dealer keeps on dealing, and the slots keep on whirring—as long as we keep betting. Obviously, someone who wins big can quit while ahead (though often doesn't!), but there is nothing intrinsic to the activity that constitutes a natural end point. Second, the cost of being present for the duration of most entertainments has a fixed price that is paid up front; tickets to the ball game probably cost too much, snacking costs even more, but extra innings or overtime are free. Gambling, on the other hand, requires continuous betting to keep playing; it charges us by the minute to participate, renting time to us, so to speak. Taking these two together, we see that casino gambling invites us into an open-ended activity in which there is a reliable probability that length of play correlates directly with our financial loss and the casino's financial gain—that's the "house edge."[11] So in the end, our dream of winning big—our greed—correlates perfectly with the casino's greed—its dream of winning all our money, one small bet at a time.

Second, we should be careful not to be misled by vocabulary. For example, lotteries use terminology of "games," "play," and "winning," but "playing" the lottery hardly qualifies as playing at all. The "game" is played *against* a faceless government, not *with* other players; it isn't social. The "playing" isn't free but is purchased, and it doesn't enact a playful experience of freedom because "players" either make no choices or response at all, or merely choose a series of numbers. It isn't *autotelic*, oriented primarily to the fun and excitement internal to the game, but *eschatological*—an externally oriented quest for the happiness that a jackpot purportedly buys. (Of course, one thing that keeps lottery players going is the high percentage

11. For a definition and discussion of "house edge," see ibid., 56–60.

of "instant wins." That brief pleasure of "winning," of having a scratch card that pays, is an internal pleasure. But it is not the fundamental motivation that causes people to play. Rather, like nicotine added to cigarettes to create addiction, small wins motivate players to *keep* playing rather than quit, even when quitting would be in their best interest.) Nor does it really require place or embodiment, drawing a temporary "magic circle" around our space and time, since scratch cards truly are about instant results anywhere, anytime, and weekly drawings are technologically mediated encounters.

In short, playing the lottery is not an embodied activity that freely seeks to make fun with others. So weekly lottery play is not a true form of play; it is more a parodic "prayer" for happiness. It is a ritual act seeking a better life, a propitiation of chance or luck for the good life that money can supposedly buy.[12] Affectively, playing the lottery enacts displeasure or resentment about one's present circumstances, a sense of longing for what one lacks, a present emptiness that covets a filled future. As such, it is an impediment to recognizing the presence of God's providence in our lives, poor training for properly Christian forms of gratitude for all of God's goodness to us. In sum, if I play the lottery, I'm not actually playing, but instead am distorting a faithful orientation toward God's provident goodness.

Finally, we should note that most forms of gambling are experiential engagements with anticipation by way of risk. Many kinds of gambling provide a succession of highly concentrated moments of uncertain outcome—blackjack or bust, win/place/show or lose, jackpot or near miss, high hand or fold. These moments themselves, or the experience of stringing them together, are one of the core pleasures for many forms of gambling, offering an adrenaline rush. So although gambling is unavoidably about money, there is an experiential dimension at its core. The kiss of the dice precedes an ecstatic abandonment of self to the caprice of chance. The starting bell initiates a fateful journey toward the culmination of the contest. The consistent flip of the deal or whir of the slot wheels effects an immersion in the ebb and flow of luck. Some of these affective dimensions apply apart from wagering: every sports fan knows the feeling of anticipation; every card player knows the excitement that attends to chance events (the deal, draw, discard, etc.). So wagering doesn't create the ecstasy of possibility or the thrill of chance, but only amplifies it. And there seems to be a correlation

---

12. "According to the Consumer Federation of America, one in five Americans think the best way to achieve long-term financial security is to gamble." Paynter, "Predatory Gambling," 74.

between the size of the risk and the rush; higher stakes or longer odds are usually thought to intensify the pleasure.

What might such experiential dimensions mean for the church? First, they remind us that our entertainment culture has strong currents that flow from the mundane toward sensational spectacles, intensified experiences, and hyperreality. Gambling is one example of entertainment that habituates us to distorted hopes and tepid gratitude. So while we may still faithfully pray "thy kingdom come," we play "my kingdom come" lotteries. And while we will still intone "give us this day our daily bread," we experience daily bread (and shelter and work and family) as a thankless white-bread existence of daily grind, tired tedium, and spiceless life in need of the stimuli of spectacle, immersion, or hyperreality. Gambling becomes one more entertainment diversion that steers us from engaging the goodness of our real lives to pursuing the excitement of imagined lives.

Second, the pleasure gamblers experience in their risky activity, in "taking a chance," always with something painful or harmful to lose, suggests that we need to revisit the place of risk in our vision of Christian discipleship. Nigel Turner notes that "part of the thrill of gambling is the potential for loss."[13] Ironically, suggests Turner, this risk of harm allows us "to momentarily forget our mortality." Flirting with luck turns players away from life's mortal horizon, however briefly. Ritualizing danger through a game of chance brings a respite from the threat of death, however temporary. This suggests that gambling appeals as a form of *ecstasis*, which includes both being drawn outside this mortal coil and being drawn into that lively sense of pure possibility. In short, gambling makes perfect sense as a coping mechanism for persons without faith in the resurrection of Jesus from the dead. But where Christian hope abounds, the genuinely thrilling engagement with death is the risky adventure of discipleship. According to Paul, disciples always risk (and sometimes suffer) the loss of all things for the sake of Christ (Phil 3:8). In a world of tepid possibilities, it isn't surprising that high-stakes gambling and extreme sports offer compensatory escapes. In the world as it really is, however, the wild God of the exodus and Easter offers a thrill ride second to none. You can bet your life on it. (After all, that's what Jesus did.)

In the end, not all gambling is created equal. There may be legitimate fun in some forms of private betting, if it is temperate, accountable, and kind. But given the wider cultural context in which such practices occur,

13. Turner, "Games, Gambling, and Gambling Problems," 34.

vigilance is essential, lest the powers inveigh and invade. When it comes to commercial gambling, all bets are off. Although we cannot blame gambling for our culture of greed, we must recognize how it participates in and exacerbates our societal lust for money. Moreover, we must recognize just what a fallen power commercial gambling is; it is determined to deplete us completely for its own enrichment, while refusing accountability for our individual good. It (mostly) doesn't cheat or steal because it doesn't have to: the lie is built into the vocabulary, the deception is part of the rush, and the edge always belongs to the house. Like psychotropic drugs, it brings ecstatic thrills to some, stupefaction to others, temporary escape from dullness and death to all. And as with the use of those drugs, it risks escalation, addiction, isolation, incapacitation, and impoverishment. But it can be a lot of fun when you're not counting the cost. Christians do, however, count the cost, risk the cross, stake their claim on a risen Lord. This suggests to me that we must say no to every form of commercial gambling.

✛ *Do you agree that Christians should say no to every form of commercial gambling? What pleasures associated with gambling-as-entertainment do you find most significant or beneficial? Are they unique to gambling?*

nine

Wii Play: Video Games

FROM "WE PLAY" TO "Wii PLAY"

THE TITLE OF THIS chapter plays with the way "we" and "Wii" sound alike. Apparently Nintendo intended that resonance, and more, when it christened its newest gaming system. Nintendo explained that "Wii sounds like 'we,' which emphasizes this console is for everyone. Wii can easily be remembered by people around the world, no matter what language they speak. No confusion. Wii has a distinctive 'ii' spelling that symbolizes both the unique controllers and the image of people gathering to play."[1]

The bulk of this chapter will show that while "Wii play" sounds exactly like "we play," it typically looks very different. And here, looks are not deceiving: "Wii play" *is* different, in profound ways, from "we play."

PACMAN GOBBLES THE MARKET

I've noticed that, positive or negative, treatments of video gaming often begin autobiographically, almost confessionally. It's as if the writer needs readers to know that he or she writes as an insider, one who truly understands video gaming from within. So here goes. In 1980, I owned the first *Pac-Man* in our town, a full-size arcade console game. It didn't live at our

1. Carless, "'Wii,'" para. 2.

house, but right beside *Asteroids* (and later *Galaga*) in my parents' convenience store. We didn't get the game for fun, but funds—a college fund for me. It was an investment, intended to entertain my peers while providing for my education, one quarter at a time.

Thirty years later, I can play *Pac-Man* for free on my laptop, or for $10 on my son's PS3™, or for $4.99 on my wife's iPhone. So quarters are not dropping as fast in the few arcades still around, but there is exponentially more money being spent on the full spectrum of video gaming. For several years, the industry has boasted sales revenues that exceed movie box-office receipts.[2] Gaming content pulled in around $15.5 billion in 2010, with another $6.29 billion for gaming hardware. This means that video gaming is BIG, and not just in its wallet. If *World of Warcraft* were a denomination, its 11.5 million "members" would exceed my own United Methodism by 48 percent. Moreover, the shared life of typical "WoW-arriors" exceeds that of typical Methodists by hundreds of hours per year.

As the prior paragraph hints, video gaming has become an incredibly diverse phenomenon. So much so, in fact, that there is scholarly debate about what to call it and how to define it.[3] For our purposes, "video games" are digitally based (hardware and software), electronically mediated, screen-focused personal entertainment games. Each of these phrases is important for understanding the loves and pleasures that video games elicit. Digital computer technology gives video games both the expansive possibilities and invisible limitations of virtuality; we can seem to be doing the absolutely real or the utterly phantasmagoric. Electronic appliances mediate video games to us, originally tethering us to stationary indoor devices, but increasingly tethering the devices to us.[4] Video screens give these games their key dimension—visuality—thereby locating gameplay "in" the world the screen displays, and consequently focusing gamers' attention

---

2. This doesn't mean that gaming is "bigger than Hollywood," however, despite what many advocates claim. Worldwide gross revenue for movies continues to exceed video games, although with the increasing hybridity between the two (along with comics), it is becoming difficult to tell them strictly apart. For example, actors' bios on the Internet Movie Database now include their video game voice credits side by side with their other acting credits. Dyer-Witherford and de Peuter, *Games of Empire*, xvi.

3. See Buckingham, "Studying Computer Games," 4–5.

4. Video games can be played on an increasing multitude of devices—dedicated gaming consoles (PS3, Xbox, Wii), desktop or laptop computers, personal gaming devices (Nintendo 3DS, PSP Go, Xperia PLAY), cell phones, higher-end calculators, e-book readers, iPods, and iPads. In their mobile form, these devices become part of the "always-on, always-on-you" category discussed by Turkle, "Always-on."

almost exclusively on the device screen rather than the other players or the ambient environment. But unlike passive screen-based entertainments (television and movies), video games require and respond to interaction— that is, like other games they are *played* by players following rules, adopting strategies, developing skills, and pursuing objectives.

There are many ways to categorize video games, none of which is entirely satisfactory. Andrew Burn and Diane Carr offer this overview:

> Thus, a game can simultaneously be classified according to the platform on which it is played (PC, mobile phone, Xbox), the style of play it affords (multiplayer, networked, or single user, for instance), the manner in which it positions the player in relation to the game world (first person, third person, "god"), the kind of rules and goals that make up its gameplay (racing game, action adventure), or its representational aspects (science fiction, high fantasy, urban realism). All these possibilities for classification coexist in games, and none are irrelevant . . .[5]

Given this variety, and the vast differences between *Angry Birds* and *Legends of Zelda*, *Second Life* and *Call of Duty*, not everything that follows will necessarily apply to every game. The goal will be to concentrate on larger trends relating to *playing* video games. But first we must deflate some of the overstatement that afflicts discussion of video gaming.

✤   *What is your history with video games? Does that history predispose you to think more positively or negatively about gaming?*

REFUSING RIDICULOUS RHETORIC

There's been a lot of hyperbole, even hyperventilation, about video gaming. On one side are those who claim that video games are a kind of plague, inciting violence, fostering loneliness, breeding addiction. Video gaming is portrayed as a catechism of cultural collapse. On the other side are those who claim that "the kids are alright,"[6] because gaming makes us better and happier people. Here are examples of the contrast. Robert Woods's criticism is milder than most: "Playing video games is fun, but it may desensitize

5. "Defining Game Genres," 16.

6. Beck and Wade, *Kids Are Alright*, xii: "The ninety million kids who grew up gaming are more social, more loyal to their teams, more sophisticated decision makers than their counterparts who didn't play video games in their formative years."

us to the lasting consequences of our choices."[7] J. Cameron Moore, on the other hand, celebrates that by playing video games "we can develop skills of moral perception and decision-making."[8] With their antithetical assessments of the moral impact of gaming, Woods and Moore exemplify just how polarized the conversation about gaming can be.

If we historicize the debate a bit, two observations are in order. First, video games are not the only entertainment medium to be indicted for "corrupting our youth" or "undermining our culture." In the twentieth century, every new medium (radio, cinema, television, the Internet) and most innovative styles and genres (jitterbug, jazz, rock and roll, rap, hip hop) have elicited condemnatory rhetoric about immorality, sexism, violence, and antisocial threat.[9] History repeating itself through reiterated rhetoric doesn't mean that critics are wrong, but it does provide a bit of perspective: these condemnatory claims often display *anxiety* about cultural change and *allegiance* to class status and American identity. With a few exceptions, this rhetoric of refusal is not oriented toward the better future that Christ brings, but toward a supposedly paradisaical past (whether the fleshpots of Egypt or the goodness of Eden, either way not the New Jerusalem). In this regard, many naysayers have an anemic eschatology that does not adequately imagine and hope in God's future (not to mention moral myopia about the failings of their own adolescent era).

Historically, the pendulum usually swings from initial condemnation through caution and acceptance to celebration. When viewed historically as a repeating pattern, this seemingly inevitable swing from refusal to advocacy ought to give us pause. Perhaps advocates of new media are just as shortsighted as opponents, although in different ways. Where critics have a jaundiced view of the present but see the past through rose-colored glasses, cheerleaders see a black-and-white past giving way to a Technicolor future.[10] Their excitement about the future's arrival may feel like a robust

---

7. Woods and Patton, "Faithful Criticism of Popular Media Technologies," 35.

8. Moore, "Moral Choices in Video Games," 74.

9. Both observations are drawn from Buckingham, "Studying Computer Games," 2–3. William Romanowski writes, "Parents concerned about the amount of time their children spend watching TV and movies or listening to music today may be surprised to find that their counterparts at the beginning of the twentieth century also worried about the effects of vaudeville theaters, the new dance halls and nickelodeons, and later radio and comic books." *Pop Culture Wars*, 25–26.

10. This kind of romantic historiography is given stunning visual representation in Gary Ross's *Pleasantville*. For a critique of his implicit eschatology, see Laytham, "You Can Do It."

eschatology that "flips the script"[11] on the anemic eschatology of the old fogeys, but in fact their eschatology is just as mistaken, because it imagines that a better future is arriving through the midwifery of technology and the ministrations of pop culture, rather than through the birth, ministry, suffering, death, and resurrection of Jesus Christ.

The most egregious illustrations I've encountered of this kind of unreflective embrace are in the book *Halos and Avatars: Playing Video Games with God*. There, Craig Detweiler speculates that if Jesus showed up today, he'd surely "grab a controller, and join the fun."[12] Here, what betters or even beatifies life is not the suffering savior but video gaming, not taking up a cross but grabbing a controller. Subtly but inexorably, claims that Jesus would be a gamer are used to validate and vindicate Jesus, trivializing his *passionate* incarnation of truth, beauty, and goodness on the cross, and ignoring the cries of the needy and the groaning of the oppressed. *Halos and Avatars* sanctifies Jesus by imagining that he w00ts gaming just as much as we do.

"Ah, you middle-aged curmudgeon," readers may now be thinking, "you are completely out of touch with 'digital natives.'" Objections like that lead to the second historical observation. Just as new entertainments have inexorably provoked rhetorics of nostalgic alarmism or naïve techno-optimism, they have also produced rhetorics of generational segmentation. David Buckingham points out that ". . . the popularity of computer games frequently reinforces a generational rhetoric that is characteristic of popular discussions of young people and new media."[13] For example, notice how a "generational rhetoric" is operative in both the title and subtitle of Beck and Wade's book *The Kids Are Alright: How the Gamer Generation Is Changing the Workplace*.[14] Generational rhetoric is also at the core of categorizations like "digital immigrants" and "digital natives" (with perhaps the nuance of

11. This phrase is used effectively by David Dark in his *Everyday Apocalypse* to expound an apocalyptic dimension in some of the best of pop culture.

12. See Detweiler, "Halos and Avatars," 16. This sentiment is repeated and amplified by Kitchen, "*Madden* Rules," 120, who writes, "If Jesus were here now, he might grab a controller and throw down in a healthy game of *Halo 3*. He wouldn't even need cheat codes. God gave us sports, video games, and a competitive spirit because he loves us and wants us to challenge ourselves and be happy doing so every day. He gave his Son for much the same reason."

13. Buckingham, "Studying Computer Games," 2–3. See the perceptive discussion of the commercial dimensions of this in Schultze et al., *Dancing in the Dark*, 3–4. They argue that generational conflict is exacerbated by patterns of generational marketing.

14. Beck and Wade, *Kids Are Alright*. Contrast that with Bauerlein, *Dumbest Generation*.

"digital settlers" thrown as a buffer in between), a matrix that assumes that *when* you were born determines, in a virtual sense, *how* you perceive, think, feel, and live, perhaps even *who* you are.[15]

The church has been entirely too careless when it comes to generational rhetoric. We have exhibited this explicitly when we have allowed such distinctions to have a primary rather than secondary or tertiary identity status. Whenever the centrally operative descriptor for planning ministry is a generational particularity, rather than common membership in the covenant community, it is likely that something has gone wrong. This sounds counterintuitive inasmuch as the people of God have since Deuteronomy been charged with transmitting the faith across generations (e.g., Deuteronomy 6). On closer examination, however, we see that what Scripture envisions is maturation through a series of generational stages—childhood, adulthood, eldership. Being young is curable; we all grow up and grow old; the point is to grow in grace, to mature in the Spirit, to "put on Christ." Thus, generational labels (Greatest, Boomers, Busters, X, Y, Millennials, etc.) should not be treated as something that rightly endures through a lifetime. Doing so gives to our history, and especially to its pop-culture dimension, a sort of astrological power of determination. The church should no more focus on Boomers or Millennials than it does on Pisces or Scorpios.

Of course, this is not to say that there are not real differences between Christians of different ages (e.g., between me and my young-adult children), differences largely traceable to the formative power of their engagement with the trivialities and principalities being studied in this book—global culture industries, technological vectors, entertainment trends. It is to say, however, that we must avoid the logical fallacy that is so often imbedded in generational rhetoric: simplistic claims that *is* implies *ought* or *must*. Put simply, there is an implicit claim that description entails prescription, that having named a distinctive quality of a generation, that quality now determines or makes inevitable the proper mode for engaging the generation: given X, it is utterly and inevitably necessary that Y. So, for example, with gaming, it is claimed that because a whole generation has grown up playing daily, that generation must be evangelized and engaged through the modalities of video gaming.

---

15. The so-called digital natives, born in 1980 and after, are sometimes described as evolution's next phase, other times as an almost entirely different species—*homo cyber* replacing *homo sapiens*. Well, if that truly is happening, then we have truly lost whatever sapience we had.

This section has tried to make three points by way of its two observations. First, hyperbolic claims about the negative or positive impact of gaming get in the way of clear-eyed theological thinking. Second, both Christian rejection and advocacy of new entertainments usually get eschatology wrong in ways that distort our proper hope in the future that Jesus Christ is bringing. And third, a century of accommodation to generational logic has made the church more tribal, its connective tissue more compromised, rather than more unified, the joints and ligaments of Christ's body robust and strong.

✣ *Do you agree that both condemnatory and celebratory rhetoric about gaming tend to misplace Christian hope? How might beginning with a focus on our hope in Christ position us to make wiser judgments about gaming and other entertainments?*

✣ *Since entertainments foster generational segmentation within the church, how might your church discuss video gaming without further dividing into generational clans?*

Let us now explore three key questions that video gaming raises.

EXODUS TO FUN AND THE PURSUIT OF HAPPINESS

✣ *Do video games pursue happiness by an exodus from the real?*

Edward Castronova has written a disturbing book called *Exodus to the Virtual World: How Online Fun Is Changing Reality*. According to Castronova, we are already witnessing the beginnings of a mass exodus from the frustrations of the real world to the fun of virtual realms. For Castronova, it's easy to account for this migration: ". . . synthetic worlds are designed to be fun all the time. The real world isn't."[16] Over the next twenty years, Castronova believes, tens or even hundreds of millions will begin to live as much of their lives as possible in virtual environments. This is because "improvements in technology will make virtual worlds into veritable dreamlands. They will be more fun, for more people. Simple economic theory predicts that in this competition, the real world is going to lose."[17]

---

16. Castronova, *Exodus to the Virtual World*, 69.

17. Ibid., 7. Of course, the real world sometimes fights back. The same week I read Castronova, hackers took down the PlayStation® Network for more than a week, leaving

I happened to read Castronova on the same day I encountered this line from Pope Benedict XVI's recommendation of *YouCat*, the new *Youth Catechism of the Catholic Church*: "This catechism was not written to please you. It will not make life easy for you, because it demands of you a new life. . . . So I beg you: Study this Catechism with passion and perseverance. Make a sacrifice of your time for it!"[18] Contrasting Castronova's invitation to "on-line fun" with Benedict's demand for offline sacrifice suggests some satirical dichotomies: *Myst* versus mass; *Halo* versus Hallelujah; *Call of Duty* versus call to worship; *Super Mario* versus serving neighbors. (Of course, parents of young gamers know that these conflicts can be quite real.) Viewed through Castronova's "simple economic theory," it begins to look like not only the real world, but especially the church, is going to lose out to the pleasures and enticements of online fun.

Happily, the contrast is neither as real nor as stark as I've made it appear. Indeed, there are three deep agreements between Castronova's analysis and Benedict's recommendation: 1) we all want to be happy, and happiness requires 2) plenty of hard work and 3) friends along the way. Let's unpack each of these claims in turn.

First, we all want to be happy. Thank God for that, because the desire for happiness is God-given and God-directed. We have it from God, as part of creation's goodness, and we have it for God, to draw us ever more deeply into the triune One "in whom we live and move and have our being" (Acts 17:28). This means, contrary to caricature, that it isn't true that a sure sign something is wrong is that it makes you happy. Of course, in a fallen world we aren't always right about what will make us happy; that second donut made me miserable instead of happy. That's one reason we need good friends along the way, wise companions to guide us and support us. We don't begin with a true sense of what happiness is, either; in our fallen state, we start out enjoying perversions and distortions of happiness, like teasing a sibling or torturing the cat. That's one reason that learning to be truly happy is such hard work (even though, from another perspective, it is as easy as receiving a gift).

Where does that leave us? It leaves us recognizing that not only video gaming but all of entertainment is part of our human quest for happiness—our deep desire for, and long journey into, the depths of God's joy.

---

eight million gamers stranded in the "un-fun real world" waiting for the restoration of their portal into cyberspace.

18. *YouCat: Youth Catechism of the Catholic Church*, 10.

Our desire for happiness is a sign of something, but not the thing itself. We can enjoy it and celebrate it for what it is—a hint of bigger and better things to come; every glimmer of enjoyment is a sign that we are meant for something more. But if we become too attached to the sign, treat it as an end point rather than an indication, we are in danger of missing the true fun, the real happiness, the genuine beatitude that is ours in Christ. Therefore, I am not suggesting that our entertainments have a quasi-sacramental function, let alone that they are now the primary locus of God's material engagement with us. Such a claim would overreach precisely by mistaking our feeble quests for true entertainment with God's faithful promise to find and claim us in baptism and Eucharist.[19] Certainly every glimmer of beauty or thrill of joy that entertainment conveys is rooted ultimately in God's transcendent glory, but sacraments make that transcendence immanently and personally available in ways that mediated entertainments cannot.

But an all-out "exodus to fun" risks destroying our happiness precisely because it mistakes a virtual world for the promised land, and mistakes gaming for God. Escapism in small doses is fine,[20] but an overdose is no fun at all. Escapism describes something that can be integrated into the rhythms of a balanced life, can serve purposes of refreshment, rest, frivolity, and fest precisely because it is occasional and complementary to the necessary rigors of making a living, caring for others, keeping promises, and doing good. (In addition to this general danger with all escapist activity, escapism oriented to a virtual world risks one further danger—development of an aversion to the real, and thus to real happiness. This will be explored in the final section of this chapter.)

Second, the pope reminds us that happiness is worth pursuing "with passion and perseverance." Gamers agree; passion and perseverance are apt descriptors of the attitude and commitment of serious gamers. Talk to them about a favorite game and you hear the passion; watch them tediously master a game level or discover a game secret and you'll see the perseverance. The happiness that comes from playing well requires hard,

19. For an extended critique of treating entertainment as sacrament, see Byassee, "God Does Not Entertain."

20. Video games are entertainment, which means they are forms of escapism. Egenfeldt-Nielsen, Smith, and Tosca, *Understanding Video Games*, 147, define escapist as "any human activity not immediately geared toward survival. In this definition, video games are certainly escapist, but so too is literature and indeed all of the fine arts. The time that is 'left over' in our struggle for survival can—and perhaps should—be filled with another reality, one that is more pleasurable and offers relief from the difficulties of living."

demanding effort (just as the happiness that accompanies the life of faith does not make life easy). Pursuing happiness requires perseverance—the sacrifice of time, precisely because we need *formation* not just information. Thus, the most obvious real-world consequence of gaming is that it requires significant amounts of time.[21] Whether gaming makes players smarter or dumber, more or less violent, antisocial or well adjusted, is highly debated. One thing that cannot be debated is this: gaming consumes lots and lots of time.[22]

So what? There are plenty of studies showing similar time commitments with television (or more recently Facebook and YouTube). Castronova and other advocates often point out that the passionate fun of video gaming is quite different from the passive state of watching television.[23] Playing a video game requires dynamic interaction with the game "environment," discovery of strategy, and development of skill. In this regard, gaming is different from the twentieth century's most significant entertainments—radio, television, cinema—which do not require much response from us. If you choose to, you can dance or sing with the radio, shout at the television, laugh and cry at the movies. But these mediated entertainments "happen" with or without your response; passivity is allowed or even encouraged. Not so with video games. They require action: the full participation of the entertained through the action of eyes and thumbs, making choices, utilizing creativity and effort. Gaming fun results in 1) learning—the acquisition of knowledge, understanding, skills, habits, and feelings, and in 2) commitment—a cultivated affection for particular games, for fellow players, and for the practice of playing.

All this suggests to me that gaming's "exodus to fun" is profoundly analogous to traditional Christian practices of *catechesis*—formation in our baptismal exodus from death to life. Both gaming and catechesis take significant amounts of time; both require "serious" effort that, paradoxically, can be great fun; both are active, responsive processes that would be destroyed by passivity; both seek to form holistic understanding that unifies head, heart, and hands in a lifelong commitment. Finally, both are thought

21. Ibid., 25.

22. Most of the recent literature on gaming suggests that most "gamers" play four or more hours per day, at least five days a week, but that they regularly report occasions of playing six to eight hours, or even more.

23. Egenfeldt-Nielsen, Smith, Tosca, *Understanding Video Games*, 1, describe the changing world of video games as a transition from a time when "most people were content with being passively entertained" to today's insistence "on a more active role."

to "take" best when engaged in adolescence and early adulthood. Two conclusions: 1) Castronova's statistics ought to shock us into recognizing that pop culture is often a more successful catechist (that is, shaper of personhood) than is the church; these days, far more "gamers for life" are being produced than "disciples forever." 2) If there is a conflict between gaming and discipleship, its root is not necessarily gaming content or the pursuit of pleasure, but simply time. The intensive natures of gaming and of discipleship suggest that we may not have time for both.

Third, happiness is best pursued in good company. Many of the most popular video games allow or even require cooperative interaction with other players. Indeed, the most popular console and computer games are either inherently social (e.g., *World of Warcraft* is a massive multiplayer online role-playing game that is most fun when played in raiding guilds) or allow for group play (e.g., *Call of Duty*, which allows for teams of up to sixteen). This means that a "typical" gamer is not isolated, stupefied, and antisocial. A happy gamer is a social creature. So is a happy Christian. Both gaming and discipleship recognize the intrinsically social nature of our quest for happiness. The key question raised by this exodus to a virtual world (as opposed to marching to Zion) is whether the good company we encounter there is real or virtual, genuine or a simulacrum. We'll explore this in the next section, noting that virtual gameplay impacts identities and relationships in ways that are often inimical to truly happy creaturely life.

✣ *How can we recognize gaming fun as a hint that God made us for happiness without sacralizing or scapegoating gaming?*

✣ *If video gaming is a kind of pop-culture catechesis, what does this suggest about how we should think about and pursue the practices of Christian formation and nurture?*

✣ *Does a sociality played out in virtual "space" according to game scripts draw us into genuine, healthy community, or a simulacrum of it? Do video games pursue happiness by an exodus from the real?*

EXCARNATED: BODIES LOST AND AVATARS FOUND

✣ *Do video games establish identity by "disappearing" our bodies?*

This section begins with a simple claim: the Christian doctrine of *incarnation* means that bodily life is good, something to be embraced and enjoyed.

Our hope in Christ is not that we can finally escape the limitations of bodiliness for the freedom of a purely mental or "spiritual" existence. It is rather that we might be freed from death and sin for a resurrected bodily life that enjoys God forever. If we look at the full trajectory of human life from birth through death to "the resurrection of the body and the life everlasting," *incarnation* can be seen as describing the full process of Jesus' life, and especially his final resurrection fullness, rather than merely a claim that from the beginning this man is God with us. So at its best, the incarnation of Jesus communicates not only the goodness of all our bodily life, but a trajectory toward its fullness and perfection.

Unfortunately, those kinds of claims are always difficult to sustain. Throughout its history, the church has needed to be vigilant against theologies that dismiss or denigrate Jesus' human body, with the consequence that our own bodies are construed as problems to be overcome rather than as the locus of our personal identity and availability. In the first few centuries, this trend was called Docetism, which existed as a religious or philosophical way of life. In modernity, however, a similar docetic trend has become part of our popular imagination. Philosopher Charles Taylor calls this trend "excarnation."[24] Think of it as a way of life that seeks to overcome bodily limitations, if not exit the body altogether. As we saw in the discussion of iPods, the "regardless power" of technology has an excarnating trend, precisely because it habituates us to enact our will regardless of bodily limitation. Similarly, video gaming involves powerful trajectories of excarnation precisely because they locate the player's actions and identity in a virtual—that is, non-bodily—realm.

First a bit of explanation. The primary focus of all gaming is the video screen; it is the *where* of the action. The player's play requires input to the game; some device is needed to translate human intentionality into the ones and zeroes of the game's program. Typically this device has been a computer keyboard for PC-based games or some kind of "controller" for gaming consoles. In some simulation games, a controller that mimics real equipment is marketed—for example, a joystick for *Flight Simulator*, a steering wheel, gas pedal, and brake for driving games, a plastic guitar for *Guitar Hero*, a pistol for first-person shooters. But mostly gamers have developed proficiency with a generic controller that requires motions that do not simulate on-screen action. This has meant that video gaming is more of a bodily activity than backgammon, but far less bodily than sports,

24. Taylor, *Secular Age*, 288.

charades, or dress-up. "People move their hands, bodies, eyes, and mouths when they play video games," says Alexander Galloway, though he admits that mostly they move their *thumbs*.[25] So video gaming is not (yet) a fully excarnate activity, but gaming has a powerfully excarnating impact, precisely because the intended "locus" and focus of one's action is not the body and the immediate space it inhabits, but the screen. Whether the game perspective is first person (looking "through the eyes" of the game character), third person (looking at the game character), or "god" (ability to see any or all of the game from multiple perspectives), the process of playing is about *en-visioning* action by *ex-carnating* our intentionality, decisions, and even our desires.

So consider the irony that one December I waited for hours at a big-box electronics store to try to buy my son the latest gaming platform for Christmas. I was planning to mark Christ's incarnation with a device built for excarnation! Am I off the hook because this particular gaming platform was the Wii, or only because it didn't arrive, so he got socks and underwear instead? Some people think that the Wii is immune from the problem of excarnation, because its various interfaces use motion sensors to input three-dimensional body motion. Typically, this allows for games that invite players to simulate real-life motions so that a simulation appears on the screen. For example, to play Wii bowling, I simulate the bowling motion with my whole arm (although not by running eight to ten feet and sliding past the foul line as I loft the sixteen-pound ball—I'm not a very good bowler).

Other gaming platforms have followed suit with interfaces that capture a full range of motion. So a critic like Kutter Callaway exults that motion capture has revolutionized gaming, moving it from a hands-only activity to one in which "a player's entire physical structure is implicated in the gaming experience through a unique user interface. Thus, as a fully embodied engagement with the virtual world, the Wii experience is an expressly *somatic* experience."[26] He is certainly right that persons who lack the dexterity or patience to master a classic video game controller can almost instantly and intuitively play Wii successfully. For example, I am nearly as adept at creating the 7-10 split with a Wii controller in the living room as I am with a sixteen-pound ball at the local bowling alley. But there's the rub!

25. Galloway, *Gaming*, 4. "What used to be primarily the domain of eyes and looking is now more likely that of muscles and doing, *thumbs*, to be sure. . . ." Galloway, *Gaming*, 3.

26. Callaway, "Wii Are In*spirit*ed," 81, emphasis original.

There's no ball to rub, hold, swing, and hurl with a Wii, only a weightless simulacrum on a high-definition screen. Though a fuller range of motion is involved, the Wii and its imitators continue the trend of excarnation precisely by substituting virtual images for material objects, a virtual environment for real space, and an avatar for me—that is, for my body.

One of my favorite parodies on YouTube makes the point better than I can. It repurposes an ad for the *Wii Fit*, a game interface that looks like a bathroom scale, but is supposed to enable a wide range of fitness activities. The parody asks in enticing tones: "Instead of having your kids go outside and play to get exercise, why not have them stand right in front of the TV?" As long as video gaming is about inputting my actions into a virtual avatar who is acting in a virtual environment, it remains a powerful form of excarnation—a fantasy of losing my body, no matter how frenetically I'm waving my hands or wiggling my hips.

There is a second vector of excarnation in many forms of video gaming—the avatar. Early video games gave no identity choices. In *Pong*, you were a "paddle"; in *Pac-Man*, you were the Pac-Man gobbling dots and fruit; in *Asteroids*, you were the spaceship shooting furiously. Today, almost every video game offers some choice of identity. For example, *Mario Kart* lets you assume one of several different characters; *Soul Calibur* lets you fight as one of dozens of different characters, with additional costume and weapon options. It is quite common in many games for playing to begin with a lengthy process of avatar selection, as players work through a series of menus offering extensive choices of species, gender, body size and shape, race, hair color and style, facial features, wardrobe, accessories, and weaponry. The number of choices is finally finite, but the possibilities *seem* endless.

Some games go much further. In role-playing games, players often design a unique character—the avatar that will represent them in the virtual world. In most role-playing and fantasy games, ". . . the basic premise . . . is to take on virtual identities that exist within the context of the game"[27] in order to *play the game*. For example, in order to play *World of Warcraft*, one must play as a relatively unique avatar. In order to play it well, one has to play that same unique avatar for hundreds of hours, acquiring gear, skills, etc. Identity formation is even more pronounced in a game like *Second Life*, where players do nothing but create and sustain a virtual identity. In some ways, such construction "games" are more like Facebook fallen down

27. Williams et al., "Gaming Cultures, and Social Life," 13.

Alice's rabbit hole than like a game, because they take virtually enhanced, computer-powered narcissism to the nth degree.

Some social psychologists see video game avatars as an opportunity for "identity play." For example, Sherry Turkle notes that Eric Erikson "said that identity play is the work of adolescence. And these days adolescents use the rich materials of online life to do that work. . . . This kind of identity work can take place wherever you create an avatar."[28] In one sense, an avatar seems similar to forms of pretend and dress-up that young children play. Video games can be seen as another form of play's "magic circle," where we can explore alternative possibilities and identities, without the threat of permanent consequence. Yet identity exploration with an avatar is subtly but significantly different from embodied identity play in multiple, excarnating ways.

First, notice how this identity play happens "outside" our most tangible identifier—our body—precisely by substituting a virtual "body"—a visually rendered three-dimensional image. This puts identity at one remove from reality: what my body *is*—me!—my avatar can at most only signify and mediate. I am my (aging, balding, weakening) body, regardless of how strongly I might wish or will it otherwise. This means, correlatively, that my avatar is not me, regardless of how strongly I might wish or will it to be so. So the first impact of doing identity work through gaming is that it will almost certainly weaken our sense that, whoever we are, we are inextricably identified with our bodies.[29] In this regard, it is crucial to recognize that Christ's incarnation is the antithesis of adopting an avatar![30] That sug-

28. Turkle, *Alone Together*, 179–80.

29. Qualitative interviews with serious gamers regularly find comments to the effect that gamers sometimes "feel" that their avatar is more their true self than their body. See Turkle, *Alone Together*.

30. In a section titled "Jesus: the Ultimate Avatar?" Craig Detweiler implies that a video game avatar is an appropriate analogue for the incarnation. He writes, "When our digital stand-in drops into a battle, we experience a bit of what Jesus may have experienced in the incarnation." *Halos and Avatars*, 195. The remainder of the section narrates the life, death, resurrection, and exaltation of the Son of God as a role-playing game in which Jesus "was eventually fragged during a deathmatch" but "respawned, took his place as Administrator, and redefined the way the game is played." George Lindbeck argues in *The Nature of Doctrine*, 118, that an "intra-textual" approach to doctrine will place the world within scriptural reality, redescribing "reality within the scriptural framework rather than translating Scripture into extrascriptural categories. It is the text, so to speak, which absorbs the world, rather than the world the text." Detweiler is an example of what it looks like when the world absorbs the text, a danger that began, ironically, with gnosticism.

gests that the directionality of Christ-likeness is into the body, more fully identifying with and embracing bodily life.

Second, because the avatar distances identity (and action and consequence) from our bodies through electronic mediation, it secures our bodily vulnerability against risk. This is true physically because our bodies, in all their vulnerability, are completely unavailable to the others with whom we play. The bloodiest first-person shooter game cannot give my body the slightest scratch, no matter how many times my avatar gets shot. This distancing also happens psychically, as avatars (and other mediations of identity) are used to protect me from 1) the unmediated vulnerability that is unavoidable with bodily presence, and 2) the uncontrollable access that my body offers. I can both distance myself from my avatar and distance you from it. In this regard, video gaming is part of a larger group of technological media (such as cell phones and social media) that are socializing us to eschew, dislike, even fear bodily immediacy to one another. Again, Christ's incarnation involved his making himself available bodily to touch us and be touched by us. It was a risky endeavor that led to a brutal death. As followers of the crucified, risen Lord, we need a trajectory that does not flee bodily availability and psychic vulnerability for the safe distance of avatars.

Third, extensive identity play through avatars (and gaming more generally) excarnates us from the drive toward embodied union, physical co-presence, sharing with love the same time and space. Notice first how patterns of identity play through gaming are excarnating in the way they separate bodies for extended periods of time. Sherry Turkle observes:

> Creating an avatar—perhaps of a different age, a different gender, a different temperament—is a way to explore the self. But if you're spending three, four, or five hours a day in an online game or virtual world (a time commitment that is not unusual), there's got to be someplace you're not. And that someplace you're not is often with your family and friends—sitting around, playing Scrabble face-to-face, taking a walk, watching a movie together in the old-fashioned way.[31]

True, some game genres draw friends into the same room—for example, player-versus-player competitions like *Dance Dance Revolution* often draw a crowd; but role-playing games typically do not lead to physical congregation. The typical participant in a twenty-person raiding party

31. Turkle, *Alone Together*, 12.

in *World of Warcraft* is probably sitting alone in a room. Thus, gaming more generally and role-playing games specifically habituate us into the false sense that "spending time together" does not require the co-location of bodies. Of course, in this era of technological mediation, the phrase "spending time together" no longer implies bodily co-presence to digital natives; they see gaming and Facebooking and other mediations as time spent together. But truly being "with" or "together" or "present" is a matter of actual bodily location and duration, not of virtual avatar mediation. If the latter were adequate, then the Word had no reason to become flesh and dwell among us (John 1:14).

✢ *What Christian practices depend on or affirm the claim "I am my body"? How does the excarnating trajectory of gaming weaken these practices? Do video games premise identity on losing our bodies?*

✢ *Does Christian discipleship invite us into relational availability and vulnerability? How does the excarnating trajectory of mediating technologies weaken this calling?*

✢ *Does Christian faith become incarnate as we "spend time together" bodily? How should we engage an activity like gaming that is social yet dis-embodied, that socializes us to be "alone together"?*

ENTRANCED: IMMERSION AND FLOW

✢ *Do video games immerse us in endless trivialization?*

"I underestimated how immersive this gaming phenomenon had become," confesses Daniel White Hodge in his article summarizing qualitative interviews with gamers.[32] He studied thirty-five "gamers between the ages of nineteen and thirty-eight. To be considered gamers, they had to play video games, on average, between twenty and forty hours a week (about three to six hours per day) for at least five years."[33] Hodge's qualitative study gives us a quantitative indication of the entrancing power of video games: there is something about video gaming that holds us for hours at a time, weeks on end, year after year. Video games "immerse and enthrall. Time-wise, video

32. Hodge, "Role Playing," 163.
33. Ibid., 164.

games garner significant investment by players. This happens in gaming to an extent not seen in other mass media. Many games are rated at sixty or eighty hours of total gameplay; some, like *Sims Online* or *World of Warcraft*, far exceed that."[34] A virtual world like *Second Life* can apparently be "played" forever, world without end.

Why and how do video games so entrance us? One answer seems to be the pleasures they bring to our experience of time, which Diane Carr describes as "immersion, engagement, and 'flow.'"[35] Pleasures differ from game to game, but many theorists suggest that a high percentage of video games offer immersion in one or both of the following forms.

Psychological immersion is about "getting into" the game; it is a form of mental engagement. Carr uses *Baldur's Gate* as an example. This game requires regular shifting in point of view, does not offer "a 'realistic' 3-D space," and uses PC keyboard commands rather than a game controller. Yet to describe playing it, she uses terms like "absorption," "engrossment," and says that "time flies" (53). A key dimension of psychological immersion is the way video games typically correlate increasing game challenge with a player's increasing skill (motifs include "leveling up," engaging new or more difficult opponents, or increasing game speed). It's as if the game starts as checkers but becomes chess as your skill improves. In psychological immersion, a "player is slowly drawn into the game world via his or her imaginative investment" (54).

Where psychological immersion meshes with game design and player skill, a condition called *flow*[36] often occurs. Carr says, "The flow state is possible when an activity involves escalating yet manageable challenges, options, decisions, risk, feedback, and achievable goals. It is an intensely pleasurable, optimum state, incorporating focus, euphoria, and high levels of motivation. Flow states have been associated with a variety of activities, including computer games . . ." (57).

34. Galloway, *Gaming*, 5. Of course, there are board games that seem to take forever (*Risk* comes to mind), and you can play successive hands of a card game forever (my wife and I are playing our children to one million points in pinochle). But those games don't enthrall us like video games do.

35. Carr, "Play and Pleasure," 52. Cited parenthetically in the next three paragraphs.

36. The key work on flow was articulated by Csikszentmihalyi. Various theorists apply it to video gaming, for example, Egenfeldt-Nielsen, Smith, Tosca, *Understanding Video Games*, 149f.; Turkle, *Alone Together*, 226, writes, "You can have this experience at a Las Vegas gambling machine or on a ski slope. And now, you can have it during a game of *Civilization* or *World of Warcraft*. You can have it playing *The Beatles: Rock Band*. You can have it on *Second Life*."

Perceptual immersion "involves the degree to which a technology or experience monopolizes the senses of a user" (53). Think about watching a movie in a plush movie theater versus catching it in the kitchen while cooking dinner. Video gaming is especially well suited for perceptual immersion, since our visual perception cannot distinguish between real and virtually simulated images. In addition to this "hot" dimension, there is a "cool" side as well. "Video games are simply too absorbing and too demanding of our attention to allow us to relate to anyone who is not in the digital world with us."[37] Whether our game immersion is psychological, perceptual, or both, it will diminish our non-game perceptions of environment and persons.

Where psychological and perceptual immersion coalesce with flow states, it becomes exceptionally difficult to stop playing. After all, playing the game is delivering "need satisfaction with immediacy, consistency, and density."[38] Moreover, the pleasure of playing creates a self who prefers game pleasures more than any that his "first life" offers.[39] Sherry Turkle gets at something similar:

> . . . if we ask, "What does simulation want?" we know what it wants. It wants—it demands—immersion. But immersed in simulation, it can be hard to remember all that lies beyond it or even to acknowledge that everything is not captured by it. For simulation not only demands immersion but creates a self that prefers simulation.[40]

As one young gamer said in a Kaiser Family Foundation report, "Studying is just, like, wasting Xbox time."[41] Beyond the entrancing effect of immersion and flow, there is another reason that video games log so much playing time: they either lack "natural" stopping points altogether,[42] or their "natural" end points only increase desire to keep playing (for example, where gameplay is stopped by "defeat," a player will usually find it

---

37. Rigby and Ryan, *Glued to Games*, 116.

38. Ibid., 102, elaborated 102–5.

39. See ibid., 97–118.

40. Turkle, *Alone Together*, 285.

41. Kaiser Family Foundation, "Profiles of Generation M(2)," video quote at 4:52–56.

42. Rigby and Ryan, *Glued to Games*, 109, note that in massive multiplayer online role-playing games, ". . . you are *always* in the middle of something, indeed usually in the middle of several goals simultaneously. . . . This creates a feeling of ever-present unfinished business."

pleasurable to immediately try again, deploying a different strategy or action inferred from the prior experience of loss).

Thus the caricature of typical gamers as addicts is largely false, although "current data suggest that 10–15 percent of gamers fall into a pattern of video game overuse or addiction."[43] What is most certainly true is that the durative, temporal pleasures of gaming make it an entertainment that players engage *extensively*—in how often and long they play, and how they regularly think about gaming when not playing[44]—and *intensively*—in the fullness of attention and passion that they give to their play.

The entrancing nature of gaming is central to its appeal. Recognizing why gaming is so pleasurable, and how those pleasures—delivered with immediacy, consistency, and density—draw us in, positions us to reflect on the need for temperate engagement with game temporality. The pleasures of intensive play are not problematic in themselves. Indeed, they can be a beneficial triviality that offers fun in the context of enjoyable agency, sociality, and competence.[45] But the pleasures of many games are designed to keep us playing, to hold us longer, to so immerse us that gaming becomes our passion, our preoccupation, our primary pursuit. In short, the trivial pleasures of video gaming sometimes want to become powerful principalities that hold us completely captive. Recognizing that, we must choose carefully not only *when* to play but *what* to play, and with whom.

The problem is, I think I'm immune, and so do you. Media theorists call this the "third-person effect." Simply put, it is the almost universal perception that each of us holds that media impacts don't affect us. We agree that iPods promote isolation for everyone except us. We agree that "broadcast yourself" is an invitation to reflexivity for everybody but me. So we nod our heads in agreement that games without natural stopping points are best avoided, and that MMORPGs that bind our "free time" to the late-night demands of the raiding party are asking too much, but all the while we mentally exempt ourselves. Notice what this means: even if gaming didn't provide the pull of immersion or the dopamine rush of flow, it would still be difficult to resist precisely because I don't really think I need to.

❖   *In what activity do you regularly experience immersion (perceptual or psychological) and/or flow states? Does that experience refresh*

43. Ibid., 98.

44. Ibid., 107.

45. Ibid., 97.

and empower you for the rest of your life, or beguile you into prefer-
ring it above everything else?

"This Is Living!"?—Another Word from Our Sponsors

A few years ago, Sony Europe ran an ad campaign for the PlayStation3 with the slogan "This is living!" Different video ads featured suggestive mini-dramas staged in an ornate hotel fraught with atmosphere. Each ad used crosscutting to weave together mysterious and mondo characters, hints of criminal intrigue and impending violence, transgressive desire and sexual innuendo, all with oblique narration by the cool Carribean desk clerk. Each ad ended with the PlayStation3 tagline, "This is living!"

In one sense, the ads weren't serious. They embodied a "wink-wink" campaign that traded on the ironic sensibilities of gamers (as well as re-lying on the more permissive broadcast regulations of Europe). It was an inside message from Sony that positioned PS3 gamers as knowing partici-pants in an enjoyable triviality that non-gaming cultural critics are taking all too seriously. The subtext seemed to say, "We get it, so we get to have the fun. They don't, which is their loss." At first glance, the campaign seems to agree with this book's perspective that entertainments are properly used as enjoyable trivialities that can enrich and enliven us. And yet . . .

The ads positioned viewers as voyeuristic consumers of a surreal sim-ulacrum of life that offered itself as more interesting than normal activity; as more engaging than real, embodied relationships; as more evocative of desire than the material world; as more provocative than present choices. In short, "This is living!" positioned the gaming life as better than real life. For all its ironic stance, Sony apparently meant "This is living!"

Unfortunately, because the best games do give us such a powerful this-is-living rush, they too easily habituate us not only to prefer gaming, but to perceive it as living at its very best. So I will conclude by suggesting that when it comes to real life and genuine living, gaming is finally impotent and alienated. Perhaps we can see this best by pairing a particularly dis-turbing portion of one PS3 ad with a comment by Douglas Rushkoff. The ad couples its musical score with visual edits to imply the sexual journey of several characters from arousal to climax. One is an athletic young man, shown wearing nothing but a jock strap, who is apparently masturbating while watching a soccer game and fondling his soccer ball. Sony's jaded punchline correlates his implied orgasm with a soccer goal. Apparently this visual double entendre wants us to laugh simultaneously at sports-related sex fetishism and at alarmists who worry that gaming promotes sexual perversion.

Instead, we would do well to laugh at Sony for graphically demonstrating the truth of Douglas Rushkoff's claim that playing a video game is "an essentially masturbatory act."[46] It is that because 1) it stimulates with simulacra of realities and fantasies, and responds with mimicry of real action. Here we have to pity the confused state of several of the contributors to *Halos and Avatars*, who assert the essential sameness of simulated activity in gaming and the real activity it simulates. Matthew Kitchen's claim comparing a video simulation of Pebble Beach to the real thing can stand in for that entire book's perspective: *"at the end of the day everyone is playing golf."*[47] No, actually they are not all playing golf, any more than the adolescent masturbating in his bedroom and the parents enjoying marital communion in theirs would lead us to say, "at the end of the day everyone is making love." 2) Gaming often pursues its pleasures in isolation, and always in mediation, meaning that even if pleasure is shared, it is not shared through the co-presence, communication, and communion of bodies. Some Wii games and *Dance Dance Revolution* might seem immune to this claim, but in fact they only mitigate it partially because engagement is visually *mediated* through a screen, rather than tactilely *immediate* to touch. 3) Finally, gaming is essentially impotent activity because it creates nothing with tangibly enduring value.[48] The one potent exception is that gaming can form or strengthen a healthy sociality; where it does, we should celebrate something with eternal value.

None of this should suggest that imaginative play is inherently sterile, nor that video games should be off-limits. Instead, it suggests that the proper limits for gaming are the intrinsic limits of our humanity—that our

46. Rushkoff, *Playing the Future*, 181.

47. Kitchen, *"Madden* Rules," 117.

48. Granted, there is a booming monetary economy that profits from virtual activity in gaming worlds, buying and selling virtual "gear" for *World of Warcraft*, offering business services in *Second Life*, etc. Thus intangible virtualities are exchangeable for money, but that does not mean they have true worth. Unlike a tasty tomato, well-made quilt, or a baby, the e-gear trading on eBay has no intrinsic worth. And unlike acts of love (Matt 25), which endure eternally, gaming will probably cease well before the last gigawatt of energy pulses away.

happiness is found in God, that our bodiliness is embraced as good, that our attentiveness remains fixed on what is real. (These three limits summarize the discussion of the last three sections.) Paradoxically, we find in the Christian Eucharist that these three limits *free us* for communion with God—as we are drawn into God's heavenly rejoicing, as we receive bodily the broken body of Christ, as we are immersed by the Holy Spirit in the mystery of faith. Truly, *this is living!*

✢ *How does our gaming fit us for the work of worship, and especially for the joy of making Eucharist together? Does "Wii play" empower or impede how we pray?*

These questions may finally be the best criteria for a faithful engagement with gaming.

ten

CosmoGirl as Cheap Grace

SEVERAL YEARS AGO I stumbled across a fashion magazine for teenage girls. While I don't normally pay attention to that genre of print media, even when stuck in a long line at the grocery store, this time was different because the magazine was *Revolve*, a contemporary translation of the New Testament published in the format of a glossy teenzine. I was dumbfounded at what seemed to me an incredibly bad idea. Yet I quickly discovered that other sincere Christians believed this was a wonderful tool for youth ministry. That disconcertingly different response was what led me toward questions of theological engagement with entertainment culture. In this chapter, we will move in three steps: from an overview of magazines as entertainment, to a closer look at teen girl fashion magazines, and a concluding consideration of *Revolve*.

MAGAZINES AS ENTERTAINMENT

For more than a century, magazines have been a part of the American ecology of entertainment. Yet today we might be tempted to dismiss them as not important enough to warrant serious theological engagement. After all, most people use broadcast media like television and radio every day, whereas they "read" magazines far less frequently, if at all (often a matter of passing the time while waiting somewhere). Clearly magazines seldom give us a "water cooler moment"—the entertainment event that everyone at work or school is talking about.

Yet magazines remain significant, as anybody who has stood in a grocery store checkout line knows.[1] And the numerous "glossies" on display there are merely the tip of an iceberg—four thousand strong. One industry association reports that its members' nine hundred-plus magazines have circulation revenue approaching $9 billion, suggesting that magazines continue to be important in the entertainment economy.[2] Though music, movies, television, sports, and video gaming all capture more of the market, it is important to notice the symbiotic relationship between them and magazines that attend to them.

For example, celebrity zines like *Us* and *People* both need and help sustain Hollywood's celebrity culture; *Rolling Stone* requires rock fans, but inspires them too; *Premier* needs cinema to call forth its crowd, but also forms the film crowd, just as *Computer Gaming World* depends on the gaming industry while also helping to constitute it. Taking *Sports Illustrated* (hereafter *SI*) as an example, it is not hard to see that in one sense the entertainment value of the magazine begins on the playing field. Yet these days most fans catch most games on television, so in some ways TV becomes the real aggregator of the *SI* audience. Moreover, television is also the reason that sports fans are so familiar with the look of their favorite teams and players. A glossy magazine full of color pictures becomes a natural accoutrement to the practice of watching the sport on television. Yet this doesn't mean that *SI* has an entirely parasitic relationship to televised sport. The relationship is far more symbiotic. *SI* can create a buzz around a particular athlete or game or rivalry that enhances the value of watching it. Moreover, reading the magazine contributes to the social identity of "sports fan." Indeed, we consider someone to be a fan regardless of whether they mostly attend the games, watch them on television, or just follow the sport through box scores (newspaper or online) and by reading magazines like *Sports Illustrated*. So overall, magazines that arise from existing entertainments function not only to sustain the larger environment of entertainment, but also to validate and direct our commitment of time, energy, money, and passion to it. Magazines assure us that being a "fan" is not *fanatical*, but a great way to live, love, and *spend*.

1. For an interpretation of the grocery store checkout line, see Lawson, Sleasman, and Anderson, "Gospel according to Safeway."

2. Association of Magazine Media, "Circulation Revenue."

❖ *Do you subscribe to any magazines? Are they symbiotic with an entertainment industry? Do they "sell" you not only stuff, but the value of the entertainment itself, and of devoting your time, attention, and emotion to it?*

Reviewing some historical changes in magazines can help us recognize two important trends in entertainment more generally. First, *segmenting*; magazines show us a common movement in entertainment media from a general or mass audience to narrower and more specialized ones. (Two other media where this has occurred are radio and cable television.) During the second quarter of the twentieth century, general audience magazines were thriving. But the strong rise of broadcast television at midcentury had a quelling effect on periodicals intended for "everyone." Advertisers saw that television offered them greater and more frequent access to consumers, so they switched media. This killed a number of successful general audience journals such as *The Saturday Evening Post*, but it didn't destroy the magazine industry. Instead, specialized magazines found a growing audience and advertisers gladly paid for access to such demographically homogenous groups. After all, it only makes sense that makers of camping gear would gladly pay for access to the readership of *Backpacker,* or that automakers would do the same for access to readers of *Car and Driver.* Today there are thousands of consumer magazines, most targeting very narrow slices of the magazine entertainment pie. (Similarly, radio, cable, and satellite television all "narrowcast" to a select and homogenous demographic defined by particular entertainment taste.)

Notice what happens with the rise of specialization in entertainment media of all sorts (not only magazines but television, film, radio, and the Web). We get used to segmentation by interest; we begin to take it for granted that preferences and tastes are an appropriate way to differentiate ourselves into groups. Our regular participation in specialized entertainments habituates us into a kind of tribalism of taste. Worse, these different tastes are usually also differentiated by age, so that specialized entertainments construct and reinforce segmentation into generations.[3] We now take it for granted that entertainment gathers homogenous groups—children's televi-

---

3. On this generational differentiation, see Schultze et al., *Dancing in the Dark*, 3–5. Vincent Miller suggests that niche marketing, which can exploit individualizing devices (e.g., personal electronics) and technologies (DVRs, Web site data collection), may bring an end to the generational identity created by midcentury marketing strategies. Miller, *Consuming Religion*, 70–71.

sion, *Not Another Teen Movie, Modern Maturity*—into a sectarianism of demographic sameness. So entertainment forms us in habits of gathering according to our differences. Obvious examples would be congregations that take it for granted that difference in musical taste is a proper rationale for multiple worship services, or the near universal notion that teenagers should be quarantined from older adults when learning and serving Jesus. These patterns of assembling are clearly antithetical to the way Jesus wants to assemble the diverse membership of his body, but many American Christians cannot see that because narrowcasting has normalized segmentation by style, taste, and generation.

✤ *Has your church organized itself in ways that take for granted segmenting by generation or taste? Is segmenting an effective strategy for enculturating the gospel, or a failure to be fully converted to the gospel?*

Second, *the triumph of image*. The twentieth century has witnessed a profound shift toward the visual. At its core, pop culture simply is a visual culture (pop music and surround sound notwithstanding); *American Idol* and its ilk would never succeed if we could not *see* the contestants sing. This shift toward spectacle was not historically spontaneous, nor was it merely a factor of technological inventiveness (though cinema, television, and digital reproduction have contributed to it). Rather, its primary catalyst was a shift in advertising strategy from verbal information to visual imagination.

Another Word from Our Sponsors

Does *Cosmopolitan* contain ads, or is it essentially one giant two hundred-page ad? Probably both. Vincent Miller provides an overview of the fashioning of visual culture through advertising. "Print advertising underwent a seismic shift in the 1890s. The sheer number of ads for a growing range of consumer goods rendered text-based ads increasingly ineffective. Advertising trade journals noted the need to capture the reader's attention, and technical advances in printing provided the means for doing so with images."[4]

---

4. Miller, *Consuming Religion*, 87. Cited parenthetically in the next two paragraphs.

Thus, instead of conveying information, advertising increasingly purveyed images that associated positive experiences or feelings with the product being sold. In the process, significance shifted from the product signified to the process of signification: the product's worth was no longer intrinsic to it, but was constructed visually through imaginations of its meaning, purchase, possession, benefits, use, or consumption. This turned consumption "into an 'imaginary' act. People are no longer primarily interested in the goods themselves, but in their images. Consumption becomes an imaginary activity whose object is the advertisement as much as the product itself" (57).

This changed the way people relate to the advertisements accompanying their entertainments. "The reading of ads becomes part of the flow of reading magazines and watching television" (58). In magazines, especially, the happy marriage of audience interest and advertisers' goods begins to blur the distinction between content and ad. Some magazines do this intentionally, by juxtaposing articles and ads about the same thing: for example, a sunscreen ad immediately follows an article on skin cancer. But even where there is no intentional collusion, "magazines offer an environment that is conducive and sympathetic to the adverts they run."[5]

Thus magazines both influence and symbolize our cultural shift toward visual modes of knowing, feeling, valuing, and deciding. They also signify the deep collusion of entertainment media with their marketing sponsors, such that the entertainment visualizes our desire for, and imagines our satisfaction from, consumption as the best way of living. The joke is on us, however, because in this process the advertisements themselves (rather than the consumable product) become the true source of our happiness. This visual culture promises what it can depict but never deliver: satisfaction, a heart resting in its true home. Ironically, though, this failure does not expose advertisements to the withering light of truth, but instead exposes us to inexorable anxieties about our lacks, wants, and failures. Visual culture parodies the gospel by promising liberation, fulfillment, and enjoyment, yet delivering bondage, emptiness, and anxiety.

5. Gill, *Gender and the Media*, 182. Something equivalent could certainly be said of the experience of watching television.

✥ *How have we been captivated by visuality, captured by the cultural shift toward images? Does a visually oriented pop culture convince us to seek satisfaction, truth, healing, and belonging through consumption rather than through congregating—participation in the human inter-relation that is Christ's church?*

All this suggests to me that discipleship might be one fruitful lens through which to critically view magazine entertainment. Specifically, since discipleship involves who we are, how we live, and what we love, it makes questions of identity, practice, and affect central. For any type of magazine, then, we can ask about identity. What kind of person does the magazine assume its typical reader to be, and what person does it urge the reader to become? We can also ask about activity. What patterns of life are recommended and what practices or disciplines are urged on readers? Finally, we can ask about affect, aspiration, or desire. What does the magazine, not just in its explicit messages but more broadly in its use, beckon us to care about, delight in, aspire to, and hope for? (Obviously these discipleship categories and questions are germane to most other forms of mediated entertainment, too.)

COSMOGIRL AS DISCIPLESHIP?

My case study for this engagement is teen girl beauty magazines like *Seventeen* (which began publishing in 1944, with circulation now at around 2.4 million), *CosmoGirl* (launched in 2000 with a 2006 circulation of 1.4 million), and *Teen Vogue* (also launched in 2000 with a 2006 circulation at just under 1 million, but claiming a total audience of over 3 million).[6] Though readership may be shifting from print glossies to the Web, there are still millions of teen girls who read these magazines weekly. One British study in 2000 reported that 80 percent of girls aged 12–19 read a magazine for pleasure at least once a week. For pleasure! Maybe also to get the latest celebrity gossip, or to see the hottest new fashion, or to acquire six more beauty tips, but also for the fun of it. These magazines are used by teen girls

6. One indication of the volatility of this market is the number of such magazines that have folded. These include *Teen* (founded 1954, with top circulation of two million, folded 2008); *Young Miss* (which became *Young and Modern* and then *YM* had a top circulation of 2.2 million, folded 2004); *Sassy* (founded 1988, folded into *Teen* in 1996); and *Elle Girl* (launched in 2001, ceased print publication July 2006, though it continues to exist as a Webzine).

as entertainment, so it is worth our while to ask what makes them fun. If we browse through several issues, the answer is not hard to see.

All the teen fashion zines have a common look and format. The cover nearly always centers on the smiling face of a young female celebrity, with the claim that somewhere inside she will reveal some of her private life. There are half a dozen other headlines, promising fashion and beauty tips to help you look better, inside information on how guys think, salacious "real-life stories," and some sort of connection with entertainment celebrities. Inside the magazine there is page after page of bright, full-page advertisements for clothing, shoes, accessories, makeup, and personal hygiene products (ads comprise 50 to 60 percent of most issues). Stuffed between the ads are not only the cover articles, but quizzes, letters to the editor, product reviews, celebrity gossip, horoscopes, and a calendar, hardly any long enough to demand more than ten minutes of casual attention. Throughout the publication the graphics are big and bold, and even the most text-laden pages usually reserve at least a quarter of their layout for a glam-shot photo. The result is an entertainment product that we "look at" rather than read, one in which advertisements are not interruptions but a crucial part of the enjoyment sought, one that focuses on how to be (or become) successfully feminine.

For seven years my theology classes have been asked to browse through such magazines in order to discern the vision of humanity (the "theological anthropology") presented there. Together we have discovered several consistent themes. Most obvious is the emphasis on looking beautiful: the magazines are filled with airbrushed photos of young women with clear skin, straight white teeth, incredibly thin and tall bodies, lustrous hair, and perfect makeup. There is a yawning chasm between this fashion industry ideal of beauty and the real looks of most high-school girls, one that raises the question of whether perusing beauty magazines significantly diminishes self-image (and perhaps contributes to eating disorders). Most studies show that seeing mediated images of "desirable others" negatively impacts human self-esteem in ways that increase our vulnerability.[7] Fashion magazines capitalize on that vulnerability, the desire to look better, by promising that purchasing the right products is the path to perfecting yourself.[8] This is the second key theme my students notice—the powerful imperative to buy

7. Dill, *How Fantasy Becomes Reality*, 18–20.

8. On the theme of how media create communities of consumption, see Schultze, *Communicating for Life*, 113–17.

the right stuff, with the promise that this is what will ameliorate that aching sense of inadequacy.

Beyond the imperatives to look good and buy things, the third common theme is the importance of relationships, of which two types really matter—peer relations with other girls (who are just like you), and romantic relations with boys (who would be impossible to understand apart from the information the magazine provides). The final theme my students usually notice is that life should be fun. Everyone in the pictures looks excited, happy, or pleased with themselves (except perhaps the model in an acne ad who failed to use the miracle cleanser). The emotional register presented is very narrow; there are hardly any depictions of what we might call negative emotions like grief, anger, or fear. Apparently, human life is about having fun and seeking pleasure; "double your joy" commands one advertisement.[9]

All of this bears directly on discipleship as identity, practice, and affect. It constructs identity around appearance, consumption, and elective relationships; I am how I look, what I buy, and who I'm with. It fosters aspirations to be beautiful, buy the right things, get the right boy, and stay happy all the time. These aspirations lead to practical disciplines: regimens of diet, exercise, and makeup; practices of dress, adornment, and accessorization; patterns of expectation, consumption, and communication.

I will focus more closely on this practical dimension momentarily, but first note just how problematic this overall vision is. The church should not countenance *any* of its disciples locating their primary identity and sense of worth in personal appearance, especially as defined by the fashion, beauty, and entertainment industries. Nor does the church want *any* of the faithful placing their primary relational aspirations in America's cultural ideology of romantic fulfillment. The fact that the target audience is adolescent girls (the mean reading age of *CosmoGirl* is sixteen) only amplifies these two objections.

More subtly, the church must challenge the notion that the good life involves homogenous relationships that we choose. It is telling that in these magazines relationships that precede our choosing—given relationships like family or teachers or church—are either omitted altogether or presented as problems to be solved by the witty advice columnist. There is never even a hint that a genuinely good life might intrinsically require

---

9. Nearly twenty years ago, Quentin Schultze et al., *Dancing in the Dark*, 7, pointed out that entertainments aimed at youth—"from MTV to films and recording" to magazines like *CosmoGirl*—"conspire to peddle alluring visions of identity and intimacy."

relationships with people we are "stuck with," with people significantly older and younger, with people who are racially, ethnically, or culturally different. The identity and aspiration presented in *CosmoGirl* is a profound distortion of a relational network that is genuinely diverse. This is segmenting in action.

Let us take up the disciplining of life in these magazines. It is usually offered as innocuous advice or expertise about some aspect of personal appearance (clothes, makeup, hair, etc.) or about relations with boys (understanding "them," getting "their" attention, getting or keeping a boyfriend). Five tips to great hair, seven tricks to look great on a budget, four ways to keep your guy, six cheats to get his attention. *Ironically*, following the magazines' directions about beautification and boyfriend-ification is presented as a surefire way to "be yourself."[10] A typical article in the October 2003 issue of *Seventeen* promised me "A Cute Butt in Three Weeks." Actually, the pictures and text suggested that the promise was not for me, but for derriere-conscious young women. Besides "three exercises for a tighter tush," this article also offered techniques for fighting posterior pimples, readers' answers to the question, "Why do you love your butt?" and a quiz to see if I could correctly identify four celebrity bottoms—all this on a single page!

Obviously a focus like this is both superficial and distracting. Less obvious than the focus of how-to articles, but entirely more problematic, is the form in which they come: simple steps offered by an expert that, with a little discipline, will effect the desired change in less than a month. The magazines promise quick results without too much effort—a presto-chango fantasy of near instant, near effortless improvement. That optimistic time frame is intrinsic to the periodical nature of this medium; young women's magazines are published monthly, so *Seventeen* needs me to finish this issue's regimen before next month's arrives. Otherwise, I might forego "Killer Thighs in Twenty-One Days," leaving the November *Seventeen* to languish at the checkout aisle, because I'm still working on a better butt.

There are several more optimisms intrinsic to these self-help features. One is that meaningful transformation is primarily a matter of technical know-how, easily summarized as bullet points and just as easily comprehended. Another is that I can effect my own transformation by simply following the directions of an expert or authority. So *Teen Vogue*'s mission

10. Gill, *Gender and the Media*, 187, points out that "the messages about being yourself, being beautiful and being knowledgeable about boys are inextricably linked in teen magazines in a way that is both profound and taken for granted." Her entire chapter on "Gender in Magazines" is quite helpful.

statement makes clear that it is the *exclusive authority* on such matters: "Style-conscious girls everywhere know there's only one source for relevant fashion and beauty news communicated in a sophisticated tone with the power of the *Vogue* brand."[11] I need expert advice, but I don't need real relationship with other people who train, guide, assist, or encourage me. Deeper still is the optimism that I already recognize in myself what needs development or transformation; all I lack is the technical information (and perhaps motivation) that the magazine provides. Ironically, the needs I supposedly recognize in myself are actually created by the articles and ads that exacerbate "insecurity by creating an atmosphere in which every aspect of the anxious self—personality, appearance, hygiene, . . . [is] subjected to ruthless surveillance."[12]

All of this optimism about self-transformation is profoundly at odds with the Christian understanding of discipleship, what Dietrich Bonhoeffer memorably termed "costly grace." Both *CosmoGirl* grace and costly grace look for personal transformation, but that is where the resemblance stops, because Christian discipleship is pricey; it costs open-ended time, learned wisdom, and shared community.[13] First, disciples of Jesus recognize that meaningful change is not a presto-chango matter of self-improvement. Rather, it is a putting to death and a coming alive over the course of a lifetime of following Jesus; there is no thirty-day shortcut to faithfulness. Second, disciples of Jesus discover that their ignorance is far deeper than a lack of information about how to fix a problem they already recognize. Most basically it is a failure to see—fully and clearly—their own sin. So their power of discernment is not innate, as if already recognizing the problem they are ready to receive "five tricks for spiritual transformation," or "seven steps to a healthy soul." Instead they must learn the wisdom of recognizing their sin and receiving God's grace. This learning the wisdom of Christ happens over time through engaging in specific practices and engaging with specific persons. Disciples are learners who submit to regimens (like worship and service) and disciplines (like prayer and fasting) for the long haul, as much to *find* as to *fix* what is broken in them. Third, disciples need something far more substantial than advice from experts; they require

11. *Teen Vogue*, "Mission Statement," para. 1.

12. Adapting Miller's general observation about the therapeutic impact of advertising, *Consuming Religion*, 87.

13. In summarizing Navone's work on early catechesis, Budde, *(Magic) Kingdom*, 69, calls attention to several dimensions, among them the "substantial investment of time," the "process of *sequential learning*," and "apprenticeship with a church member."

ongoing immersion in Scripture and conversation with the saints, ideally saints of their own congregation. Some of these saints will offer wisdom to guide the process of recognition and transformation; others will offer encouragement and accountability.

In the end, *CosmoGirl* and all the rest offer cheap grace: they construct identities around appearance, consumption, and elective relationships, and they constrict imaginations (and discipline bodies) with a vision of the good life as the pursuit of beauty, boyfriends, and fun. Even though many teenage girls treat them as "just fun" or "harmless fantasy," the church should still be quite charry about its adolescent disciples having a subscription to *Seventeen*. If you aren't convinced, consider that *Seventeen* "once had an advertisement featuring a young girl holding a new issue with the caption: 'Her Bible.'"[14]

✤ *Overall, this section has suggested that fashion magazines are a power to be resisted. Is there any appropriate way to "enjoy the triviality" of teen girl fashion magazines? Or are they utterly malignant?*

HER BIBLE

✤ *Would anything important change if the teenzine in question were not* CosmoGirl, *but a contemporary translation of the New Testament produced to look like a fashion magazine?*

Apparently millions of American evangelicals would answer "yes," if we judge by the sales statistics for *Revolve*. The basic premise of *Revolve* is to distribute the text of the New Testament in the form of a beauty magazine for teenage girls. As the Web site promoting it said some years ago, *Revolve* can go where girls would be unwilling to take a "big black Bible"—to school or practice or sleepovers.

Its format resembles *CosmoGirl* in a number of ways. Its appearance is designed to make it almost indistinguishable from other fashion zines; it has the same shape, layout, graphical intensity, and bevy of photographs of happy, attractive young women (almost all white). When I include it in an inductive exercise where my students are fanning through different fashion magazines, they sometimes take as long as five minutes to notice that it is "different" from *Teen Vogue* or *Elle Girl*. Its special features mimic other

---

14. Mattingly, *Pop Goes Religion*, 158.

teenzines: there are lists, calendars, quizzes, beauty secrets, relationship tips, and a "Guys Speak Out" section.

Of course the content is different. *Revolve*'s "Beauty Secret" sections always have a picture that implies a tip about appearance, but text that turns the focus from outer looks to inner attitudes. For example, the tip on plucking your eyebrows suggests that, just as applying a warm washcloth first eases the pain of plucking, so giving a hug first will ease the pain of telling a friend bad news. Perhaps the "Beauty Secret" that most clearly encapsulates *Revolve*'s strategy is the one that tells readers to "remember that your inner beauty can shine through better when you're not so focused on your outer beauty."[15] This helpful advice is placed directly under the glossy picture of a traditionally beautiful, smiling young woman. Clearly this medium is at odds with its message. It takes a severe case of "Media Manipulation Denial Syndrome"[16] to believe that the trite words the eye reads can overpower the visual message it sees, especially when that seeing has been shown to impact self-esteem directly apart from rational reflection.[17]

To step back, if beautyzines generally suggest that personal transformation can be accomplished quickly, easily, and alone, won't *Revolve* inevitably do the same thing? Generally, I think that it does, even though it does not intend to do so. Indeed, *Revolve*'s introduction begins with the claim that "*this* Bible is about radical devotion . . ." (emphasis added). Unfortunately, claiming that *this* Bible is radical already suggests that some other Bibles aren't, an implication that seems natural to an entertainment medium premised on segmenting audiences by taste and age. Moreover, the implication seems to be that it is the surrounding text—notes on "Radical Faith" and "Learn It and Live It"—that makes this Bible radical, not the scriptural words themselves nor the Christian community that reads and obeys them. Lest you think I am overstating the case, here is the publisher's online advertisement for *Revolve*: "the New Testament in *a magazine format* continues *showing teen girls that the Bible is entirely understandable and relevant to their lives*" (emphasis added). If you read only the words I've italicized, it sounds like the revealing work is being done by the magazine's format, not by the Holy Spirit illuminating the words of Scripture through the church's faithful interpretation.

15. *Revolve*, 69.

16. For a humorous elaboration of MMDS, see Dill, *How Fantasy Becomes Reality*, 20.

17. Ibid., 18–19.

This leads to a second and central criticism. *Revolve* has trouble presenting the true cost of discipleship because it cannot transcend the limitations of the teenzine format. Like the other fashion zines, it uses lists, bullet points, and captions to convey its message. The question is whether scriptural "truth" can be squeezed into this genre without taking on the presto-chango sensibility that I can transform myself quickly and easily by understanding a few simple facts and by following the advice of experts. *Revolve* never says that radical discipleship is quick and easy; indeed, it says that discipleship is deliberate and demanding. But *Revolve's* format suggests otherwise precisely by making discipleship something we instantly recognize on our own rather than slowly learn in the company of other Christians. *Revolve* implies that I can understand Scripture, God, and myself by reading a brief paragraph here, a caption there, or the occasional brief list.

The "Learn It and Live It" sections are the quintessence of this presto-chango approach to faith formation. The "it" we learn is a single propositional sentence drawn from Scripture. Apparently we don't need to read these sentences in the larger contexts of the verse, chapter, letter, testament, and canon in which they are set. Rather, they mean what they mean as free-floating facts, and anybody who reads them should be able to understand them immediately. And understanding "it," they can then "live it" by following simple advice, usually one or two sentences. Thus the "Learn It and Live It" features suggest that scriptural wisdom is acquired by the simple process of reading words on a page, not by the hard task of attentive learning in community, and that scriptural wisdom can be embodied by the simple decision to "live it," rather than by struggle, temptation, and prayer. The editors promise that "God never intended the Bible to be too difficult for his people," which is true enough, but only if we faithfully and corporately engage it. But the format of *Revolve* inevitably makes the Bible too simple and individualized, precisely by reducing it to simplistic truths I can understand and embody by deciding to, without transformation, support, or accountability.

Here's an example: in 2 Corinthians 12:7-10, Paul reports that when he implored the Lord three times to remove a tormenting thorn in the flesh, he received this answer: "my grace is enough for you. When you are weak, my power is made perfect in you" (New Century Version, the translation used in *Revolve*). Paul goes on to say in his weakness, "Christ's power can live in me. For this reason I am happy when I have weaknesses, insults, hard times, sufferings, and all kinds of troubles for Christ. Because when

I am weak, then I am truly strong" (NCV). In context, that final sentence has everything to do with the promising presence and perfecting power of Jesus Christ. But *Revolve*'s "Learn It and Live It" prints only this: "When we are weak, we are strong." [18] Ostensibly this is a faithful translation of 2 Corinthians 12:10. But because it lacks the contextualizing promise of verses 8–9, it turns a very specific promise about hardships and weakness in Christ into a general claim about weakness that simply isn't true. The teen readers of *Revolve* aren't likely to notice that falsification because of three decontextualizations. First, this "Learn It and Live It" is not printed on the page containing 2 Corinthians 12, but on the page for Acts 7. So a curious girl would have to fan eighty-four pages further to read the full promise in context. Second, she's unlikely to do that since regularly "reading" fashion magazines has already habituated her to prefer and trust captions, headings, and short declarative sentences, rather than more complex written material. Finally, whether intended or not, the bright yellow background and two smiling teens are so much more visually gripping than the typography of the biblical text itself. In the end, while *Revolve* claims to be an improvement on the "big black Bible" teen girls are embarrassed to carry to school, it continues to make the actual *Bible* small, black, *boring* print. Given these three decontextualizations, it seems unlikely that this kind of Bible will greatly enhance biblical literacy or fluency among adolescent girls.

Finally, turning the Bible into a fashion zine risks transforming our engagement with Scripture into a form of casual entertainment rather than disciplined devotion. If you read *Elle Girl* for fun, then reading a Bible that looks, feels, and communicates like *Elle Girl* will likely (inevitably?) pull you into that same pattern of engagement. Moreover, as one researcher notes, in these magazines most articles are a page in length, and most content is conveyed as bullet points or captions, so reading them is not a particularly demanding activity that requires intense concentration or sustained attention. This is a genre of entertainment meant for intermittent use in the spare moments of our lives. The danger is that teen girls will approach *Revolve* with identical reading habits, assuming that radical devotion to God can be practiced through casually scanning God's Word. It can't, and creating Bibles that look like it can is just one more instance of being seduced by a principality.

18. *Revolve*, 181.

✛ *Are you persuaded that refusal is the correct response to Revolve or other similar efforts to load Christian content into an existing pop culture form? Do you believe that the impact of a detrimental cultural form or practice can be mitigated by replacing "bad" content with "good"?*

✛ *Can practices of discipleship ever adopt the form or format of entertainment without being reshaped by entertainment's agenda and constrained by entertainment's limits?*

eleven|

What Would Bono Do?

CELEBRITIZING SCRIPTURE

"Stars Contribute to the New Audio Bible" proclaimed the headline in *Radiant* magazine's "Faces and Places" section. The accompanying news nugget informed us that

> More than 80 black celebs are teaming up . . . for The Bible Experience—an audio Bible project created to reach a new urban generation with a modern and accessible approach. The artistic 70-hour Genesis-through-Revelation reading aims to bring the Scriptures to life with the help of Cuba Gooding Jr., Angela Bassett, Queen Latifah, and Kirk Franklin. Denzel Washington and his wife, Pauletta, will read Song of Songs.

The 79-CD set was released to what the publisher described as "unprecedented consumer satisfaction and national recognition."[1]

There are at least two things to celebrate here. The first is how a newer entertainment modality can beckon us to engage Scripture in the way it was originally encountered—as an oral event, rather than a written text. Ezra arranged for the Torah to be read aloud to the people (Nehemiah 8); Jesus read aloud from the scroll of Isaiah (Luke 4); Paul clearly expected local leaders to read his letters to the entire congregation (1 Thess 5:27). So when

---

1. Zondervan, "Bible Experience," para. "Description."

digital technologies invite us back to an auditory encounter with the God who speaks, we should celebrate the shift.

We can also celebrate that a publisher with a largely white marketing demographic wants to reach across ethnic and cultural lines. The church is catholic, not Caucasian, so it is very good to hear the Word in tones and inflections other than white. But notice what connects Christians here. Not the uniting waters of baptism, or the reconciling balm of the Holy Spirit, or the Bible as shared Scripture, but the common culture of celebrity. Because celebrity is everywhere in our media-dominated, entertainment-saturated culture, it seems normal, even natural, that such a project should be undertaken. In the United States of Amusement, we are habituated to regard celebrities as common ground.

Not that celebrities are common. They "coolify" everything, which is why Cuba and the gang can "bring the Scriptures to life." Traditionally, enlivening Scripture has been Holy Spirit work. But in a culture of celebrity, we're already conditioned to believe that stars can vivify anything, even the Bible. Who needs the Holy Spirit when you've got Queen Latifah?

I don't want to be glib. Denzel probably reads Scripture better than most people in my congregation. (James Earl Jones probably reads it better than God! Okay, that was glib.[2]) But that gets at another of the rubs here: Scripture is meant to be read aloud in the midst of the worshiping assembly.

✣ *If celebrities read me the Bible on my car stereo, is that worship, Bible study, or entertainment?*

This question gets at a key issue in thinking about entertainment: the relationship between medium and message. Does Marshall McLuhan's observation that "the medium is the message" apply here? Is a star-powered, digital Bible entertainment or discipleship? Notice three dimensions of this particular "medium"—technologies, habits, and mediated relations. The audio Bible involves *technologies* (both digital recordings and the devices that play them) that we own and use primarily for entertainment purposes. The audio Bible counts on *habits* of listening to digital recordings (in particular places and times that I choose for myself) that are developed through practices of entertainment. Increasingly, entertainment technologies and habits shape our vision of the good life. "Old and young people alike increasingly believe that entertainment-oriented leisure provides the basic reason for

---

2. But if you wanted to check it out, there is a 16-CD boxed set titled *James Earl Jones Reads the Bible*, published by Topics Entertainment in 2002.

living. Happiness consists of having a quiver full of electronic gadgets that give sensate pleasure during all non-working hours."[3] That claim is accurate, but incomplete; we need a second quiver filled with celebrities.

The audio Bible also counts on our mediated relationship with *celebrities*. Regardless of how faithful Denzel is in his local AME congregation, we know him first and primarily (probably only) because he entertains us in movies, appears in interviews, smolders on magazine covers, and all the rest. The social reality of celebrity is just as important a component of modern entertainment as are technological innovations and leisure habits. Granted that there would be no New Audio Bible if not for the invention and marketing of inexpensive recording technologies, there would likewise be no New Audio Bible without celebrities; they are just as much a part of the package as technologies and habits.

Therefore, in the end, the real meaning of a celebrity audio Bible has more to do with entertainment in general, and celebrity in particular, than it has to do with devotion and discipleship. The Word of God becomes another "credotainment" commodity appealing to my desire for entertainment.[4] Once a "live" reading in the midst of a gathered community committed to live what it hears, Scripture has become one more venue for the stars to come out and shine. Celebrity mediation displaces the flesh of Christ's body. That's entertainment.

❖ *Do you think a "celebrity audio Bible" is dangerous to discipleship? What other instances of credotainment or celebritizing have you noticed in the church? Do you think it's odd to use "consumer" to name our relation to Scripture?*

CELEBRITY CHEESE WHIZ

Celebrities are the flags that the attention economy waves to catch our eyes. They are the cheese whiz on the entertainment mousetrap. If you don't believe me, consider how often a particular celebrity's face alters your behavior: you pick up a magazine, or unmute a commercial, or pause your channel

---

3. Schultze, *Dancing in the Dark*, 10.

4. "Credotainment" is the neologism that Lawrence and Jewett use to condemn the trend toward "the recreational religion phenomenon," which has a "stronger emphasis on inner states rather than acts in the community." *Myth of the American Superhero*, 286–87.

surfing, or buy a movie ticket because of star power. Celebrities catch our eye, and the entertainment economy profits from our attentiveness.

So celebrity has become intrinsic to entertainment. It has become so pervasive and normalized in this culture of mass-mediated entertainment that we mostly take for granted that:

1. Constantly encountering celebrity names and faces is normal, and through such encounters we come to assume that we "know" the celebrity.

2. Celebrities are better at something than ordinary people are. Everything can be made better through celebrity presence, participation, or association.

3. Because celebrities are also ordinary people (in the most important senses), their attitudes, aspirations, and actions make good models for our own.

4. Therefore, it is good when celebrities permeate all aspects of our lives, and that can happen through entertainment and consumer choices.

5. Therefore, we should not be too worried about the ceaseless efforts of marketers and media to celebritize our lives.

✛ *How many of these five statements about celebrity do you take for granted? Does celebrity distort our ability to think well about life's proper goal and how to reach it? Is it possible to have truthful public conversations with communications media as celebritized as ours?*

If these assumptions were all good and true, then we would be in beautiful shape. But we are in terrible trouble, because as most readers of this book will recognize, each of these presumptions about celebrity is either a major distortion or else a demonstrable falsehood. Yet we mostly avoid that realization by colluding with popular culture's swindle: as long as we are allowed to exercise our personal taste and judgment about particular celebrities, we will refuse to recognize the fraudulent nature of the whole cult of celebrity.

A STAR IS MADE

Celebrity might seem to be a natural effect of loving football or movies or music. We are entertained by people who are truly excellent, and we want to see and hear more of them in order to get more quality entertainment.

So if Peyton Manning becomes a celebrity, it is because he gives us so many good football games to watch. If Cate Blanchett is a star, it's because she regularly offers stunning performances. If Bono is a pop idol worldwide, it's because he is an amazing musician. True enough. But even in the case of such obvious talent, there is always more to celebrity. For example, Manning's fame includes not only his skill at passing, but also his persona in television commercials. Blanchett's stardom is produced and sustained by structures, processes, and practices far beyond her movies. And Bono became a rock idol not just because he can sing, but because fans love his showmanship. The regular presentation of their personas outside of their primary entertaining activity captures our attention, becomes itself a form of entertainment, and convinces us along the way that we know and like the "real person" whose persona we continually consume.

Star is probably our most important term for celebrity. Watch the Oscars and you'll see that star means Hollywood, and Hollywood means stars. Certainly there are also music and sports stars, and even occasionally politicians or clerics who achieve a kind of crossover fame (Bill Clinton and John Paul II come to mind). But the cinema (along with its younger sibling, television) is the original and primary domain of the celebrity we call stardom. Indeed, we could hardly imagine movies without movie stars. Yet it was not so in the beginning.

No one "starred" in early movies, for two reasons: 1) cameras couldn't focus on faces, so 2) movie marketing didn't focus on individual actors. Only when camera lenses were invented that could focus closely on an actor's face, and then directors began using that technology to shoot "close-ups," was it possible to transform actors into stars. Why? Because audiences could now recognize and identify with particular actors. Our brains are hardwired to recognize familiar faces as members of our "in group," someone who is significant for our well-being.[5] The close-up, therefore, created a sense of personal relationship and identification—not so much with the character in the movie, but with the actor—*the face*—who played the role. The well-known face creates a sense, a feeling, that we know and are related to the famous person.

That can impact what seems normal in the church. Consider Tim Stafford's description of the technological structure of worship in many megachurches. "Where once churches displayed Jesus in stained glass,

5. Carlin Flora, "Seeing by Starlight," 38, notes that evolutionary psychologists "point out that when our brains evolved, anybody with a familiar face was an 'in-group' member, a person whose alliances and enmities were important to keep track of."

now many display the pastor in JumboTron. The pastor's face is the key image. . . . Seeing his winsome smile, we feel that we know him personally, even if we are sharing the view with 3,000 other 'friends.' He speaks to us less as an oracle of God than as a persuasive friend."[6] Stafford alerts us to the way the technological instrumentality of celebrity has infiltrated our churches. Through the technology of the close-up, we can now feel as close to our pastor as we do to . . . Oprah. And the qualities of that relationship are likely very similar: a sense of authenticity, of caring, and of familiarity that borders on intimacy. The video close-up and its concomitant habits of feeling are integral to the rise of celebrity, whether in Hollywood or in megachurches meeting near you.

But that is only half the story of the development of stars. Stardom required more than a cinematic technique that engendered audience identification. It also required economic practices that manufactured and marketed a star's persona. First, Hollywood producers began to make and market movies around stars rather than stories (the so-called star system). Second, Hollywood studios developed public relations armies (sixty to one hundred strong) whose entire focus was to invisibly create and control the unique image of each star.[7] That image is semiotic; the persona of the actor becomes a sign of meaning. Because Jim Carrey means lovable wisecracker and Matt Damon means tough guy with a heart of gold, their presence in a movie brings those meanings to their film role, and transfers our affection for the star to the movie itself. Thus, the best stars are "bankable," never guaranteeing the commercial success of a film, but coming close.

Today, a massive, profitable mediascape entertains us by ceaselessly re-presenting each star's persona to an adoring public. Stars have so completely infiltrated our world that avoiding them for even a short while would require complete media isolation. Most of us consider it normal to have mediated encounters with multiple stars dozens or even hundreds of times a day. We simply cannot imagine a world that is otherwise, even though that "otherwise world" existed up until the 1920s.

In sum, the phenomenon of movie stars required a technological capacity (close-up lens) along with a set of cinematic decisions (shooting and editing, casting and marketing), an audience affinity for particular personas, and an economic system that constantly mediated relation between stars and fans. This means stars are *made*, not born or "discovered." Stars

---

6. Stafford, "God Is in the Blueprints," 81.

7. Gamson, "Assembly Line of Greatness," 263.

are produced—by the confluence of technologies of mediation, economies of distribution, and affinities of audience reception.

✤ *Is it possible to pass a single day without multiple encounters with celebrity? Would it improve our lives if we developed ascetic practices of fasting from celebrity? What would that look like?*

✤ *Does living amidst the constant manufacture of personas diminish our commitment to and capacity for the formation of Christian disciples?*

LIFE STARS ME

The celebritization of entertainment both fosters and reinforces the individualism that permeates late consumer capitalism. Celebrity theorist David Marshall writes:

> The interactions of celebrities as reported on television and radio and in magazines and newspapers establish a code of individuality that is central to the meaning of celebrity. Generally, celebrities' behavior is representative of the expression of individual preferences and desires and the acting on those preferences and desires. *The celebrity is the independent individual par excellence; he or she represents the meaning of freedom and accessibility in a culture.* The close scrutiny that is given to celebrities is to accentuate the possibility and potential for individuals to shape themselves unfettered by the constraints of a hierarchical society. . . . As a system, celebrities provide a spectacle of individuality in which will itself can produce change and transformation.[8]

How does stardom reinforce individualism? Partly through the many stars who publicly live lives that are visibly individualistic, even narcissistic.[9] But more basically, stardom reinforces individualism through the images, descriptions, and narratives that make and sustain it. There are two common scripts that lie underneath most celebrity publicity, and both scripts are necessary to sustain the economic practices that stardom serves.

8. Marshall, *Celebrity and Power*, 246, emphasis added.

9. Pinsky et al. suggest in *The Mirror Effect* that celebrities are more narcissistic than the rest of us, and that attending to celebrity influences the impressionable (teens and young adults) toward narcissism. Ironically, Pinsky himself is one of the new breed of celebrity—a "media personality" famous for hosting the nationally syndicated radio show *Loveline* and various reality shows focusing on celebrity rehab.

One script is that fame is deserved, not manufactured. The image makers (public relations) who manufacture the star's persona, and the myriad media that purvey it, collude to endlessly reproduce the narrative that stars are born this way. Of course they have to be "discovered" or get a "break," but the underlying narrative of most twentieth-century stardom has been that stars merit their fame, that celebrity is intrinsic to a "star quality," or an "authentic, gifted self" that was simply discovered.[10] Our democratic sensibilities demand that the stars who shine above us are understood to be there for deserving reasons. Otherwise, if their renown is manufactured and their celebration orchestrated, why should we continue to watch or care *or pay*?

Ironically, this mythology of deserved celebrity and discovered "star quality" is actively manufactured and managed by the massive public relations industry that creates and sustains each star's persona.[11] Over the last few decades, many consumers have begun to recognize this. But that recognition has not produced any mass exodus from popular culture; instead, it has engendered a jaded, ironical audience, who now thinks that winking along with the fraudulence is part of the fun. The net effect of the wink may well be that we continue to believe that beneath the *celebratus apparatus* that manufactures fame lies a person who is nonetheless genuinely individual and innately qualified for celebrity.

This first script justifies the attention we pay to stars. It reassures us that a given star is worthy of our leisure time and worth our consumer investments. But writing that script requires that relationships, organizations, communities, and families become entirely secondary in the star's storyline. Fame cannot be a group project, or else the game is up. We imagine a star's identity apart from any significant community or relationship. At best other people are accoutrements and accessories for a star, as important and permanent as their wardrobe or hairstyle. At worst, others disappear entirely from view.

Thus this first script inculcates an individualistic approach to personhood in which a person's core identity is thought to be prior to relationships, communities, and choices. "I" precedes "all" in ways inimical to the gospel, which locates our authentic identity in relation to and election by Jesus Christ. Even where we are not enamored of celebrity and refuse to aspire to stardom, we nonetheless engage in identity construction in a

10. Gamson, "Assembly Line of Greatness," 266.

11. On this, see the description of Gamson in ibid., 262–65.

context that alienates us from the true core and context of self. Our being awash in a sea of stars makes the virus of individualism both harder to see and nearly impossible to eradicate.

The second script the image makers purvey is that each star is unique, an individual whose personality and talents make him or her utterly unlike any other star. The narratives and images that create and sustain this unique persona do several important things, all serving the bottom line. First, these individualizing projections target the interests and desires of specific consumers. Second, these stories differentiate the star from other stars, thereby justifying our attention and affection. Third, over time these projected images work to shape our desires and affections for the celebrity.

Notice that the star's individualized persona is a very powerful kind of product. Its main economic purpose is not to be sold per se, but to sell everything else. Though stardom began as a product whose purpose was to sell particular movies to the cinema audience, it didn't take long to discover that stars can also sell cars, insurance, perfume, wars, talk shows, books, monthly magazines, and now even audio Bibles. A key reason for this is that stars capture our attention, but they also confer feeling and meaning. We feel a particular way about a star's persona. So for Scripture's central love poem, it's Denzel reading the Song of Songs rather than Chris Rock or Tracy Morgan, precisely because Denzel means a sexy feeling.

The larger issue here is not how we feel about Denzel, but the powers and processes that shape our affections and individualize our imaginations. The two scripts of celebrity taken together constitute a powerful form of expressive individualism. Living amidst culture industries that continuously propagate these scripts means that we dwell within a formational process, for these scripts do far more than just create and sustain particular stars. They capture our imaginations, colonize our longings, and shape our actions such that we become—not stars, certainly—but expressive individuals determined to display innate uniqueness and to demonstrate original personality. Celebrity culture functions as a catechesis that shapes lives and devotions antithetical to the gospel. Pulling back the curtain on how it works suggests that the problem is not the moral failings of a particular star, nor is it the material excesses of the industry as a whole; the problem is the marketing mythology that undergirds the entire process. That problem can't be cured by adoring Miley rather than Madonna (the singer, not the mother of Jesus).

I am suggesting here that inhabiting a star-scape means that we are always in the midst of a counter-formation, one that captivates our hearts and habituates our minds toward patterns other than the mind of Christ. In the end, the only cure is Christ, and that cure has a particular locus and pattern. Christianity has a long tradition of recognizing that our desires can and must be shaped over time in Christlike ways. That shaping occurs in and through community, as together we engage in practices of worship, spiritual disciplines, and service. This habituation of feeling and action is the fruit of the Spirit, a putting on of Christ. As such, it is the antithesis of celebrity's scripts that "I'm absolutely amazing," that "I'm utterly unique," so naturally "life stars me."

✣ *Does the "I deserve my fame" script diminish our capacity to recognize and embrace the relationships that make us who we are?*

✣ *Does the "I'm a unique individual" script shape us as expressive individuals?*

WHAT WOULD BONO DO?

In the 1990s, members of my church youth group regularly sported WWJD bracelets of various colors. Today, they are far more likely to be wearing the white bracelets of Bono's One Campaign. Noticing the bracelets can help us notice the growing influence of celebrity activism and the ongoing dynamics of celebrity culture. The question, "What Would Bono Do?" invites reflection on the possibilities and the limits of celebritizing the Christian moral life. At stake is whether it provides a sufficient guide to faithful discipleship.

But first, "What Has Bono Done Already?" He is consistently mentioned as one of the top two or three celebrity advocates for programs of justice and compassion. Bono was at the heart of the Jubilee 2000 campaign for third-world debt forgiveness by first-world creditors; he cofounded the Africa relief organization DATA (Debt, AIDS, Trade, Africa); he helped found ONE: The Campaign to Make Poverty History, and also the Product (RED) movement, which raises money to fight AIDS, tuberculosis, and malaria.[12] So the answer to the question of Bono's involvement and efficacy is "quite a bit!" His efforts have led to $50 billion in annual debt forgiveness to the world's poorest countries,[13] to a justice coalition of more than 2 million people, to more than $150 million in direct contributions to fight

12. One Campaign, "Board of Directors," para. 1–4.
13. Hicks, "Star Power," 23.

disease in Africa. As people who recognize God's call to love mercy, do justice, and walk humbly with God, we cannot help applauding.

We're not the only ones applauding. In 2005, Bono shared the cover of *Time* with Bill and Melinda Gates as the magazine's "persons of the year." *Time's* cover article said that in 2005 ". . . Bono charmed and bullied and morally blackmailed the leaders of the world's richest countries into forgiving $40 billion in debt owed by the poorest. . . ."[14] Bono did this with wit and passion and intelligence, but the secret ingredient in his recipe for meaningful social change was almost certainly his celebrity. As the article pointed out, "such is the nature of Bono's fame that just about everyone in the world wants to meet him—except for" Bill Gates.[15] What Bono symbolizes, therefore, is the larger phenomenon of celebrity culture increasingly exerting its power in efforts to mend the world.

FOCUS OR FROTH?

The "power" that celebrities bring to their advocacy work resides in their capacity to focus our gaze. Because we are so well trained to look at celebrities, we are also ready to look at whatever they look at. In an attention economy, celebrity has the power to capture and focus our attention—even on matters that we would rather not see. *Time* titled its persons-of-the-year cover "The Good Samaritans,"[16] a reminder that compassion is always first a matter of *seeing* neighbors. In our contemporary equivalent of the road from Jerusalem to Jericho, with much of Africa lying in the ditch, hurt and bleeding, it is harder to "pass by on the other side of the road" if a celebrity keeps pointing our attention toward the suffering (Luke 10:25–37).

Giving ear to Bono's cries for justice, we take for granted a world in which we pay attention to him *because he entertains us so well*. The "celebrity currency" he spends has accrued to his account, not because he is holy or his cause is true, but because we love U2's music, and because its front man has captured and captivated our media gaze for three decades now. I think Bono is a good person who is entirely right in his passion for justice, but that's not why I know his name, recognize his face, or listen to his message. It all depends on the celebritization of entertainment. Our habits

14. Gibbs, "Persons of the Year," 44.

15. Ibid., 44.

16. Kelly, "Good Samaritans," 8.

and practices of entertainment are the necessary structures for creating and sustaining this phenomenon.

We might wish things were otherwise. Bono himself gets at the absurdity with his quip that "there's nothing worse than a rock star with a cause."[17] Bono is voicing the fact that celebrities always have access to cameras and microphones, and thus have the capacity to influence media content. Whether it's NBC or NPR, CBS or PBS, we're more likely to hear about the slavery of sex trafficking if stars tell us the story, and we're more likely to see the poverty of water shortage if celebrities are also in the picture. Bono certainly knows that we listen to him and attend to his causes not so much because he is good and holy, or even because his causes are just and true, but because he entertains us so well. Nonetheless, he presents those causes to us because they are good and right, and in hopes that finally we will be more captivated by their truth and justice than by his celebrity. But will we?

✢ *Are we capable of developing faithful convictions about justice and of sustaining truthful conversations about poverty that are rooted in something more substantial than celebrity?*

The answer depends on whether we engage in practices and community that are "thick" and rich enough to form a "gospel gaze" that imagines the world on God's terms. Jesus told the parable we call the Good Samaritan to do far more than give us a cultural reference for philanthropists and other do-gooders. In one sense, calling Bono a Good Samaritan gets at a key aspect of Jesus' parable: the surprising way Jesus locates the faithful embodying of God's will in someone considered a disreputable outsider. Just as the Jewish lawyer would want the hero of Jesus' story to be a leader of God's people (the priest or the Levite), so I as a Christian theologian want the hero of compassionate ministry in Africa to be a leader of Christ's church—a wise bishop or a courageous layperson—indeed, anyone but a God-loving, church-critiquing rock idol. Precisely for that reason, Bono serves perfectly in a modern paraphrase: "Which of these three do you think proved to be a neighbor to the continent that fell into the robbers' hands?" "The celebrity who showed mercy." And Jesus said, "Go and do likewise."

The parable is a gift of Christ to the church that is intended, through its exquisite details and startling reversal, to shape our perception and form our compassion. Contemporizing it in light of Bono's celebrity activism will only work if we remember that the parable is part of a larger story of grace

17. Falsani and Powell, "Bono's American Prayer," 41.

in which Jesus embodies the parable's truth. Put another way, this parable in Luke 10 would be nothing more than a memorable pep talk about compassion if it were not embedded in the larger story of Jesus. He is compassion incarnate, whose suffering love led not to the ditch but the tomb, and whose risen life is compassionate care for the wounded. Ideally, celebrity activism would only remind us that we, the church, are the embodiment of Christ's compassion, and that he has poured out God's Spirit on us precisely to *activate* our just and merciful care. In other words, both how we see and act should flow from what we are—the body of Christ.

HOPE FOR CHANGE: STAR OR SPIRIT POWERED?

Barry Taylor joins the applause for Bono by summarizing the star's advocacy work, and then suggesting that Bono uses his "powerful celebrity to effect change."[18] That remark gets at a certain sensibility that surrounds Bono, and celebrity more generally. We have come to think that celebrities are change agents par excellence. David Marshall points out that celebrities function as "proxies of change" in our culture.[19] The more powerless we feel, the more likely we are to believe in their power to make a difference. Marshall thinks that this dynamic is one reason that so many stars have "become spokespersons for political causes and issues."[20] They are simply playing the role that we expect of them.[21] And given the dynamics of celebrity in an attention economy, they often can effect genuine forms of change.

But for us there are at least three problems with giving our proxy to celebrities when it comes to change. First, this tends to dislocate hope. Bono's accomplishments might just tempt us to believe that the path to a mended world is better blazed by celebrities than fired by the Holy Spirit. To say that Bono's activism tempts us to trust him more than the Holy Spirit may be simplistic, but just barely. For the Spirit's power is made perfect in the midst of weakness rather than strength (2 Cor 12:9–10), and God has chosen those without standing and renown to be subjects of the gospel's transforming power (1 Cor 1:26–31). Celebrity culture, on the other hand, is all about renown and the power that it brings. It invites us to imagine that Bono and Oprah and Bill and Melinda Gates are the most powerful people or forces

18. Taylor, *Entertainment Theology*, 152.

19. Marshall, *Celebrity and Power*, 243–44.

20. Ibid., 244.

21. Or perhaps they want their lives to be about something more meaningful and less narcissistic than their own celebrity. I owe this insight to Melissa Laytham.

in the world, and therefore have the wherewithal to fix it. *Time* quotes Bono as saying about Bill Gates, "He's changing the world twice." The emphasis here is on power—the power of wealth, intelligence, and creativity.

We can work with Bono, and we probably should join the One Campaign, but finally we need to recognize that it will be God who mends the world, not celebrities. Our calling is not to save the world, for that has already been done by Christ. Thereby, he saves us from the desperate sense that *we* must redeem the world, that it is all up to us. In Christ, the world's Savior, our calling is to serve the world with a cruciform love that witnesses to God's infinite compassion and creation's coming glory.

✛ *Does the ecology of celebrity tempt you to focus hope in celebrities' power to do good? How does that obscure recognition of God's power working amidst weakness and obscurity?*

TALK OF CHANGE: CELEBRITY OR CATHOLICITY?

Second, we need to recover a much more robust moral conversation in the church. The politics of celebrity activism works in sound bites aired on *Entertainment Tonight*, in captioned pictures inside *People* magazine, in Web-based coalition building and celebrity "expert testimony" before politicians. If this becomes the source and guide to the church's moral imagination, then we are destined to be blown by the winds of fancy rather than to become a community of moral discernment guided by the Holy Spirit. In the end, faithfulness will require that we develop the capacity to reason together, that we recover genuinely "public" discourse from the self-interested hands of media. We, the church, will have to learn to *converse together* about matters that matter.

At present our power to know and understand the needs and concerns of persons around the globe seems almost entirely subject to the mediation of the culture industries. Virtually everything I "know" about AIDS in Africa comes to me via the celebritized mass media that constitute the attention economy. The same would be true of my knowledge of extreme poverty and racism in Louisiana, except that my children were part of a weeklong mission that built relationships while rebuilding houses destroyed by Katrina. Turning away from our reliance on celebrity, radio, television, newspapers, magazines, and the Internet, all of which mediate "reality" to us, requires the alternative called church. Thus the *catholicity* of the church provides an appropriate alternative to celebrity mediation. Christians are called to participate in an ecclesial communicative network that 1) shares information about distant circumstances, unknown needs, and unseen concerns, 2) prays this information to God, and 3) then acts in correspondence with its praying.[22]

> ✣ *Is moral conversation in your church energized by celebrity attention and mediated by the culture industries, rather than flowing from and through the church?*

ACTIVISM FOR CHANGE: SHOPPING OR STOPPING?

Finally, we cannot give our proxy for change to celebrities because they cannot and will not change the system that produced them. Star advocacy too easily becomes yet another prop in the celebrity system. A star's advocacy for charitable causes becomes just one more way to differentiate herself from other stars, and to elevate herself above ordinary mortals. That doesn't mean that celebrities are disingenuous about it, only that this is the overall effect of the system. So don't expect celebrities to advocate for cultural changes that would bring celebrity to an end. In a 2003 interview with Bono about his "Heart of America" tour, *Christianity Today* reported that Bono said we are "just blind" if we cannot read Scripture and see there God's preferential concern for the poor. Bono referenced the 2,103 verses about the poor "as he rode in a chauffeured SUV down Fifth Avenue in midtown Manhattan."[23] Whatever causes celebrities take on, they will almost certainly not be those that require a fundamental turning away from entertainment culture, and from the leisure and affluence that make it possible. No wonder the Product (RED) campaign allows us to fight poverty in Africa by shopping in America. There is no sacrifice asked of us, other than choosing this Gap® product rather than that one. Certainly there is no engagement with the more basic question of whether lavish Western lifestyles (by which I mean my middle-class existence, not a celebrity's megamillionaire one) are implicated in global poverty.

Perhaps as problematic as the implication that we can shop our way to global justice are concert-ed forms of compassion. Benefit concerts have

22. Consider how many of Paul's letters interweave information, intercession, and imperative.

23. Falsani and Powell, "Bono's American Prayer," 43.

been around for centuries. A local church I attended had a monthly concert to raise money for building renovations. In the mid-1980s, however, celebrity activist Bob Geldof put the benefit concert on steroids with Live Aid (1985), a two-continent benefit for Ethiopian famine relief. What was remarkable about this event, beyond the hundreds of millions of dollars (and pounds) it raised for a worthy cause, was the vast numbers of music idols it managed to put on the London and Philadelphia stages. The U.S. portion of Live Aid concluded with "We Are the World" performed as an anthem by dozens of celebrities. (The song itself was already a multi-idol, multi-platinum benefit hit of U.S. artists for Africa.) Watching the anthem is revealing; it is difficult to decide whether the primary vision being communicated is compassion for the impoverished or celebration of the celebrities. Being on stage at that moment was as much about being "in," being "big," being a musician who matters, as it was about children starving in Africa, though the latter is what allowed everyone to walk away feeling sentimental and satisfied. And "walk away" is the right term, since such concerts leave the performers and the audience largely unchanged. The world is changed a bit, for a moment. One hundred fifty million pounds can do some significant good in a starving country. But *we* are not changed. So when Product (RED) invites me to save the world by attending concerts, it is complicit in the oldest bait and switch around: the notion that the world can be changed without changing me, the swindle that compassion comes cheap and easy, the smooth path that entertainment is the road to the kingdom of God.

A 2006 *Christian Century* article put it like this: "Do benefit concerts send not one but two lessons to concertgoers? Although fans may learn to show concern about extreme poverty and sign up for the One Campaign, they may also receive the message that an economically privileged lifestyle, in which they buy CDs (promoted shamelessly by some of the performers) and enjoy expensive iPods, is morally acceptable. What if material excess is as harmful to us spiritually as absolute material poverty can be for the poor? Bono cannot lead that fight."[24]

✤ *Do you think using our consumer and entertainment habits to "work for justice" is a step in the right direction, or just another way to feel good about enjoying ourselves in an unjust world?*

24. Hicks, "Star Power," 24.

SACRIFICING AUTHENTICITY FOR FIDELITY

Having broached the question of sacrifice, let us consider it from a different angle. We all recognize that there is a distinction between the actual person who becomes a celebrity and the celebrity's *persona*, their personal image, which is ceaselessly produced, managed, communicated, and celebrated. Celebrity theorists Deena and Michael Weinstein say that becoming a celebrity requires a willingness to sacrifice one's personhood for one's persona.[25] One ritual for this laying down of one identity to be taken up into another mediated one is the renaming that is so common in celebrities. This parallels the renaming that occurs with the election of a new pope, or with taking monastic vows. In all these cases, it signifies a willingness to lay aside the present self in order to become a better self. But that is where the similarity ends, despite the parallels that Barry Taylor and others want to draw between celebrities and saints.[26] The would-be celebrity dies to self in order to be elevated into fame; the would-be disciple dies to self in order to be raised with Christ. The different objective is far more significant than the similarity of self-sacrifice. Nothing reveals that difference better than the criterion by which the transformed identity is judged. The culture of celebrity prizes nothing more highly than "authenticity." The mythology of celebrity—that the mediated persona of a star is their genuine person, truly as human as we are, and truly as excellent as we are not—means that the celebrity's persona must be "real," that her behavior must be "honest," that his image must be authentic. The *mythos* of the gospel, on the other hand, invites us to be conformed to Christ—dying and rising with him—so that the standard of our behavior and the focus of our identity is not being true to ourselves, but rather being faithful to Christ. Fidelity rather than authenticity is the standard, and its measure lies outside our self, beyond our devising and control and capacity.

Given this fairly stark contrast between authenticity and fidelity, we can return to the question, "What Would Bono Do?" While celebrating all of the good that Bono continues to do, we ought to refuse the idea that celebrity is the way God intends to mend the world. As fellow Christians, we can make common cause with him to seek justice in the midst of global

25. Celebrities become celebrities "by sacrificing recognition of themselves to recognition of their images; they become icons and idols that are reproduced endlessly through the media. . . ." Weinstein and Weinstein, "Celebrity Worship," 299.

26. Taylor, *Entertainment Theology*, 149–52. Detweiler and Taylor, *Matrix of Meanings*, 89–124.

poverty, and to bring compassion to African neighbors. But Bono is not a fellow Christian whom I'm ever likely to meet. Our relation to him is "para-social," which means that it feels like we know him when in fact we don't, and more importantly he doesn't know us. The most important work we need to do around justice and compassion will involve real conversations with fellow Christians, those in our congregation and others from around the world. Let's call these conversations, and the relationships of which they are a part, *Christi*-social as opposed to para-social. That is to say, because we are in Christ, we *are* in relationship with one another, so we *must be* in conversation with one another. These real, concrete relations and conversations are the proper context and syntax for discerning how to go about the work of doing justice, loving mercy, and walking humbly with our God. In other words, the *medium* that ought to draw us together in felt compassion and to send us forth in compassionate action is and ought to be Jesus Christ, not the phenomenon of celebrity in general, nor the force for good that is Bono.

This means that the biggest problem with the "What would . . ." method of ethics is not whether the next name is Bono or Jesus. The biggest problem is that I ask and answer the question as an individual, whose "personal" relationship—whether with Jesus or Bono—leaves me unencumbered by community in my discerning and deciding. Whether it's African poverty or global warming, whether WWBD or WWJD, I decide, I choose, I act as an individual; and then I am responsible to myself to judge the results, which I mostly do according to how I feel about it. Just like whether it's U2 or Nirvana, whether it's television or Netflix, whether it's iPod or Wii, I decide, I choose, I act as an individual; and then I am responsible to myself to judge the results, which I mostly do according to how I feel about it.

✢ *Is there "space" for the communion of saints in a popular culture filled with celebrities? How can we celebrate Bono's good work while also celebrating the saints in our church?*

✢ *Does star-powered advocacy tempt us to hope too much in Hollywood power and too little in the weakness of crossbearing? To trust too much in celebrity and too little in the church? To believe that we can make a difference without becoming different?*

twelve

The Church of Oprah?

BIG, LOVING QUEEN OF THE SMALL SCREEN

How big is Oprah? For starters, she is a one-name celebrity—someone so famous that we don't need the surname to differentiate her from the crowd.[1] In earnings and power, she is unparalleled. *Forbes* magazine publishes an annual listing of the top one hundred celebrities. (This alone is proof of how enamored we are of celebrity, and of celebrity's intrinsic relation to consumer capitalism.) Oprah has been in the top three for seven of the last ten years, and never lower than ninth. No one else has even come close to this kind of sustained success. In media reach, Oprah is the biggest. Besides her daily talk show, which before retirement reached 113 million

---

1. David Marshall contrasts Oprah with (Tom) Cruise, suggesting that first name versus last "indicates a gendered difference in the construction of celebrities and also a difference in institutional construction of celebrities" (*Celebrity and Power*, 144). For Marshall, first name indicates the familiarity and intimacy that attach to television and the feminine, whereas last name fame indicates a more masculine aura and the mystery of film. While Conan and Dave (Letterman) might support Marshall's point about medium, what about Leno? And while Angelina and Madonna (does she have a last name?) might further his point about gender, what about Tiger, Lebron, Kobe, Tupac, Leonardo? The truth is that most male movie stars have extremely generic first names like Tom (Cruise or Hanks?), Ben (Stiller or Affleck?), or Robert (Redford or Downey Jr.?). I would suggest that because celebrity requires differentiation of each star from every other, the celebrity who can become a one-name star will typically do so via whichever name is most distinctive.

worldwide,[2] Oprah helms the most powerful book club in America, OWNs a cable television network (OWN, for Oprah Winfrey Network), publishes her *O* magazine (guess whose picture graces every cover?), and runs Harpo Productions, Inc., a multimedia production company, and a high-traffic Web site (oprah.com).

So here is one of life's little ironies. I went to a coffee shop to work on this chapter on Oprah. Unfortunately, I had to leave because they had *Oprah* on at a volume so loud that I could not concentrate. Notice how this exemplifies one of the taken-for-granted transitions of the past several decades: a proliferation of televisions in public spaces (bars, airports, airplanes, coffee shops, college dining rooms, elevators, gas pumps, grocery checkout stands, lobbies of all sorts) matching the proliferation of televisions in our homes (from living room to kitchen, bedroom, study, even bathroom, not to mention the cell phone in my pocket). Television has become not just a necessity we cannot live without, but a constant companion we can hardly escape. It might like our full attention, but often settles for partial; typical users are more likely to turn it on like the lights—when they enter the room—than like the oven—when they want to consume something particular.

The focus of the show was *The Twilight Saga*, and it allowed us to meet the young stars of the movies. In less than ten minutes, I saw three different clips that are typically Oprahesque. One was Oprah's hushed-tones conversation with experts about the social and psychological significance of *Twilight*. Clearly Oprah has the authority to set our middle-aged minds at ease about the benignity of girls gushing over cross-creaturely romance. A second vignette was an intimate camera journey into a college sorority so smitten by *Twilight* that they read the books daily, watch the movies weekly, and live in hope of encountering the series' stars face to face. The segment culminated in one of Oprah's typical surprise gifts: the surprise appearance of Taylor Lautner in the flesh as the sorority sisters sat together watching *Twilight*. Clearly, Oprah has the power to make our dreams come true. Finally, I saw Oprah talking with the movie's stars about what they do on a typical Saturday night. Obviously, as their fame brought younger eyeballs to Oprah, so her celebrity legitimized theirs. While this latter vignette is common across the spectrum of talk shows (Leno, Conan, Letterman, Ellen, etc.), the first two are Oprah's personal corner on the market. She is

2. Marshall, *Celebrity and Power*, 132.

the trusted guide to matters moral and especially spiritual. And she is the beneficent donor of joy and contentment.

No wonder Kathryn McClymond begins her essay titled "The Gospel According to Oprah" with the quip "Oprah loves you and has a wonderful plan for your life. Well, maybe not a plan—but Oprah Winfrey has a core set of values that she repeatedly shares with her viewers."[3] McClymond's parody on door-to-door evangelism may sound cheeky or unfair. But it is remarkably similar to how Sirius XM Radio promotes its Oprah station: "Oprah Radio helps you live your best life."[4] Thus, insider and outsider alike recognize that Oprah Winfrey is an evangelist whose aim is the personal transformation of her audience.

To unpack what this might mean, I will look at the form and the format that produces Oprah's celebrity, and finally at how her celebritized spirituality invites us to kick the religion habit and join the church of entertainment. While the focus of this chapter is Oprah, the subject matter is television—its format and formative power and impacts.

FORMING THAT FAMILIAR FEELING

People just love Oprah. They have a sense that she is the kind of friend who is on their side and wants the best for them. In this section I will show that these feelings for, and ideas about, Oprah have as much to do with the particular format of her entertainment medium as they do with the particular shape of her personality. (Though of course I wouldn't discount the importance of her personality.)

Many people may not remember that Oprah was nominated for a best supporting actress Oscar for *The Color Purple* (1986), but few will be surprised that she has won multiple Emmys for her daytime talk show. Though Oprah's fame now extends far beyond television, that medium is its primary source and has continued to shape the particular features of her celebrity. Generally, we feel closer to TV stars than we do to movie stars. There are multiple causes for this: we generally watch television in the familiarity of our home, whereas we often watch movies in the formality of the cinema. "Big screen" means something very different at a theater versus in the living room, giving a different scale to the face that we face.[5]

3. McClymond, "Gospel According to Oprah," 173.

4. Sirius XM, "Oprah Radio."

5. See Nayar, *Seeing Stars*, 33.

These general claims about television are amplified by the talk-show format, and amplified even more by some of the distinctive features of Oprah's show. Most basically, and unlike the star of a sitcom, soap opera, or drama, the role of a talk-show host is to play herself. Oprah does that with alacrity. But there are built-in structures that help: real-time filming without edits or retakes; the presence of a live audience in the studio; and the self-revelation that constitutes some (or much) of the host's conversation.

Commentator Marcia Nelson reflects on her experience of watching a year of Oprah in order to write *The Gospel According to Oprah*: "I was surprised at how much I felt *a part* of the show's culture rather than *apart from* it."[6] Nelson means this as a reflection on the relevance of the show's content and the "realness" of its host. What Nelson fails to calculate is the degree to which the show's structure and mode of presentation are also at work to create that sensibility. Talk shows are mostly taped, but they are broadcast to simulate live programming. Thus, they project a sense of immediacy, of being together in time even if the host is there in the studio and I am here in my living room. Moreover, the focus of each episode can be nearly as fresh as the daily news. Thus, even though we recognize at some level that a massive production apparatus (people, technologies, and processes) separates us from Oprah, the format and appearance of the show provide a feeling of immediacy and relevance. Successful talk shows—and Oprah's has been the most successful ever—construct for us a feeling of presence and communion. I am with Oprah and she is with me. Regular watchers have the added feeling of familiarity—with the appearance and structure of the show, and more importantly with its steadfast central character, Oprah.

WE'RE HER POSSE AND SHE'S OUR FRIEND

A second factor that constructs the personal, sympathetic relation with the talk show celebrity is the "live studio audience." In important ways, the audience is our proxy. By their presence, they embody our shared feeling for Oprah, our common acknowledgment of her celebrity status. By their applause and laughter and shouts of support they voice our solidarity with Oprah.[7] When Oprah "enters" the audience, sits with them, invites their questions and responses, and holds their hands, her enacted intimacy with them becomes vicariously an intimacy with us. This is a departure from

6. Nelson, *Gospel According to Oprah*, 95, emphasis original.

7. Marshall makes this point in *Celebrity and Power*, 135.

earlier talk shows, where the hosts stick close to the guests and keep a distance from the audience. Marshall suggests that it is a populist ritual that helps construct Oprah's populist persona.[8] When Oprah permits individual spectators to voice their fears and hopes, to ask questions or vent outrage, to enter the public discourse of the show, she is not merely empowering particular individuals, but all of us, inasmuch as these participants serve as our representatives.[9] Without the ritualization of relationship that Oprah performs with the audience on every episode, we would not feel anything like the degree of sympathetic identification with Oprah that we do, and thus she would not be anything like the degree of celebrity that she is. Seeing Oprah in the crowd every day ritually enacts the claim that "Oprah loves you and has a wonderful plan for your life."

This means that "we" are part of her identity, and she is part of ours. After analyzing Oprah's relationship to her audience, David Marshall concludes that "Oprah Winfrey has made the audience itself, as expressed through the live studio audience, part of her identity as a celebrity."[10] Just as Diana was the "people's princess"—someone whose persona was constructed by her emergence from and utter dependence upon "the people"— so Oprah is the "people's pastor," someone whose persona is constructed daily by her "pastoral" engagement with her studio and television audience. Nelson points out that the public memorial service twelve days after 9/11 was presided over, not by Billy Graham or some other religious official, but by Oprah, "an entertainer" who nonetheless occupies a kind of pastoral role in the United States.[11]

For Oprah's fans, traffic also flows the other way: they are not only part of her identity as America's pastor, but she is part of their identity as persons (usually middle-aged, middle-class women) struggling for a better life. They are persons with affection for, and trust in, Oprah. As one fan site put it, of all the one-name celebrities in the world, ". . . there's only one that we all know intimately. Oprah is not just another famous entertainer. She's a friend to the world and a role model for all people. . . ."[12] This language of intimate knowledge and true friendship is precisely the language of identity construction. And that is true not just of "fanatics" who develop Oprah

8. Ibid., 140.

9. This analysis is based on ibid., 134–35.

10. Marshall, *Celebrity and Power*, 135.

11. Nelson, *Gospel According to Oprah*, vii–ix.

12. Oprah Winfrey Fansite, "Frontpage," para. 1.

Web sites; it is the reality of the average fans who make Oprah a regular part of their lives.

OPRAH INCARNATE

The final structural factor that builds our connection with Oprah is the incarnational narrative at the core of most shows. Here, Oprah is our proxy; in her, our hopes and fears take flesh and find answers. Where earlier daytime talk shows were meant to capture partial attention, *Donahue* and *Oprah* were designed to command complete attention. *Oprah* regularly does that with a narrative arc that moves from problem to solution: guests present some kind of problem or crisis, the studio audience chimes in with its thoughts, experts are consulted, and the solution is given. As the problem is presented, Oprah embodies concern; as the audience gets its say, Oprah channels its energy; as the experts deliver the solution, Oprah "makes it plain" by rewording "the professional's advice into language of practicality and usability for the audience."[13] Oprah takes us on a vicarious journey through the problem—from confusion, through comment, then analysis, to a usable solution. We are especially willing to allow Oprah to represent us in this way because 1) the show consistently focuses on topics about which she is passionate, 2) the show regularly focuses on a topic that Oprah has personal struggles with—such as weight, or poverty, or sexual abuse, and 3) she has already embodied in her own life the empowerment of overcoming disadvantage and the prospect of positive transformation through good advice and willpower. David Marshall highlights how this works:

> In the case of Oprah, this familiarity leads to a sympathetic form of identification and is buttressed by occasional program episodes that have personal relevance to her life. Occasionally, episodes of her show have focused on themes directly related to her "private battles" concerning her history as an abused child or, alternatively, her battle with diets and weight loss. Oprah as hero is presented as vulnerable and subject to weaknesses that others suffer. Audiences are thus constructed to be loyal and therefore regular viewers of her program; they are drawn to her candor, which allows her to move seamlessly from the public sphere to the private in

13. Marshall, *Celebrity and Power*, 136–37.

her presentation of self. . . . Her power as a sympathetic hero is dependent on her presenting herself as both honest and open.[14]

So because Oprah seems to embody her show's motto, "Live your best life," we allow her to represent us in our own struggles for the good life. And so each episode is a bit like going to church. Marcia Nelson suggests that Oprah's TV show "has a morning [worship] service feel to it. Go to this house of worship and sit down for an inspiring hour that will engage you and give you a lift."[15]

Noticing the narrative structure of each sixty-minute episode ought to give us pause, however. Can all of the world's problems be presented, analyzed, and solved in sixty minutes, minus commercial breaks? Hardly. Nor does Oprah try. Her focus is largely, almost exclusively, the personal, relational, familial, and spiritual. Oprah may have ventured into politics by supporting Obama in 2008, but the problems her show highlights must be personal in ways that exclude a focus on larger realities like politics, economics, and education, problems like war and government-sanctioned torture, like mass transit or agricultural policy or strip mining, like the morass of public education. Oprah's problem-resolution structure is at most interpersonal in scope and intensely individual in focus. In respect to [fill in the problem of the day], what can you (singular) do to "live your best life" right now? Even here, the Christian tradition of disciplined devotion to God, of slow growth in holiness through disciplined practices, ought to suggest to us that many of the most needed personal transformations are too big to be analyzed in a sixty-minute show and too hard to be solved with informative advice and willpower. Regimens of transformation, apart from traditions of sanctity, simply empower and expand forms of narcissism.

PORCH OR PEW: HOW FAR DOES OPRAH TAKE US?

In this regard, the church of Oprah may be like celebrity culture more generally, a form of what Mark Edmundson calls "easy transcendence"— a transcendence that requires so much less of us than art or religion.[16] It is, after all, entertainment. Marcia Nelson hastens to add, however, that Oprah is

14. Marshall, *Celebrity and Power*, 190–91.

15. Ibid., ix.

16. Gabler, *Life the Movie*, 168.

entertainment *with* values. That's not religion. But it's compatible with religion. My friend Phyllis Tickle . . . says Oprah is entertaining in the atrium outside the houses of worship where real religion, with doctrine, practices, and community, lives, breathes, and prays. A viewer may—or may not—go from that entryway into the house of worship.[17]

Over the centuries, Christianity has sometimes identified certain phenomena as "preparation for the gospel." Is Oprah a propaedeutic (the technical term for a preparatory process) to Christian conversion? Does Tickle's image of Oprah as the church's front porch suggest that we should celebrate Oprah's celebrity spirituality? Answering these questions will likely depend on whether the phenomenon in question works more like yeast that leavens an entire batch of dough, or an immunization that inoculates against actually developing the condition. Let's look at specific dimensions of Oprah's gospel.

First, let's notice how Oprah's life story embodies her gospelesque slogan: "Live your best life." To her fans, Oprah embodies choosing and living the good life. She does this not in terms of her astounding net worth (estimated as high as $1.3 billion), public popularity, or media power, but precisely in terms of her empowering triumphs over adversity and her ennobling practices of generosity.

Oprah embodies the conviction that we can and should choose to enact better lives. She has not allowed poverty, sexual abuse, body image issues, racism or sexism to deny her happiness. To differing degrees, she has overcome each of these conditions that regularly crush human flourishing. She is an amazing woman. Especially in relation to gender and race, Oprah's public persona represents "symbolically the potential of empowerment of women, [and] of marginalized groups within the American system."[18] No wonder Carlin Flora suggests that watching a celebrity like Oprah is like receiving spiritual guidance; it helps us "muster the will to tackle our own problems."[19] The empowerment that Oprah's own life story embodies is something she seeks to engender in her millions of viewers.

Oprah also embodies and preaches a clear sense of the basic shape that a better life will take. Its fundamental pattern will be generosity—to oneself, to loved ones, and to persons in need. This involves cultivating

17. Nelson, *Gospel According to Oprah*, 94–95, emphasis original.

18. Marshall, *Celebrity and Power*, 142.

19. Flora, "Seeing by Starlight" 34.

habits of gratitude, of giving, of forgiving, and of serving.[20] Though the compatibility of such "values" with Christian conviction is obvious, Oprah does not espouse a particular faith. Instead, she appears to craft a message that is more intentionally generic, suitable to the religiously plural environment of her national and global market. While she is willing to credit "God" with having a positive influence on her life, her benevolent deity does not appear to have a specific name or a defining story.

So we might say that Oprah is yet another American who is "spiritual but not religious." Oprah herself uses such language. A 2007 *Washington Post* story reports that Oprah answered a question about whether she has any doubts in this way:

> No, I don't have any doubts. I really don't. Because I live in a very spiritual space—not a religious space, but I live in a spiritual space where I understand the connection that we all have with each other. It's not just rhetoric for me. I really do understand the common denominator in the human experience.[21]

In this claim, I hear a worrisome overconfidence in self that risks pride, and a troubling underappreciation for communal faith that risks sloth. Yet the quote demonstrates that Oprah's self-understanding is congruent with her fans' confidence. If "Oprahism" were ever to start holding religious services, surely the first anthem would be "Nobody Knows Me Like ~~Jesus~~ Oprah."

Perhaps now we are in a better position to evaluate the question:

✢ *Is Oprah a proper propaedeutic to the gospel, a pathway to hardcore discipleship?*

The next three sections suggest that there are three reasons that the answer is no, though each one begins with something genuinely positive about Oprah's "ministry." The problem is that her "ministry" stops short, or more accurately, that in stopping short it implies that a way station is the final destination.

---

20. These four habits are chapters 5, 8, 9, and 10 respectively of Nelson, *Gospel According to Oprah*. Nelson is more comfortable with the language of values than habit.

21. Robinson, "Can Oprah Boost Her 'Favorite Guy'?" 80.

cOmmunity ISN'T CHURCH

First, we should appreciate the degree to which Oprah creates affective community. Celebrity itself has developed out of the isolation and loneliness of mass society; it is a "para-social" form of relationship that compensates for lack of nourishing relationships in everyday life. While most critics of celebrity would see a good deal of fandom as diminishing our humanity rather than enhancing it, they would be much harder pressed to render such judgments against the community that gathers around Oprah. It coalesces around a shared group of values; it affirms a shared set of activities (there are *Oprah-tivities* like watching the show and talking about it afterwards, reading the magazine and book club selections, and surfing the Web site; and there are *Oprah-tunities* like giving back to the community, etc.); and it effects a shared sense of identity (even if you don't join the book club or wear an "I heart Oprah" T-shirt). Even if persons never went to the shOw, Oprah impacts their believing, their behaving, and their sense of belonging. In an increasingly fragmented world, none of these forms of cOmmunity should be denigrated.

But for inheritors of Ezekiel's vision of the reconstitution of the valley of dried bones (Ezekiel 37), neither should we celebrate cOmmunity as the ideal form of life together. Oprah helps us feel connected (and hopeful and thankful), but she does not help us become accountable or interdependent. In other words, what Oprah offers is largely affective community without accountable interdependence. We were created and redeemed for more. Consider that the spirit who blows the dry bones back to a living body is the Holy Spirit who gifts each member of Christ's body the church. These gifts are given to each for the good of all, in such a way that no one has all the gifts that make for healthy community and happy life. Instead, we must depend on one another for what we ourselves lack, trusting in the fullness of the Spirit's giving to all, rather than in a complete giving to each. There is a sufficiency, indeed an abundance, but it lies in the interdependent exercise of our gifts rather than in independent activity.

This makes our relationship to one another something quite different from voluntary community around shared taste, something far more than a chosen, supplemental relation that enriches our already existing personhood; it suggests that "live your best life" is impossible without a genuine community of shared gifts. Thus, the interdependent distribution of gifts entails accountability for their deployment. They are not given for my gain, but for the common good, and thus my responsibility, my obligation, is to serve others by exercising my gifts. I am *obliged*, that is bound, by the reception of Spirit-gift. This binding is not first to a particular activity or exercise of the gift, but a binding by the Spirit to the Father through the Son, and thereby a binding by the Spirit to the community of the Son.

So in the end, while we Christians may celebrate Oprah's community as a better alternative than loneliness and despair, it is not a step toward Christian community precisely because Christian community does not begin with recognition of a shared affection (for Oprah or the Cubs or whatever), but with the reception of a bonding, binding Spirit. Oprah's community may be real, but it isn't interdependent at its core, and—given its location in entertainment culture—it isn't accountable at all. Oprah herself is the quintessence of both. She has no interdependence on specific members of the Oprah community. She needs her fan base, sure. But she does not depend on particular fans for their unique gifts. Nor is she accountable to the community for her own exercise of gifts. Rather, as a businesswoman she minds the bottom line and watches the ratings. Community Oprah-style is altogether too likely to be a prophylactic to Christian community rather than a propaedeutic to it. In other words, cOmmunity can too easily be a fence rather than a gate.

mOrality NEEDS CHURCH

Second, we should appreciate the way that Oprah offers moral guidance. Unlike so many celebrities whose tabloid escapades model destructive behaviors and immoral choices, Oprah is all about improving lives—hers and ours. Unlike too many talk shows, of which *Jerry Springer* may be the worst, Oprah's focus is moral uplift rather than providing a forum in which to leer at, if not promote, human degradation.[22] Toward that end, her talk show "advises viewers on virtually every area of their lives: marriage, family, work, finances, emotional and physical health, and spirituality."[23] Her book club selections are meant to teach a life lesson, one that can then be rehearsed on the episode devoted to the book. Oprah isn't a utilitarian who thinks that what works is what's right. Rather, she genuinely believes that doing the right thing—giving, forgiving, serving—will lead to becoming better persons.

22. See chapter 4, "YouTube and U2charist."
23. McClymond, "Gospel According to Oprah," 178.

Fair enough. The problem for Christians is that Oprah relocates moral authority from Christian community to herself and to each individual. Let's consider her many shows on forgiveness as an example. On the one hand, these first-person accounts of forgiving horrific acts carry an inherent moral authority. There is something compelling about truthful witness to the power of forgiveness. But on the other hand, these episodes also show us some of the limits to Oprah's moral guidance. Specifically, they alienate us from traditioned moral community—from reasoning together about how we should live in Christ.

Oprah has the first word. The stories that are shown, issues that are addressed, the guests that are invited, the experts that are consulted, and the shape of the program are all selected and scripted by Oprah (and her people) according to Oprah's own moral sensibility. In this sense, what counts as forgiveness and what exemplifies forgiving well are entirely governed by Oprah. She decides, without accountability to particular canons of authority, without communal discernment in a wider moral community, without displaying her own process of moral reasoning (though occasionally she may decide to stage that process as a vicarious model of what we should undergo).

Oprah also has the last word. Literally, she has the final word on every show, which is what always grants the final positioning of, the ultimate benediction on, moral matters. More importantly, she is the one who renders the summary judgment of what an "expert's advice" or a guest's experience means. The implication is that we don't quite know what it means, why it matters, or what to do about it, until Oprah summarizes it for us. So in one sense, Oprah relocates moral authority from Christ and his story, from the Bible and its tradition of interpretation, from the church and its processes of adjudication, to herself.

In another sense, the irreducible fact that her show is a show—that is, an entertainment—means that finally I am as alone with my moral decision as I am with my remote. Choosing whom and whether to forgive becomes analogous to choosing what and whether to watch. I could just as well play Wii, and there's no one with a right to counsel me otherwise. Learning life lessons in an entertainment modality suggests that I could just as well harbor a grudge, or seek revenge, and there's no one with a right to counsel me otherwise. The best Oprah can do—in an entertaining style—is to try to persuade me that forgiving is in my own best interest, that I will be glad I forgave, just as I am glad I tuned in to her show. In other words, in an entertaining program about the value of forgiving, the basic structure of entertainment consumption as a personal lifestyle choice gets mapped on to the question of whether and how to forgive: it too becomes a personal lifestyle choice, subject to the authority of my own interests and desires and goals, but not to something larger—like a community of the forgiven faithful, or a canonical revelation of a God of mercy, or a risen, forgiving Lord.

So far, the dislocation of authority that I am suggesting would be true whether I was watching Oprah or Billy Graham—it is intrinsic to the entertainment practice of watching television. There is a more specific way that Oprah strips from me the authority of traditioned moral community. Her show positions forgiveness (or whatever value or practice is being considered) as something we can understand outside of specific moral traditions like Judaism, Christianity, or Islam. Doing this sometimes requires her to reshape how stories of forgiveness get told. Oprah guests "Chip and Jody Ferlaak told a magazine that they had been asked by producers to avoid specifically Christian language in relating their story so that its message of forgiveness would be apparent to people of different faiths."[24] In other words, the Ferlaak's normal way of telling their story of forgiveness would entail specifically Christian language that embodies core Christian convictions. But the "suggestion" by Oprah's producers that they tell it differently implies that the Christianity is not really an intrinsic part of the story. In effect, this implies that a faith tradition may provide *motivation* to forgive, but that the specific stories, doctrines, and practices of faith are not intrinsic to perceiving, understanding, and enacting forgiveness. But is that true? Should the children of Abraham agree that they can truly understand forgiveness apart from Isaiah and Hosea? Should the followers of Jesus of Nazareth accede to the notion that they can understand forgiveness apart from his life, death, and resurrection? Whatever Oprah's reason for excluding particular faith talk, its net effect is to diminish significantly the moral authority of that faith tradition, and to replace it with the moral authority of my subjective experience—what feels right to me, and my personal judgment—what seems true to me. Of course, Christianity has always demanded that my experience and judgment be involved in moral discernment and decision, as the tradition of conscience proves. But conscience is properly formed by the particularity of the church's reasoning together about Christ, and conscience is properly exercised in the context of Christian prayer and practice.

24. Nelson, *Gospel According to Oprah*, 67.

To say this as clearly as possible, in moral matters Christianity is called to measure all things against the standard of the incarnate Son of God, to see all things through his compassionate eyes. Oprah's moral compass may be reasonably accurate. But she robs us of the very capacity to know that by replacing the moral authority of the One who will rise in the East with her judgments and my decisions. That trade is not worth making.

✢ *Are you convinced that Oprah's celebrity has a pastoral shape, and that her media network functions as a quasi-church? Has Oprah changed your life, directly or indirectly?*

✢ *A "typical Christian" could spend more than* five *hours a week with the "church of Oprah," probably less than* two *in the church of Jesus Christ. How problematic is that disparity? What might it entail for Christian Oprahites? What might it mean about Christian practices of entertainment more generally?*

transfOrmation ISN'T HOLINESS

Finally, we should appreciate the way Oprah wants to fix things. Her philanthropy is extensive. Her advocacy is powerful. Most importantly, her media focus has been and remains that of helping improve lives. Oprah wants to change us, and the world, for the better. Remember, "Oprah loves you, and has a wonderful plan for your life."

Oprah's plan includes helping you choose the right stuff. See the "O list," a regular feature in *O* magazine. Oprah's plan includes providing you with the information you need in an easily understandable form. Oprah's plan includes clear, doable processes for improving your life. "Want to unstick a relationship that disappoints? Repeat the phrase, 'He's just not that into you.'"[25] She offers a ritual practice for inculcating gratitude—the "gratitude journal." Oprah is too good a friend to command "live your best life" without commending ways to do it.

It would be easy enough to charge Oprah with Pelagianism, the Christian heresy that expects that we have the power and the will to heal ourselves. I do not think, however, that Pelagianism is the best way to analyze Oprah's plan to give us a makeover. Instead, we would do well to remember

---

25. Ibid., 42.

that some transformations are not as entertaining as others, and that every transformation requires not only techniques and exemplars, but standards.

As to the former, Phillis Tickle reminds us that "if entertainment required sacrifice and discipline, it wouldn't entertain."[26] In that regard, the transfOrmations that Oprah urges are typically user-friendly: presentable in sixty minutes; understandable by the nonexpert (as long as Oprah translates); achievable by every woman who is willing to try; amenable to clear, sequential actions, with a simple and inviting first step. "Want to lose weight? Take ten thousand steps a day, starting with one."[27] And the exemplars of transformation—guests (and sometimes Oprah herself) who testify that this process "works"—are far more likely to tell us how doable this change was than they are to warn us about the depth of sacrifice or the stringency of discipline that it required. "I did it, so of course you can, too" is the basic message. Such transformations can be valuable: I'd be better off with lower cholesterol, higher energy levels, etc. But such Oprah makeOvers—indeed all the transformations the popular culture promotes—float above the most basic transformation that constitutes the Christian life: dying to self and living in (and for) Christ. That transformation entails a regimen for the whole self over a whole lifetime (even then, it will require a resurrection). It is the disciplined discipleship of bearing crosses, the sacrificial service of forgiving enemies—transformative work that isn't very entertaining by the standards of mass media. So while Oprah's gospel promises to change us for the better, it stops far short of making us whole or new or free or holy. Change like that finally requires church.

The latter concern about Oprah's agenda to improve our lot is that she shows us how to change, and she shows us people who have changed, but apart from a proper conversation about the standards for achieving and assessing change. What are we aiming at? Is it anything larger than to become more like Oprah and her wonderful guests? As Christians, we have a legacy that must not be forgotten. For us, regimens of transformation are attached to traditions of sanctity. For us, the Scriptures tell us how we should change and whom we should become. For us, the saints show us how we should change and whom we should become. I speak of "traditions of sanctity" precisely because the holy character of God is so rich that it shines forth in a myriad of diverse but saintly lives; it is called forth through a myriad of disciplined, sacrificial practices. There are multiple traditions of conforming

26. Quoted in ibid., 86.

27. Ibid., 42.

to and embodying Christ's holiness. They are not competing versions of holiness, but complementary visions of Christ. Together, they comprise standards by which the goals and processes of transformation must be judged. Apart from such standards of sanctity, every regimen of transformation risks narcissistic absorption with oneself, and solipsistic (self-absorbed) evaluation by and of oneself. Thus, I am suggesting that Oprah's consistent focus on transformation is less dangerous as a Pelagian claim that "I can do anything," but far more dangerous as the narcissism of transforming myself and the solipsism of supervising my own transformation.

So, in summary, Oprah fosters a kind of community, but not the empowered and empowering fellowship of the Holy Spirit, with its interdependent accountability. Oprah focuses on moral uplift, but in doing so she orphans us from the household of God with its canons of authority, traditions of guidance, and community of discernment. Oprah furthers personal transformations, but not the conformation of dying with and dwelling in Christ that can only transpire on pilgrimage with all his saints. Thus Oprah is good; indeed, she is far better than Springer or Geraldo, better than Donahue was, better than *The View* is. But Oprah isn't best. Church is. The church of Jesus Christ, for all of its failings, is the best place to experience community, to realize goodness, to pursue holiness. If there is a problem with Oprah, it is that she gets us close enough to what is best that we may be content to stay there, to keep tuning in tomorrow, rather than hungry enough to walk through the church's door seeking to receive (and live) our best life now.

The church of Oprah is great entertainment, the very best. That's exactly why it is such lousy church.

✛ *If the church offers something entertaining television cannot—gifts of mutual interdependence, canons of moral authority, and regimens of holy transformation—how important is each of these in the life of your congregation? What changes in practice would be required to "tune in" on them? Would turning off television—even or especially "better" television like Oprah—be an important step?*

thirteen

Love the Cinema, Hate the Sin?

MY PLAYFUL TITLE TRADES on a staple of my early Christian training: we were taught to "love the sinner, but hate the sin." In one sense, that's godly advice—intending for us to emulate both God's overwhelming love for us (John 3:16) and God's unflinching wrath against sin (Rom 1:18). So "love the sinner, hate the sin" was a counsel to love everybody, even and especially those who reject the gospel, without approving or overlooking their sinful deeds.

But in another sense, "love the sinner, hate the sin" is theologically dubious advice because it almost inevitably distorts our account of sin in several ways. First, even though the phrase uses the singular term *sin*, it seems to think about sin as a collective noun for *sins*, and it seems to define sins as outward actions that break God's law (or maybe just as actions that break the rules). While it is true enough that sins contradict God's will, plenty of them fall outside the paradigm of the individual dastardly deed—for example, sins of omission like not feeding the hungry, sins of attitude like pride or envy, and sins of social structure (e.g., see chapter 6 on sports). If we forget that, then we're likely to hate only some sins, some of the time, rather than hating all sin all the time. Let's call this mistake *moralism*.

Second, while it is true enough that when we say *sin* we should also think about sins, since they are inextricably related, that doesn't mean we should equate the two or focus primarily on the latter. Just as the real problem in illness is the disease rather than the symptoms, so the real problem here is sin rather than sins. Sins and sinning manifest an underlying condition that holds us captive, destroys our wholeness, and foments enmity between us and just about everything else. This is the real problem, and it is harder to see and harder to fix than we wish it were. So we succumb to the simpler focus on sins, and try to "love" sinners by urging them to try harder to stop their sinning, as if the problem of sin could be cured by trying to commit fewer sins, as if lung cancer could be cured by coughing less. Let's call this mistake *pelagianism*.

Third, the adversative *but* in the middle of "love the sinner, but hate the sin" suggests that a sinner and his sin are so easy to differentiate that there is no worry that in hating the sin we might end up hating the sinner a bit, too. Such a clean separation between agents and their actions comes at considerable theological cost, a cost that we ought not to pay. Sometimes it costs us a positive view of our bodies by identifying the sinner-that-we-love as the soul or mind or "self," while locating the sin-that-we-hate in bodily desires and actions. That kind of thinking puts our body on the enemies list (right beside sin, death, and the devil) as something God needs to defeat or destroy, rather than redeem through resurrection. It splits our humanity in two, reckoning sin to a baser bodily dimension, and reckoning holiness to a nobler spiritual one, in the process implying that our turning away from sin will require a turning away from the body and its desires. Let's call this mistake *angelism*.[1]

Other times, the adversative thinking leaves our humanity intact but costs us the unity of creation itself. This happens by simplistically splitting reality into pure good and utter evil, with both being pretty easy to spot. That would suggest that instead of gradations, evil comes in only one flavor—absolutely terrible—and goodness is just the opposite—absolutely terrific. Let's call this mistake *dualism*. The problem with dualism is that it implies that the only reason anyone would ever choose to do evil is because they were evil and wanted evil. A sinner like that would be hard to love, even harder to empathize with.

Interestingly, Christian responses to Hollywood have often resembled hating the sin far more than loving the sinner. I think we can see all four misunderstandings at work—moralism, pelagianism, angelism, and dualism.

Christians have a long history of disliking, deploring, and generally defaming the movie industry. Though very early there were positive

---

1. For an excellent account of this mistake and its corrective, see Clapp, *Tortured Wonders*.

assessments of the possibilities of film, by 1920 or so the church was beginning to oppose publicly what to its mind was the excessive immorality of many movies. Things shifted into high gear in 1933 with the creation of the Legion of Decency, which invited Christians to take a pledge to avoid any and all movies deemed indecent. Unfortunately, the benchmark for decent/ indecent had far less to do with God's character as revealed in Jesus Christ than it did with American character as embodied in bourgeois culture. So it isn't much of an exaggeration to say that the Legion focused on respectability rather than righteousness, mores more than motives. So Hollywood developed the Hays Code, which regulated what movies could say, do, and show according to a moralistic list of rules that implied that goodness was a matter of outward conformity rather than inner transformation.

Today that kind of moralism is no longer a matter of Hollywood regulating itself, but it is still at work where Christians use the MPAA's rating system (G, PG, PG13, R, and NC17) as a moral guide. Unfortunately, PG13 and R are pretty blunt instruments for making moral distinctions. Sin may be foulmouthed, but so was Martin Luther. Sin can be sexy, but so is the Song of Solomon. Sin certainly breeds violence (read Genesis 4), but most of the Christian tradition has refused to equate all violence with sin.[2] Moralism doesn't usually make us holy; it just makes us feel holier-than-thou.

Some Christians push the moralism to an all-out dualism. For them, Hollywood is not just a fallen power but an utter evil. Robert K. Johnston offers this quote from Herbert Miles' 1947 book *Movies and Morals*: movies "are the organ of the devil, the idol of sinners, the sink of infamy, the stumbling block to human progress, the moral cancer of civilization, the Number One Enemy of Jesus Christ."[3] While a dualism that extreme is relatively rare these days, there are still quite a few Christian organizations and leaders that depict Hollywood as Satan's elite squadron in a culture war against God's children of light, or that suggest that a particular movie will be a "Death Star" wielded to destroy Christ's embattled church. That kind of rhetoric evinces a disabling ethos of fear that is utterly unfitting for the people of a risen Lord.

Finally, where Christians focus mostly or even exclusively on profanity, violence, and sex in their moral evaluation of movies, they evidence both

---

2. For the best overview of how to think about this claim, see Bell, *Just War as Christian Discipleship*.

3. Johnston, *Reel Spirituality*, 57. Miles' comment is especially ironic coming just a few years after the Holocaust.

pelagianism and angelism. There is some compelling evidence that what we see impacts us, so I am not suggesting that it is silly to give discerning thought to what we watch. I am suggesting, however, that it is pelagian to assume that avoiding such influences will somehow keep us pure. We aren't pure to begin with, but fallen, and seeing that truth rendered cinematically just might help us. Worse, the concentration on bodily acts like profanity, violence, and sex too easily gives hostage to angelism's claim that our bodies are finally the source of the problem, rather than being one of the zones where sin comes to expression.

In short, the theologically distorting view of "love the sinner, but hate the sin" all too easily produces an adversarial stance of "hate the sin, and hate Hollywood while you're at it." Yet anyone who has seen *The Mission* or *Romero*, not to mention *Lars and the Real Girl* or even *Billy Elliot*, has to acknowledge that there is more to movies than dualistic moralism or pelagian angelism. Indeed, one of the most theologically interesting aspects of the movies is how hate and love and the full gamut of human emotion can come to expression there.

✢   *Are there particular emotions that you regularly feel at the cinema?*

MR. LUCAS STRIKES (MR. LINDBECK) BACK

In chapter one, we introduced Mr. Lucas to Mr. Lindbeck, suggesting that theology's work is finally to be a shaping wisdom or cultural grammar for Christian living. This book has mostly focused on entertainment practices in relation to theology as a grammar of conviction, or as enculturated agency, desire, and perception. Along the way, we noticed the inadequacies of cognitive construals of theology as ideas in our head, and of experiential construals of theology as expressing feelings in our hearts.

Perhaps it's time for the empire known as Lucasfilm, Inc., to strike back, by letting Mr. Lucas remind Mr. Lindbeck—and us!—that *Star Wars* (and *Indiana Jones*) were blockbusters because movies are about feelings! People go to the movies for fun—the fun of being grabbed in the gut by a story, the fun of identifying with a character, the fun of sympathizing with another's hopes and fears, loves and hates, dreams and disappointments.[4]

---

4. For a positive account of the "visceral" impact of movies, see Johnston and Barsotti, *Finding God*, 26–28.

Here I want to use Mr. Lucas as a foil to invite us to seek a fuller account of the importance of emotion and desire than we have heretofore had. Let's be honest: Christian antipathy toward "sex in movies" roots in the anxiety that sexual desire will be aroused in movies, with lustful behavioral consequences. And Christian antipathy toward "bad words" roots in the anxiety that verbalizing powerful emotions will exacerbate rather than purge them, with profaning consequences. And more fundamentally, Christian antipathy toward depicting what is "bad" or "evil" seems to root in the anxiety that doing so in an entertaining format will result in "sympathy for the devil." So the first principle of the Hollywood Production Code of 1930 was that "no picture shall be produced that will lower the moral standards of those who see it. Hence *the sympathy of the audience* should never be thrown to the side of wrongdoing, evil, or sin."[5]

Yet perhaps sympathy is precisely what we need to inculcate—sympathy in the sense of *feeling with* characters the depths of our shared, fallen humanity, and in the sense of *feeling for* their struggles, failures, and captivities. I am convinced that various narrative arts—drama, cinema, novels—have the power to nurture in us a sympathetic imagination, a capacity not only to understand but to feel with and feel for others. Let's explore that cinematically (rather than theoretically).

The *Star Wars* movies have long been recognized as westerns translated to outer space, sometimes called "space operas." Thus, they are part of a genre that is long on action and adventure, short on subtle characterization or nuanced understanding. If anything, such movies may contribute to dualistic understandings of the relation of good and evil, and to pelagian interpretations of moral agency. Yet in spite of the limitations of its genre, the *Star Wars* movies work to show us that the attractions of "the dark side" can root in our desire to do good, that succumbing to evil is an incremental progression of the disordering of our loves, and that redemption is receiving the gift of another's love. None of this is realistic, given the cartoonish conventions of space operas and the melodramatic acting of the cast. So Jason Byassee's forty-eight viewings of *Star Wars* didn't make him more holy, loving, or kind. But it may well have positioned him to grow in sympathy for the pull of sin and the plight of sinners.[6]

My point here isn't "Hollywood to the rescue!" There are plenty of movies that don't know the first thing about motivation, so they can show

5. Quoted in Johnston, *Reel Spirituality*, 47, emphasis mine.
6. Byassee, "God Does Not Entertain," 110.

us nothing about why we humans sometimes fail to do the good we want to do. There are lots of films that don't know the first thing about relation, so their revel in debauchery or celebration of evil shows us nothing about how our sinful alienations are intensified or overcome. But watching the lives of others displayed in good movies—movies with heart!—may just broaden our sympathetic understanding, and indeed our love, of ourselves and others. How do I know that? I saw it happen in *The Lives of Others* (2006), the Oscar-winning story of the humanizing transformation of a Stasi officer assigned to surveil a playwright and his lover in East Germany. We watch the journey of Captain Gerd Wiesler from heartless automaton of the communist police state, whose understanding of human psychology is focused entirely on subjugating others without any sympathy, to passionate protector of his victims, willing to risk everything for their sake. What we watch happen to Captain Wiesler as he watches the unfolding lives of others is a parable of what can happen to us as we watch the lives of others unfold—our sympathy grows in ways that might finally equip us to love the sinner, but hate the sin.

❖ *What movies have nourished your sympathy—your capacity to feel with and feel for those who seem most alien to you?*

The remainder of this chapter will seek to remedy the distorting power of moralism, pelagianism, angelism, and dualism by reflecting on the sympathizing power of specific films or genres. Or to be more precise, I will attempt to describe how watching these films could have that effect, while acknowledging that verbal descriptions of what we see is a poor substitute for actually going to the movies!

MORALISTIC UGLINESS AND *AMERICAN BEAUTY*

Moralism reduces goodness to outward conformity to rules of behavior that look virtuous, yet do not make us better people. Let's look closer by considering what *American Beauty* can show us about being good.

American Beauty (1999) won critical acclaim as well as five Oscars for its depiction of . . . well, that's the key question, actually. What is *American Beauty* about? The movie was rated R for strong sexuality, language, violence, and drug content. Those elements aren't gratuitous in the film, but actually are *in some sense* what the film is about—sexuality as it relates to desire and disappointment, language as impediment to or conveyor of truth, violence as destruction of goodness, and drugs as a (false) path to freedom and happiness.

Moralism will almost certainly conclude that "from drugs and sex to hatred and death, this film revels in sickness."[7] The logic of this moralistic condemnation appears to develop as follows: 1) the film shows transgressive behavior—people breaking the rules; 2) the transgressions are mostly either unpunished or even rewarded; 3) the film seems to sympathize with the motivations and the plights of the transgressors; and thus 4) watching the film makes us participants in or accomplices to the transgressions. Specifically, characters in the movie 1) lust and fornicate, 2) seem to enjoy it without apparent consequence, 3) seem to deserve their enjoyment, which means that 4) we're lusting, too, if we watch and enjoy this storyline. Moralism's bottom line with a movie like *American Beauty* is *don't look!*

But what if we were to adopt the movie's tagline and "look closer," attempting to explore it with moral sympathy rather than moralism? This approach will, I think, discover that the movie is attempting to show us, sympathetically, a great deal of truth. First, *American Beauty* intends to show the truth that beneath its glossy veneer, the American dream of suburban success is empty, ugly, and ultimately fatal. Second, *American Beauty* seeks to show the truth about male lust. Men do become infatuated with women (or girls) that ought to be out of bounds for them, either because they are already committed to another relationship, or because the object of their infatuation is inappropriate. The movie portrays the intensity of its protagonist Lester's midlife male sexual infatuation and erotic fantasy without explicit nudity, using scenes with symbolic images and music. Thus, what we see and hear invites us to see and recognize two things simultaneously: that the young girl whom Lester desires is truly desirable, and that Lester's desire for her is truly ludicrous—an understandable but tragic distortion of their human sexuality. In other words, the film shows us something not only understandable but pitiable. It invites our sympathy for the movie character whose desires are betraying him, and through him for others and even ourselves when we are caught in similar situations. It does

---

7. Focus on the Family, "American Beauty," para. 8. It may seem judgmental to call this review moralism. But throughout the review there is a caustic cataloging of rule-breaking behaviors in the movie, none of which is situated in the movie's overall narrative arc or in each character's development or decline. I refer to "moralistic ugliness" in the title of this section precisely because I believe that there is nothing about such moralistic condemnations that is comely or attractive enough to draw sinners toward the beauty of Christ.

all this, however, without approving of the actions and attitudes for which we are developing sympathetic understanding. Moralism will entirely pre-empt that possibility, by refusing to watch what it cannot approve.

I think the movie also seeks to show the truth about the relationship of beauty and vulnerability. When Lester (and the movie) finally does "look closer" at the girl Angela's body, that moment is portrayed as transforma-tive for Lester (and thus potentially transformative for us). In that moment, Lester's gaze changes from that of lecher to that of father; Angela is revealed to him as both beautiful woman and vulnerable girl, an appropriate object of someone's desire, *but not of his desire*. This is moral progress, and we should celebrate it.[8] The camera work does not undercut the message by continuing to voyeuristically present Angela as object of erotic gaze. Rather both camera and Lester work to refocus our gaze from Angela's body to her person. Thus, the brief nudity serves the movie's overall narrative purpose of making clear the transformation that occurs in Lester.[9] *American Beauty* is not a celebration of midlife crises, nor is it an invitation to enjoy erotic fantasies of sexual license. Instead, it is a depiction of some tragic distor-tions—and one gracious redemption—of desire, intended to expand our vision of the beautiful gift of life. Along the way, it serves as a cautionary tale that moralism is a poor substitute for goodness, beauty, and truth.[10]

PLEASANT PELAGIAN FANTASIES AND *THE MISSION* OF REDEMPTION

Pelagianism rests transformation on the engine of the self, and thus under-estimates our plight and misdirects our hope. There are plenty of movies that are pelagian to the core, expressing a cultural optimism about indi-vidual powers of transformation. But some of our best movies finally show us that although we cannot hope to heal ourselves, we can nonetheless hope—in the redemptive giving and forgiving of others.

---

8. Now admittedly, Lester still proclaims a sub-Christian ethic that assumes that An-gela should offer the gift of her virginity to someone her own age without concern about marriage covenant or mutual self-giving.

9. The nudity also serves the movie's thematic concern with the way our typical "gaze" fails to see true beauty, but instead constructs our world and other people according to our own desires or according to society's definition of beauty.

10. For my argument that *American Beauty* draws us toward a hopeful eschatology, see Laytham, "Time for Hope."

Pleasantville (1998) is a movie I like a lot. It is funny, fun to watch, and showcases two generations of great actors. Unfortunately, *Pleasantville* is also profoundly bad theology, precisely because it embodies the central dogma of its genre—fantasy's fantasy that we can fix ourselves. Like *The Wizard of Oz*, on which it riffs, *Pleasantville* is a fantastical journey to find one's way home, a fantastical journey that is really about *finding oneself*—not Oz or Pleasantville or anywhere else—and about getting home not with the aid of someone else's magic, but by the *self-discovery* that "you've always had the power."[11]

The fundamental plot of almost all fantasies is what William Romanowski calls "the Wizard of Oz syndrome," the belief that all of us have, within ourselves, the power to secure our own happiness.[12] That's the gospel that David, the protagonist of *Pleasantville*, discovers and proclaims: "It's inside you!" he tells anyone who will listen. At its core, fantasy suggests "it may seem like you're in a fix, but you can fix it yourself!" The "fix" that creates dramatic tension can vary—it can be the alternate time line where you never lived (*It's a Wonderful Life*), or an endlessly repeating February 2 (*Groundhog Day*), or being magically transported to a fantastical alternate reality (*Oz* or *Pleasantville*). Regardless of the dramatic setting, however, fantasies typically offer a three-step pelagian plot: *I* find myself "caught" in a fantastical situation, *I* discover that my real problem is not *where* I am but *who* I am, and finally *I* choose to change and live happily ever after.

Such fantasies are pleasant to watch, but disastrous to live. While we Christians do not believe that humans are utterly evil or essentially sinful, we do believe that humanity has been so thoroughly distorted by sin that *I* cannot finally redeem *myself*, that *I* cannot find *my* way back to a happy home by *my own* power. That doesn't mean we should avoid watching fantasies, however. I think that

> fantasies do battle with a defeated pessimism that believes "people can't change," and a weary cynicism that says "even if they could change, most people won't." Moreover, good fantasies are fun, and even if they wrongly school our minds to be optimistic,

---

11. This is Glenda's exposition to Dorothy at the end of *The Wizard of Oz*.

12. "Instead of portraying the frailty of human experience and the need for a source of redemption outside of ourselves, the classical Hollywood mythology invests humans with everything they need to secure their own destiny and salvation." Romanowski, *Eyes Wide Open*, 114.

they rightly school our emotions to want and expect the joy of transformation.[13]

So watching and enjoying fantasies is not the problem. Living fantastically is.

I think the antidote to pelagianism is not hearing or reading about its theological perils (in spite of the preceding pages), but *seeing* the alternative: gracious redemption through the agency of another. Of course, if it's true that we cannot save ourselves, then we must truly see that in "real life." But movies can help, precisely by showing us in their unrealistic ways what is real. The gamut of movies that depict a redemption more realistic than pelagianism runs from the sweetly silly *Lars and the Real Girl* to the brutally real *21 Grams*.

I know of no movie that shows our hope of redemption more clearly than *The Mission* (1986), in a stunning, ten-minute sequence that begins with the declaration, "For me, there is no hope." Rodrigo (Robert De Niro) is a mercenary slave trader who, in a fit of jealous rage, killed his brother in a duel. Untouchable by the law, he seems to be beyond the reach of redemption—trapped in a cell of self-loathing and despair. The missionary Jesuit Father Gabriel (Jeremy Irons) dares him to try for redemption, to seek what he declares cannot be found. Rodrigo dares.

The remainder of the sequence is an agonizing, difficult ascent. Literally, the small Jesuit band is climbing a precipitous slope beside the tallest waterfall in South America. We see Rodrigo struggle to keep up; he is pulling behind him a bundle of the armor and weapons he used to enslave and destroy others, including the rapier that impaled his brother. Symbolically, we hear the musical articulation of Rodrigo's dogged quest. The deep driving tones of the bassoon render Rodrigo's determination. Sight and sound combine to tell us that he is willing himself up the mountain, yet without hope. To an uncritical eye, this seems precisely to be pelagianism, the notion that doing good can undo evil, that struggling can free, that redemption is an option we choose. Yet in the end, when Rodrigo tops the summit, we see that he remains bound by a past he cannot undo, isolated by enmities he cannot reconcile; caked with mud and futility, exhausted in body and spirit, he kneels helplessly. He is set free by the hand of another, disburdened of his rapacious past by one of his victims acting on the authority of their king. At the head of the falls, pelagianism is drowned in the cleansing waters like Rodrigo's muddy bundle plunging into the mighty river.

13. Laytham, "You Can Do It," 34.

CAN A *CITY OF ANGELS* CURE ANGELISM?

Angelism probably isn't our worst temptation, but we are constantly harried by its niggling whisper that perhaps our better life or our best self will be found beyond the body. Nothing says "no" to that like the robust proclamation of the gospel of the resurrection of Jesus. Ironically, angels bookend the story of the saving work of the Son of God by annunciating his bodily incarnation of Mary (Luke 1:26) and announcing his bodily resurrection from the tomb (Luke 24:4)! These angels may not cure our angelism, but they certainly point us towards its defeat.

Perhaps movies can serve as lesser messengers of the goodness of materiality, of the beauty of being a body, of the truth that physicality is not our problem—sin is. We must go carefully here, for there are aspects of the practice of watching movies that may diminish the body. But at their best, some of our best movies can cause us to exult in the goodness of bodily life. For example, this can happen in a story like *Billy Elliot* (2000), where a coal miner's son discovers that his body is made for ballet rather than boxing. Along the way, the movie invites us into the joyous discovery that bodily life, despite its challenges and mystery, is where goodness happens. We see that in the movie's opening sequence, which shows a gangly Billy bouncing up and down on his bed, dancing wildly in slow motion, to the music of "Cosmic Dancer" by T-Rex. Here is the exuberance of a youthful body, the freedom of unencumbered motion, the joy of spontaneous dancing. But there's more. As the music continues, Billy runs to the kitchen to finish fixing breakfast for his senile grandmother, whom he finally tracks down in a field outside the house. In his tender touch to turn and guide her toward shelter and sustenance, we recognize that bodies are the central site of our vulnerability and our care. Love requires a body. By the end of the film, we have seen that grace, too, requires a body, as do beauty, delight, and fidelity.[14]

One of my favorite movies to affirm the goodness of bodily life is *City of Angels* (1998), a movie that is theologically superior to its melodramatic plot and the mediocre acting of its leads. Ostensibly a story about an angel named Seth (Nicolas Cage) who chooses to "fall" into bodily existence because he has fallen in love with Maggie (Meg Ryan), the movie shows better than it says. It *says* that Meg Ryan is more attractive than God, that

14. For my extended analysis of *Billy Elliot*, see Laytham, "Theology Goes to the Movies," 3–15.

"one breath of her hair, one kiss of her mouth, one touch of her hand" is better than an eternity with God. That kind of schmaltzy dialogue should certainly be fair game for criticism when the emotion hasn't been earned, but it is unfairly denigrated in good movies with terms like "tearjerker" or "weepy." One thing is sure: there has been a sexist bias against emotional movies that codes emotion as "female" and "bodily," and denigrates it as a form of weakness or dependence. Thus, even a middling example of melodrama like *City of Angels* helps us notice that angelism is at work in patriarchal aspirations to independence and indifference!

City of Angels shows, on the other hand, that the attractions of bodily life are signs of the attractive goodness of God. Fat and balding Nathan Messinger (Dennis Franz) is a self-described "Glutton. Hedonist. Former celestial body, recent addition to the human race." Throughout the movie we watch Seth watch Nathan as he revels in the myriad joys of bodily life, delights that we too easily take for granted. Watching a watcher watch heightens our consciousness of what we are constantly experiencing but seldom noticing: the goodness and power of human touch, the delights of flavors and aromas, the exuberance of exertion and the tranquility of rest, the beauty and tenderness of familial love. The cinematography of John Seale is the artistic high point of the film, amplifying the power of a plot convention that inevitably invites us to join in Seth's desire for what he does not have *but we do*—bodily existence. And in the end, the movie does tell the truth that this goodness includes pain and death. It offers a strong inoculation against angelism.

DUELING DUALISM TO DEATH

Hollywood regularly represents back to us our underlying convictions about ourselves. Unfortunately, one of our modern prejudices is that some people are inherently evil and thus unredeemable, meaning the rest of us are almost entirely good, at least in all the ways that really count. Movies serve up this kind of dualism in classic action duels: Jedi against Sith, elves battling orcs, and even the ill-fated *Cowboys and Aliens*! Here's the classic tell for a movie that espouses dualism: if by the end of the story it is clear that for the world to be safe the villain's defeat is not enough, he must die, then we're watching dualism writ large. The world is not safe if Hannibal Lecter, if Sean Miller, if Hans Gruber, if John Doe, if the evil other lives.[15]

15. The arch-villains respectively in *Silence of the Lambs, Patriot Games, Die Hard,* and *Se7en.*

Dualism reassures us that the only thing really wrong with the cosmos is a few sociopaths, the occasional fascist, terrorists of all sorts, and the devil and his minions. In any case, dualism consoles us, *we are not the problem.*

Of course there are three problems with such a dualistic account of evil, and the cinematic duels it spawns. First, dualism isn't true. Living like it is produces problems two and three. That is, living as if the divide between good and evil occurs *between* rather than *within* persons, leads inexorably to underestimations of my own sin, and of my enemy's redeemability. And that leads inexorably to overestimations of the role of violence in mending the world. It may feel profoundly cathartic to watch the bad guy get it in the end, but it won't draw us deeper in self-knowledge, won't drive us further in self-sacrifice, won't show us shalom.

Happily, Hollywood is capable of far more sophisticated understandings of evil, and often renders them in its most artistically powerful forms. It can show us, for example, that evil is often greater than the sum of its contributing parts. *Fargo* (1996) renders in a bleak comedic palette how the amplifying interactions of weakness of will, selfishness of spirit, mistakes and miscues, and misanthropy culminate in a destructive cataclysm that is exponential rather than additive. *Munich* (2005) renders in subtle dramatic tones the humanity of some of the terrorists who plotted the 1972 Olympic massacre, and of the team of Masad agents who wrought Israel's vengeance. The movie does not diminish the reality that the terrorists perpetrated hateful acts, but neither does it allow that to occlude their unmistakable humanity. Steven Spielberg goes the extra mile to show us the dehumanizing impact of orienting one's life to the mission of vengeance. Instead of a dualistic duel, the movie offers us a dual perspective—showing both the valor and vanity of our efforts to right wrongs with violence.

One of my favorite examples of undermining dualism is Paul Haggis's *Crash* (2004), a movie that intentionally offers two views of nearly every character in its ensemble cast, showing us both their best and their worst. For example, we see that Officer John Ryan (Matt Dillon) can be both a spitefully despicable racist and a tenderly loving son. Indeed, we begin to see how intertwined are his hates and his loves. We see that Jean (Sandra Bullock) can be both a lonely, victimized wife and a harsh, victimizing employer. Worst of all, we see that Officer Hansen (Ryan Phillippe)—a noble, idealistic reformer—can perpetrate one of the story's greatest evils precisely as a result of his overconfidence in his own virtue. It isn't pretty. But then, neither are we. That's the gritty beauty of *Crash* and other films that have the courage to puzzle over that same puzzling ambivalence we know in ourselves: no one is entirely good or bad, only some mixture of both at the same time. And often what makes us the very best also tempts us to the worst.

✣ *What particular movies have shown you the complexity of our humanity, or have revealed redemptive paths that eschew violence?*

So in the end, refusing moralism, pelagianism, angelism, and dualism with a little help from Hollywood, perhaps we really can love the cinema, hate the sin. I certainly hope so. Pass the popcorn!

Bibliography

American Gaming Association. "Gaming Revenue: 10-Year Trend." Online: http://www
.americangaming.org/industry-resources/research/fact-sheets/gaming-revenue-10-
year-trends.

Anker, Roy. "Rugby and Reconciliation." *Books and Culture* 16:2 (2010) 22–24.

Ashby, LeRoy. *With Amusement for All: A History of American Popular Culture since 1830.*
Lexington: University of Kentucky Press, 2006.

Association of Magazine Media. "Combined Circulation Revenue Estimates for all
ABC Magazines: 1988–2010." Online: http://www.magazine.org/CONSUMER_
MARKETING/CIRC_TRENDS/16136.aspx.

Barron, Robert. "YouTube Heresies." *America,* May 25, 2009, 21–23.

Bauerlein, Mark. *The Dumbest Generation: How the Digital Age Stupefies Young Americans
and Jeopardizes Our Future.* New York: Penguin, 2008.

Beck, John C., and Mitchell Wade. *The Kids Are Alright: How the Gamer Generation Is
Changing the Workplace.* Boston: Harvard Business School Press, 2006.

Bell, Daniel M., Jr. *Just War as Christian Discipleship.* Grand Rapids: Brazos, 2009.

Boorstin, Daniel J. *The Image: A Guide to Pseudo-Events in America.* New York: Vintage,
1992.

Borgmann, Albert. *Power Failure: Christianity in the Culture of Technology.* Grand Rapids:
Brazos, 2003.

Breuer, Sarah Dylan. "What Is a U2charist?" Online: http://www.sarahlaughed
.net/u2charist/whats_a_u2charist/.

Buckingham, David. "Studying Computer Games." In *Computer Games: Text Narrative
and Play,* edited by Diane Carr et al., 1–13. Cambridge: Polity, 2006.

Budde, Michael. *The (Magic) Kingdom of God: Christianity and Global Culture Industries.*
Boulder, CO: Westview, 1998.

Bull, Michael. "No Dead Air! The iPod and the Culture of Mobile Listening." *Leisure
Studies* 24:4 (2005) 343–55.

————. *Sound Moves: iPod Culture and Urban Experience.* London: Routledge, 2007.

Bunyan, John. *The Pilgrim's Progress: from this world to that which is to come delivered
under the similitude of a dream.* New York: Heritage, 1942.

Burgess, Jean, and Joshua Green. *YouTube: Online Video and Participatory Culture.* Cambridge: Polity, 2009.

Burn, Andrew, and Diane Carr. "Defining Game Genres." In *Computer Games: Text,
Narrative and Play,* edited by Diane Carr et al., 14–29. Cambridge: Polity, 2006.

Byassee, Jason. "God Does Not Entertain." In *God Does Not . . . ,* edited by D. Brent
Laytham, 107–30. Grand Rapids: Brazos, 2009.

————. "What You're Looking For." *Christian Century,* November 27, 2007, 11.

Bibliography

Callaway, Kutter. "Wii Are Inspirited: The Transformation of Home Video Gaming Consoles (and Us)." In *Halos and Avatars: Playing Video Games with God*, edited by Craig Detweiler, 75–88. Louisville: Westminster John Knox, 2010.

Carless, Simon. "Breaking: Nintendo Announces New Revolution Name—'Wii.'" Online: http://www.gamasutra.com/php-bin/news_index.php?story=9075.

Carmody, Denise Lardner. "Big-Time Spectator Sports: A Feminist Christian Perspective." In *Sport and Religion*, edited by Shirl J. Hoffman, 105–9. Champaign, IL: Human Kinetics Books, 1992.

Carr, Diane. "Play and Pleasure." In *Computer Games: Text Narrative and Play*, edited by Diane Carr et al., 45–58. Cambridge: Polity, 2006.

Castronova, Edward. *Exodus to the Virtual World: How Online Fun Is Changing Reality.* New York: Palgrave, 2007.

Catechism of the Catholic Church. Mahwah, NJ: Paulist, 1994.

Clapp, Rodney. *Border Crossings: Christian Trespasses on Popular Culture and Public Affairs.* Grand Rapids: Brazos, 2000.

———. *Tortured Wonders: Christian Spirituality for People, Not Angels.* Grand Rapids: Brazos, 2004.

Dark, David. *Everyday Apocalypse: The Sacred Revealed in Radiohead, The Simpsons, and Other Pop Culture Icons.* Grand Rapids: Brazos, 2002.

Deford, Frank. "The Word according to Tom." *Sports Illustrated*, April 26, 1976, 54–69.

DeNora, Tia. *Music in Everyday Life.* Cambridge: Cambridge University Press, 2000.

Detweiler, Craig. "Introduction: Halos and Avatars." In *Halos and Avatars: Playing Video Games with God*, edited by Craig Detweiler, 1–16. Louisville: Westminster John Knox, 2010.

Detweiler, Craig, and Barry Taylor. *A Matrix of Meanings.* Grand Rapids: Baker Academic, 2003.

Dill, Karen. *How Fantasy Becomes Reality: Seeing through Media Influence.* New York: Oxford University Press, 2009.

Dyer-Witherford, Nick, and Greig de Peuter. *Games of Empire: Global Capitalism and Video Games.* Minneapolis: University of Minnesota Press, 2009.

Egenfeldt-Nielsen, Simon, Jonas Heide Smith, and Susana Pajares Tosca. *Understanding Video Games: The Essential Introduction.* New York: Routledge, 2008.

Evangelical Lutheran Church in America. "Gambling and the Godly Life." Online: http://www2.elca.org/socialstatements/economiclife/gambling/session2.html.

Falsani, Cathleen, and Mark Allan Powell. "Bono's American Prayer." *Christianity Today* 47:3 (2003) 38–44.

Fleming, Julia. "State Lotteries: Gambling with the Common Good." *Christian Reflection: A Series in Faith and Ethics* 40 (2011) 29–38.

Flora, Carlin. "Seeing by Starlight." *Psychology Today* 37:4 (2004) 36–40, 87.

Focus on the Family. "American Beauty." Online: www.pluggedin.com/videos/1999/q3/americanbeauty.aspx.

Fraser, Peter. *Images of the Passion: The Sacramental Mode in Film.* Westport, CT: Praeger, 1998.

Gabler, Neal. *Life the Movie: How Entertainment Conquered Reality.* New York: Knopf, 1998.

Galli, Mark. "Something Noble and Good." *Christianity Today*, May 13, 2005. Online: http://www.christianitytoday.com/ct/2005/mayweb-only/52.0a.html.

————. "Spectating as a Spiritual Discipline." *Christianity Today*, March 11, 2005. Online: http://www.christianitytoday.com/ct/article_print.html?id=34659.

Galloway, Alexander. *Gaming: Essays in Algorithmic Culture*. Minneapolis: University of Minnesota Press, 2006.

Gamson, Joshua. "The Assembly Line of Greatness: Celebrity in Twentieth-Century America." In *Popular Culture: Production and Consumption*, edited by C. Lee Harrington and Denise D. Bielby, 259–82. Malden, MA: Blackwell, 2001.

Gardella, Peter. *Domestic Religion: Work, Food, Sex, and Other Commitments*. Cleveland: Pilgrim, 1998.

Garvey, Catherine. *Play*. Cambridge: Harvard University Press, 1977.

Giamatti, A. Bartlett. *Take Time for Paradise: Americans and Their Games*. New York: Summit, 1989.

Gibbs, Nancy. "Persons of the Year." *Time*, December 26, 2005, 38–45.

Gill, Rosalind. *Gender and the Media*. Cambridge: Polity, 2007.

Godawa, Brian. *Hollywood Worldviews: Watching Films with Wisdom and Discernment*. Downers Grove, IL: InterVarsity, 2009.

Hanby, Michael. "The Culture of Death, the Ontology of Boredom, and the Resistance of Joy." *Communio* 31:2 (2004) 181–99.

Hauerwas, Stanley. *Christian Existence Today*. Durham: Labyrinth, 1988. Reprint, Eugene, OR: Wipf & Stock, 2010.

Herzfeld, Michael. *Anthropology: Theoretical Practice in Culture and Society*. Malden, MA: Blackwell, 2001.

Hicks, Douglas A. "Star Power." *Christian Century*, March 21, 2006, 23–24.

Hodge, Daniel White. "Role Playing: Toward a Theology for Gamers." In *Halos and Avatars: Playing Video Games with God*, edited by Craig Detweiler, 163–75. Louisville: Westminster John Knox, 2010.

Hoffman, Shirl. "Whatever Happened to Play?" *Christianity Today* 54:2 (2010) 20–25.

Huizinga, Johan. *Homo Ludens: A Study of the Play-Element in Culture*. Boston: Beacon, 1950.

Jenkins, Erik. "My iPod, My iCon: How and Why Do Images Become Icons?" *Critical Studies in Media Communication* 25:5 (2008) 466–89.

Jenkins, Henry. *Convergence Culture: Where Old and New Media Collide*. New York: New York University Press, 2006.

Johnston, Robert K. *Reel Spirituality: Theology and Film in Dialogue*. Rev. ed. Grand Rapids: Baker Academic, 2006.

————. "Visual Christianity." In *The Conviction of Things Not Seen*, edited by Todd Johnson, 165–82. Grand Rapids: Brazos, 2002.

Johnston, Robert K., and Catherine M. Barsotti. *Finding God in the Movies: Thirty-Three Films of Reel Faith*. Grand Rapids: Baker, 2004.

Juhasz, Alexandra. "Learning the Five Lessons of YouTube: After Trying to Teach There I Don't Believe the Hype." *Cinema Journal* 48:2 (2009) 145–50.

Kahney, Leander. *The Cult of iPod*. San Francisco: No Starch Press, 2005.

Kaiser Family Foundation. "Profiles of Generation M(2)." Online video: http://www.kff.org/entmedia/hr012010video.cfm.

Kallestad, Walt. *Entertainment Evangelism: Taking the Church Public*. Nashville: Abingdon, 1996.

————. "'Showtime!' No More: Could Our Church Shift from Performance to Mission?" *Leadership* 29:4 (2008) 39–43.

Kelly, James. "The Good Samaritans." *Time*, December 26, 2005, 8.

Kitchen, Matthew. "*Madden* Rules: Sports and the Future of Competitive Video Games." In *Halos and Avatars: Playing Video Games with God*, edited by Craig Detweiler, 108–20. Louisville: Westminster John Knox, 2010.

Kubey, Robert, and Mihaly Csikszentmihalyi. "Television Addiction Is No Mere Metaphor." *Scientific American Special Edition* 14:1 (2004) 48–55.

Lawrence, John Shelton, and Robert Jewett. *The Myth of the American Superhero*. Grand Rapids: Eerdmans, 2002.

Lawson, Jeremy D., Michael J. Sleasman, and Charles A. Anderson. "The Gospel according to Safeway: The Checkout Line and the Good Life." In *Everyday Theology: How to Read Cultural Texts and Interpret Trends*, edited by Kevin J. Vanhoozer et al., 63–80. Grand Rapids: Baker Academic, 2007.

Laytham, D. Brent. "Theology Goes to the Movies: Screening *Billy Elliot*." *Covenant Quarterly* 63:2 (2005) 3–15.

———. "Time for Hope: *The Sixth Sense, American Beauty, Memento,* and *Twelve Monkeys*." In *The Gift of Story: Narrating Hope in a Postmodern World*, edited by Emily Griesinger and Mark Eaton, 69–83. Waco: Baylor University Press, 2006.

———. "You Can Do It: The Fantasy of Self-Creation and Redemption in *Pleasantville*." *Cultural Encounters* 5:1 (2009) 33–52.

Lears, T. J. Jackson. "Beyond Pathology: The Cultural Meanings of Gambling." In *Gambling: Mapping the American Moral Landscape,* edited by Alan Wolfe and Erik C. Owens, 301–22. Waco: Baylor University Press, 2009.

Levy, Steven. "iPod Nation." *Newsweek*, July 25, 2004. Online: http://www.thedailybeast. com/newsweek/2004/07/25/ipod-nation.html.

Lindbeck, George. *The Nature of Doctrine: Religion and Theology in a Postliberal Age.* Philadelphia: Westminster, 1984.

Linn, Susan. "A Royal Juggernaut: The Disney Princesses and Other Commercialized Threats to Creative Play and the Path to Self-Realization for Young Girls." In *The Sexualization of Childhood*, edited by Sharna Olfman, 33–50. Westport, CT: Praeger, 2009.

MacIntyre, Alisdair. *After Virtue*. 3rd ed. Notre Dame: University of Notre Dame Press, 2007.

Marshall, P. David. *Celebrity and Power: Fame in Contemporary Culture*. Minneapolis: University of Minnesota Press, 1997.

Mattingly, Terry. *Pop Goes Religion: Faith in Popular Culture*. Nashville: W. Publishing Group, 2005.

McCluhan, Marshall. *Understanding Media: The Extensions of Man*. New York: McGraw-Hill, 1964.

McClymond, Kathryn. "The Gospel According to Oprah: A Canon for Contemporary Living." In *Religion as Entertainment*, edited by C. K. Robertson, 173–92. New York: Peter Lang, 2002.

Miller, Vincent. *Consuming Religion: Christian Faith and Practice in a Consumer Culture*. New York: Continuum, 2004.

———. "The iPod, the Cell Phone, and the Church: Discipleship, Consumer Culture, and a Globalized World." In *Getting on Message: Challenging the Christian Right from the Heart of the Gospel*, edited by Peter Laarman, 173–91. Boston: Beacon, 2006.

Mohrmann, Douglas. "Megachurch, Virtual Church." In *Religion as Entertainment*, edited by C. K. Robertson, 27–46. New York: Peter Lang, 2002.

Moore, J. Cameron. "Making Moral Choices in Video Games." *Christian Reflection: A Series in Faith and Ethics* 38 (2011) 69–77.

National Association of Theater Owners. "Total U.S. & Canada Box Office Grosses." Online: http://www.natoonline.org/statisticsboxoffice.htm.

Nayar, Pramod K. *Seeing Stars: Spectacle, Society and Celebrity Culture*. New Delhi: Sage, 2009.

Nelson, Marcia. *The Gospel According to Oprah*. Louisville: Westminster John Knox, 2005.

Novak, Michael. *The Joy of Sports: End Zones, Bases, Baskets, Balls, and the Consecration of the American Spirit*. Lanham, MD: Hamilton, 1988.

One Campaign. "Board of Directors." Online: http://one.org/us/about/oneboard.html.

Oprah Winfrey Fansite. "Frontpage." Online: http://www.oprah-fansite.com.

Paynter, Suzii. "The Harm of Predatory Gambling." *Christian Reflection: A Series in Faith and Ethics* 40 (2011) 73–77.

Pinsky, Drew, et al. *The Mirror Effect: How Celebrity Narcissism Is Seducing America*. New York: HarperCollins, 2009.

Rahner, Hugo. *Man at Play*. New York: Herder & Herder, 1967.

Ratzinger, Joseph. *Eschatology, Death and Eternal Life*. Translated by Michael Waldenstein. Washington, DC: Catholic University of America Press, 1988.

Revolve: The Complete New Testament. Nashville: Thomas Nelson, 2003.

Rigby, Scott, and Richard M. Ryan. *Glued to Games: How Video Games Draw Us in and Hold Us Spellbound*. Santa Barbara, CA: Praeger, 2011.

Robinson, Eugene. "Can Oprah Boost Her 'Favorite Guy'?" In *Celebrity Culture in the United States*, edited by Terence J. Fitzgerald, 79–80. New York: H. W. Wilson, 2008.

Rodman, George. *Making Sense of Media: An Introduction to Mass Communication*. Boston: Allyn & Bacon, 2001.

Romanowski, William D. *Eyes Wide Open: Looking for God in Popular Culture*. Rev. ed. Grand Rapids: Brazos, 2007.

———. *Pop Culture Wars: Religion and the Role of Entertainment in American Life*. Downers Grove, IL: InterVarsity, 1996.

Rushkoff, Douglas. *Playing the Future: What We Can Learn from Digital Kids*. New York: Riverhead, 1999.

Ruth, Lester. "A Rose by Another Name." In *The Conviction of Things Not Seen: Worship and Ministry in the Twenty-First Century*, edited by Todd Johnson, 33–52, 216–18. Grand Rapids: Brazos, 2002.

Sage, George. *Globalizing Sport: How Organizations, Corporations, Media, and Politics Are Changing Sports*. Boulder, CO: Paradigm, 2010.

Saliers, Don. "Afterword: Liturgy and Ethics Revisited." In *Liturgy and the Moral Self*, edited by E. Byron Anderson and Bruce T. Morrill, 209–24. Collegeville, MN: Liturgical, 1998.

Sayre, Shay, and Cynthia King. *Entertainment and Society: Audiences, Trends, and Impacts*. Thousand Oaks, CA: Sage, 2003.

Schultze, Quentin J. *Communicating for Life: Christian Stewardship in Community and Media*. Grand Rapids: Baker Academic, 2000.

———. *Habits of the High-Tech Heart: Living Virtuously in the Information Age*. Grand Rapids: Baker Academic, 2002.

Schultze, Quentin J., et al. *Dancing in the Dark: Youth Popular Culture and the Electronic Media*. Grand Rapids: Eerdmans, 1991.

Bibliography

Simun, Miriam. "My Music, My World: Using the MP3 Player to Shape Experience in London." *New Media and Society* 11:6 (2009) 921–41.

Sirius XM. "Oprah Radio: Live Your Best Life." Online: http://www.siriusxm.com/oprahradio.

Smith, James K. A. *Desiring the Kingdom: Worship, Worldview, and Cultural Formation.* Grand Rapids: Baker Academic, 2009.

Stafford, Tim. "God Is in the Blueprints: Our Deepest Beliefs Are Reflected in the Ways We Construct Our Houses of Worship." *Christianity Today,* September 7, 1998, 76–82.

Strangelove, Michael. *Watching YouTube: Extraordinary Videos by Ordinary People.* Toronto: University of Toronto Press, 2010.

Taylor, Barry. *Entertainment Theology: New-Edge Spirituality in a Digital Democracy.* Grand Rapids: Baker Academic, 2008.

Taylor, Charles. *A Secular Age.* Cambridge: Belknap Press of Harvard University Press, 2007.

Teen Vogue. "Mission Statement." Online: http://www.condenastdirect.com/corpmediakit/tv/index.cfm.

Thompson, William M. *The Struggle for Theology's Soul: Contesting Scripture in Christology.* New York: Crossroad, 1996.

Turkle, Sherry. *Alone Together: Why We Expect More from Technology and Less from Each Other.* New York: Basic Books, 2011.

———. "Always-on/Always-on-You: The Tethered Self." In *Handbook of Mobile Communication Studies,* edited by James Katz, 121–38. Cambridge: MIT Press, 2008.

Turner, Nigel E. "Games, Gambling, and Gambling Problems." In *In the Pursuit of Winning: Problem Gambling Theory, Research and Treatment,* edited by Masood Zangeneh et al., 33–64. New York: Springer, 2008.

Turner, Victor. *From Ritual to Theatre: The Human Seriousness of Play.* New York: Performing Arts Journal Publication, 1982.

United Methodist Church. "The Social Principles of the United Methodist Church," 163.IV.G, "Gambling." Online: http://www.umc-gbcs.org/site/c.frLJK2PKLqF/b.3713153/k.FC2F/182163_IV_The_Economic_Community/apps/nl/newsletter.asp.

Vacek, Heather. "The History of Gambling." *Christian Reflection: A Series in Faith and Ethics* 40 (2011) 88–93.

Wadell, Paul J. *Becoming Friends: Worship, Justice, and the Practice of Christian Friendship.* Grand Rapids: Brazos, 2002.

Wauters, Robin. "YouTube Turns 6 Years Old, Daily Views Shoot Up To 3 Billion (Yes 3 Billion. Daily)." TechCrunch Blog. Online: http://techcrunch.com/2011/05/25/as-youtube-turns-6-years-old-daily-views-shoot-up-to-3-billion-yes-3-billion-daily/.

Webb, Stephen. *The Divine Voice: Christian Proclamation and the Theology of Sound.* Grand Rapids: Brazos, 2004.

Weinstein, Deena, and Michael Weinstein. "Celebrity Worship as Weak Religion." *Word and World* 23:3 (2003) 294–302.

Williams, J. Patrick, et al. "Introduction: Fantasy Games, Gaming Cultures, and Social Life." In *Gaming As Culture: Essays on Reality Identity and Experience in Fantasy Games,* edited by J. Patrick Williams et al., 1–18. Jefferson, NC: McFarland, 2006.

Williams, Rowan. *Lost Icons: Reflections on Cultural Bereavement.* Edinburgh: T. & T. Clark, 2000.

Woods, Robert H., Jr., and Paul D. Patton. "Faithful Criticism of Popular Media Technologies." *Christian Reflection: A Series in Faith and Ethics* 38 (2011) 29–36.

YouCat: Youth Catechism of the Catholic Church. San Francisco: Ignatius, 2011.

Zondervan. "Inspired By . . . The Bible Experience: The Complete Bible." Online: http://www.zondervan.com/Cultures/en-US/Product/ProductDetail.htm?Prod ID=com.zondervan.9780310926306&QueryStringSite=Zondervan#productdetails.

Index

actor. *See* performer

advertising, 3, 25, 34, 36–37, 40, 52, 60, 62, 64–65, 68, 90, 105, 130–31, 135–37, 139–40, 142–43

American Beauty, 187–89

angelism, 183–85, 187, 192–93

appliance, entertainment. *See* entertainment device

ascesis, 53

attention, 5–7, 14–15, 25, 28–29, 47, 52, 54–57, 59, 65, 71, 72, 79, 84–86, 90–91, 95–96, 103, 111–12, 128–29, 135–36, 146, 152, 155–56, 158, 162, 167, 171

attention economy, entertainment as, 1, 5, 15, 57, 150, 158, 160–61

audience, 7, 11, 17–18, 44, 58, 61–62, 65, 67, 69, 75, 79–80, 86, 134–35, 137–40, 144, 152–56, 163, 168–71, 186

authenticity, 36, 60, 153, 155, 164

autotelic, 77–80, 106

avatar, 123–6

baptism, 35, 59, 61, 65, 68, 118–19, 149

baseball, 30, 44

basketball, 15, 31, 75, 79, 85, 88, 95, 98, 101, 103

beauty, 9, 14–15, 18, 29, 36, 46–47, 49, 56, 66, 71, 85, 92, 95, 98, 114, 118, 188–89, 192–94

Billy Elliot, 185, 192

body, 12, 37, 64, 74, 77, 82, 85, 89, 121–26, 132, 183, 192–93

Bono, 68, 152, 157–65

Boorstin, Daniel, 5

boredom, 15, 47–48, 70, 72, 80, 91

broadcast, 7, 15, 17, 24–26, 41–43, 51, 56, 58, 89–90, 130, 133, 135, 169

"broadcast yourself," 52–53, 58–61, 129

Borgmann, Albert, 20, 38–40

Bull, Michael, 34, 40–1, 47–48

Castranova, Edward, 116–17, 119–20

catechesis. *See* formation

catholicity, 89, 149, 161–62

celebrity, 28, 51, 71, 83, 93, 95–97, 105, 134, 138–39, 141, 148–65, 166–75, 179

Christian community. *See* church

church, 3, 5, 17–18, 20, 35, 61, 71, 98, 115–16, 136, 144, 150, 160, 175–79, 181

cinema. *See* movie

City of Angels, 192–93

clutter, 15, 25, 57

cocktail party effect, 57

Colbert, Stephen, 3–5

Index

Index